Open Economy Macroeconomics

Open Economy
Macroeconomics

RUDIGER DORNBUSCH

Basic Books, Inc. Publishers   *New York*

Library of Congress Cataloging in Publication Data

Dornbusch, Rudiger.
    Open economy macroeconomics.

    Includes bibliographies and index.
    1.   International finance.   2.   International
economic relations.   3.   Macroeconomics.   I.   Title.
HG3881.D66   339   80-66308
ISBN: O-465-05286-X

To Eliana

Contents

Preface   ix

PART 1   *Introduction*
     1. Modeling the Open Economy   3
     2. Some Basic Relations   12

PART 2   *Employment, the Trade Balance, and Relative Prices*
     3. Income Determination and the Trade Balance   33
     4. Relative Prices, Equilibrium Output, and the Trade Balance   57
     5. Intermediate Goods and Nontraded Goods   82
     6. Home Goods and Traded Goods: the Dependent Economy Model   93

PART 3   *Money and Payments Adjustment*
     7. Money, Prices, and Payments Adjustment   119
     8. Money, Exchange Rates, and Employment   143
     9. Monetary and Exchange Rate Policy for Macroeconomic Stability   161

PART 4   *Assets Markets, Capital Mobility, and Stabilization Policy*
     10. Stabilization Policy Under Fixed Exchange Rates and Capital Mobility   175
     11. Flexible Exchange Rates and Capital Mobility   193
     12. Monetary Stabilization, Intervention, and Real Appreciation   215

PART 5   *Portfolio Balance and the Current Account*
     13. Exchange Rates, Assets Markets, and the Current Account   239
     14. Growth, the Balance of Payments, and the Exchange Rate   260

Index   279

Preface

This book has grown out of research and teaching in the field of international monetary economics. At the borderline of a treatise, a text, and a monograph, it is none of either and a bit of each. It shares with a text the concern for a broad coverage of the topics in the area of international monetary economics, but it falls short of a complete coverage because many topics are plainly unexciting. With a treatise it shares the preoccupation for an integrated analytical framework and an emphasis on basic concepts, but it lacks some of the dust, age, and perspective. Finally, it is in the nature of a monograph in that it chooses and picks its topics and approaches, but also because it takes more liberties than a text or treatise would permit. With all this in mind, the book is designed as a statement of the main body of international macroeconomics.

My generation of international economists owes a great debt to those who, in the 1950s and 60s, redirected the field and gave it a new shape and formal structure. But I owe a special debt, having been a student of Harry G. Johnson, Lloyd Metzler, and Robert Mundell at the University of Chicago. Robert Mundell, as a teacher and friend, has shaped my economics quite irrecoverably.

Over the years I have been running large deficits with Karl Brunner, Jacob Frenkel, Ronald Jones, Michael Mussa, Paul Samuelson, and Alexander Swoboda and have enjoyed listening to Franco Modigliani. Stanley Fischer takes a special place for his patience, kindness, and great collaboration.

Of course, the book would not stand as it is, had I not had the excellent teaching and research advantages of the Massachusetts Institute of Technology and the exposure to many of my contemporaries' ideas at conferences, seminars, through oral tradition, and through the mail. It is hard to give credit to each influence, but I trust that they will be quite apparent throughout the book.

Beyond the general appreciation, I would like to thank in particular William Branson, Matthew Butlin, Bram Cadsby, Robert Cumby, David Germany, Lance Taylor, and Michael Veal for their close reading of the manuscript, as well as John Huizinga for his tireless efforts.

Part 1

Introduction

CHAPTER

1

Modeling the Open Economy

The title of this book—*Open Economy Macroeconomics*—reflects an attempt to integrate closed economy macroeconomics with the topics and problems arising in the economics of foreign trade and payments. Openness is an essential modification that qualifies many of the established policy precepts of a closed economy. For traditional "international monetary economics," with its flavor of partial equilibrium analysis and the quantity theory, application of macroeconomic concepts and modeling provides fresh insights in addition to formal discipline.

This introductory chapter sketches the approach developed in this book. It presents an outline of the contents as well as the motivation for the choice of material and its illustration.

I. THE MACROECONOMIC TRADITION

There is plenty of ancestry for macroeconomics of the open economy. Ever since the income-adjustment process became part of balance of payments theory, there has been a formal link between the two areas, which was recognized and developed in the analysis of the foreign trade multiplier.

The big step forward, though, came not with the integration of openness in the theory of income determination along the lines of the foreign trade multiplier, but with the integration of relative prices and income determination. Relative prices, tariffs, and devaluation had been primarily dealt with in partial equilibrium models, but it was not until the work of Alexander, Harberger, and Laursen-Metzler that the connection between international monetary economics and macroeconomics became firmly established.

They approached the question of the effects of depreciation on the balance of trade from different perspectives. The main point to emerge was the recognition that the balance of trade equals the excess of income over spending. Accordingly, the analysis of various disturbances in their trade-balance effects could not bypass an explanation of the aggregate income-expenditure balance.

James Meade's work is the definitive integration of value theory and income theory. His book demonstrates the need for a good dose of formal macroeconomics in the discussion of standard open economy questions, from tariffs to capital controls. Meade's work also made a basic imprint on the field by casting questions in the context of policy choices. The concepts of internal and external balance were used to identify the potential of various policies and the possibility of policy dilemmas.

Meade's theory and, of course, the much broader literature that took off at the time, pointed the way toward macroeconomics and away from partial equilibrium and informal analysis. The change of emphasis included modeling and recognition of aggregate budget constraints, identities, balance sheets, and interdependent equilibrium conditions—in sum, all the things we now cheerfully take for granted. Meade is the leading example of this new force, but one would certainly add the work of Trevor Swan and Harry Johnson, each of whom contributed in important ways to the integration of open and closed economy macroeconomics.

By the early 1960s macroeconomics had become firmly established as an approach to open economy questions. The standard analysis was one of comparative statics in a model with income demand determined and with the exchange rate setting relative prices. The following years brought the highly influential work of Robert Mundell, who created models and concepts that rapidly became the Volkswagens of the field—easy to drive, reliable, and sleek. Mundell drew on the Canadian experience to point out the striking implications of capital mobility for the conduct of stabilization policy. He pursued that question in several directions—the proper assignment of instruments, policy under fixed and flexible exchange rates, and the role of exchange-rate margins. But his innovation went beyond posing important new questions in that he created simple, forceful models to serve as organizing frameworks for thought and policy and as springboards for posing new problems.

The integration of assets markets and capital mobility into the open economy macroeconomic model was not Mundell's only contribution. His other work, which remains controversial, was a revival of monetary considerations in the interpretation of balance of payments problems. Drawing on the work of Lloyd Metzler, in particular his *Wealth, Saving and the Rate of Interest*, Mundell developed a further line of formal models—and students —that emphasize money creation, deficit finance, external imbalance, monetary interdependence, and inflation. Clearly, these were the appropriate models for the world economy at the close of the 1960s, when the Bretton Woods System collapsed.

Toward the early 1970s the field opened up in many directions. The formal orientation had led to interest in empirical work, and soon questions of capital mobility, or trade and payments adjustment, were becoming popular areas of applied research. This development may seem less exciting than the coining of new models and concepts, but it is no less important. The testing of theories and the progressive development of a body of stylized facts about equations and parameters has, in all likelihood, been the outstanding contribution of macroeconomics in the 1970s. Credit is due in many quarters, but it would certainly include important research efforts at the Federal Reserve and at the International Monetary Fund.

The 1970s were more than a period of empirical research. Floating exchange rates soon provided an impetus for a vigorous rebound of modeling, old ideas in better clothes, and some new concepts to go along. Following Stanley Black's work, rational expectations quickly made their way into open economy macroeconomics. The asset market approach came to challenge orthodox approaches to the balance of payments, but in turn would soon be displaced by those emphasizing the current account. Unlike the pure theory of trade, open economy macroeconomics had become an applied and policy-oriented area of study. Models increasingly formulate the issues of the day—overshooting, real-wage resistance, supply shocks, and virtuous and vicious circles. Moreover, as theories made their appearance, they soon had their painful encounters with empirical testing. Perhaps this is an optimistic picture of our field, but it does seem alive and kicking.

II. MODELING THE OPEN ECONOMY

International economics has long been a field with restricted entry. Entry has been restricted by such devices as "offer curves," for which only the initiated know which is whose, but also by the sheer variety of models and effects that appears much more abundant than in other areas of applied economics. This book is no exception to that tradition; hence some guidance is appropriate.

The complexity arises from the fact that for most issues there is an option of at least two regimes. Closed economy macroeconomics looks perforce at one country, while in the open economy we have the choice to incorporate or neglect interdependence and repercussion effects. And while closed economy macroeconomics is aggregative, looking for the most part at a one-commodity world, open economy macroeconomics is concerned not only with the level of prices, but with relative prices as well. There are import prices and export prices and the distinction between traded goods and nontraded goods, imported intermediates, and final goods. To round out matters we have the option of fixed and flexible rates—or dirty floating—in between. Capital may be mobile or immobile, and exchange-rate expectations may be there or not, rational or otherwise.

It becomes immediately apparent that the variety of assumptions allows for many permutations and some rather complicated scenarios. There are two ways, then, to skin a cat. We shall follow the other way. Throughout we choose simple models that seize an essential aspect of the problem at hand. In discussing the effectiveness of monetary policy under fixed exchange rates, for example, it is important to decide whether assets are traded or nontraded. It matters little, however, whether goods are traded or nontraded. To give another example, in discussing the effects of a quota, it matters a lot whether we have full employment or a period of economic slack. It matters relatively little whether capital is mobile or immobile. A first criterion, then, is to strip models of unnecessary and frivolous generality.

A second criterion in developing the material in this book has been to build analytical blocks that are relatively self-contained, each of which can be fitted together in various general equilibrium scenarios to accommodate the requirements of a more general or complete analysis. This criterion is particularly adopted in the gradual buildup of models. Starting from simple models of relative prices and output determination, the analysis proceeds from there to more complex models that consider problems of interacting goods and assets markets or expectations. Since at no time is there an attempt to "put everything together," there will always be the lingering doubt that perhaps ultimate generality has not been achieved. True, but the alternative is too cumbersome and is a matter not for theory, but rather for empirical estimation and simulation in large-scale models.

Even with this vow of simplicity we do not escape some degree of complexity. But this is entirely warranted, because we do want to leave room in our models for various channels or effects to play their role. There is a minimal framework that makes a model sufficiently eclectic to represent alternative views and cures of a policy problem. It is essential that these alternatives be brought into a common framework, so that their relative importance can be emphasized. For example, the competing merits of monetary, elasticity, and absorption approaches to devaluation are best illustrated in a model where both relative prices and a monetary sector are present.

Complexity is not the only choice to be made. We could attempt to develop most topics within a single, simplified model. That choice is not made here. We freely change models, as one purpose of this book is to teach both the subject matter and modeling of the open economy. Even so, there is considerable uniformity, which arises not from the assumptions about the world, but rather from the formal structure of models—the way they are set up and exploited. It is in this area that theory yields its greatest rewards, because it becomes rapidly apparent how isomorphisms can be readily applied across circumstances.

III. AN OVERVIEW OF THIS BOOK

This book is organized in five parts. The organization reflects the progressive widening of models to increase the range of interacting markets or the inclusion of dynamic or expectational problems. Each part presents substantial unity with respect to the issues discussed, although a diversity of models are used to serve that purpose.

After part 1 sets out basic concepts, we turn in part 2 to the determination of equilibrium output, abstracting from asset markets and monetary considerations and developing the topic entirely in Keynesian terms. Part 3 adds money as a determinant of spending, but does not yet allow for alternative assets. Again we look at output and the role of relative prices, but now we have the added complication of a monetary adjustment process.

Parts 4 and 5 add alternative financial assets and thus bring into the analysis interest rates, international capital mobility, and exchange-rate expectations. In part 4 a first approach develops these topics in an extension of IS-LM macroeconomics. Part 5 goes further by incorporating the link between the current account, changes in wealth, and the resulting adjustment in asset yields and aggregate spending.

What are the main themes? Chapter 2 discusses identities that turn out to be central to open economy macroeconomics. Among these we find the relation between the current account and the change in net foreign assets, as well as the relation among changes in money, credit, and the balance of payments. A last link is that between the current account, saving, investment, and the government budget. Because these relations are identities, derived from budget constraints or balance sheets, they are the uncontroversial and general tools that we use all along our way.

Part 2 introduces income determination and the role of relative prices. Chapter 3 opens the topic of income determination, developing the foreign trade multiplier, repercussion effects, and an analysis of macroeconomic interdependence. The foreign trade multiplier, derived here, remains one of the cornerstones of open economy macroeconomics because of the demonstrably large cyclical influence on the balance of trade.

Chapters 4 through 6 extend the model by bringing relative prices into play. Three questions are relevant here: First, which are the relative prices we are interested in? We look in chapter 4 at the terms of trade or the relative price of exportables in terms of importables. In chapters 5 and 6 the menu is increased to allow for intermediate goods and nontraded goods.

The second question is how relative prices can be changed. Here commercial policies are discussed—tariffs, export subsidies, or quotas—as well as exchange depreciation. A central issue, in this context, is the ability of exchange depreciation to change the terms of trade or competitiveness. The analysis leads naturally to the issue of real-wage resistance.

The third question concerns the channels through which a relative price change affects demand, output, and the balance of trade. The important distinction between income and substitution effects is drawn, and we see that income effects are the source of stability problems. The concepts of internal and external balance are developed in these chapters, in which it is shown that adjustment to disequilibrium generally requires both a change in absorption and a change in relative prices.

Only in part 3 does money enter the discussion. Until this point aggregate spending was a function only of income. Now money is introduced as a determinant of aggregate spending and thus of the external balance. Chapter 7 presents a monetary economy on the assumption of constant relative prices.

Modeling the Open Economy

Within that framework, the monetary adjustment process is developed for the case of fixed exchange rates. The further analysis addresses the question whether relative prices will change in the adjustment process. The crucial conceptual framework here is the analogy to the transfer problem.

Chapter 8 moves to a more complete model of the real side by drawing on Ricardian trade and payments theory. In a many-commodity model one of the variables to be determined by the interaction of real and monetary factors is the competitive margin between exportables and importables. The same model is used to study the effect of changes in aggregate demand on relative price levels and the implications of alternative exchange-rate regimes for the transmission of external shocks. The chapter serves as a demonstration that quite rich models of the real side can readily be integrated into a macroeconomic model in order to make an endogenous determination of a host of variables, from relative wages to the competitive margin, that are not typically part of one and the same model. In providing this integration, chapter 8 draws together much of the earlier analysis.

The concluding chapter of this part offers two very different models of money, exchange rates, and stabilization policy. In chapter 9 we demonstrate the conventional case for managed money and managed exchange rates for an economy in which wages are slow to adjust. Monetary and exchange-rate flexibility are a means for achieving real-wage flexibility and full employment. An alternative approach to the question of stabilization policy asks whether accommodating monetary and fiscal policies, while stabilizing output, tend to destabilize prices.

The question is posed in the context of Fischer-Taylor long-term overlapping wage contracts with rational expectations. It is shown that accommodating monetary policy and exchange-rate rules that tend to validate price disturbances do indeed destabilize prices. There is thus a trade-off between the stability of relative prices and that of output.

Part 4 focuses on the international integration of capital markets and the implied limitations or potential of stabilization policy. Chapter 10 opens the discussion with a careful definition of capital mobility and asset market equilibrium. Within the context of fixed exchange rates we develop the implications of asset market intervention when securities are alternatively traded in the world market or are nontraded. Chapter 10 concludes with an analysis of the determinants of capital mobility and sterilization possibilities.

Chapter 11 turns to flexible exchange rates. The essential feature of flexible rates is the exogeneity of money. The Mundell-Fleming model, which is developed here, shows the effectiveness of monetary policy and the crowding out induced by fiscal expansion. Interestingly, the crowding out takes the form of a current account deterioration. Exchange-rate expectations are then introduced as an important modification of the model. The case of rational expectations is developed along with the exchange-rate dynamics, which involves an overshooting in the adjustment process to a monetary expansion.

Fixed and flexible rates are diametrically opposed cases in the assumptions that are made about exchange market intervention and the money stock. The mixed case of a managed float is addressed in chapter 12. This chapter integrates the earlier chapters by offering a flexible structure: the degree of capital mobility that can be less than infinite and exchange-rate policy, through intervention, can vary from fixed to flexible rates. The model is applied to the issue of inflation stabilization and the problem of monetary control. The link among exchange depreciation, interest differentials, capital flows, intervention, and money creation is the cornerstone of this model. Clearly, these linkages have been at the center of exchange-market turbulence over the last few years and are well worth studying.

The book concludes in part 5 with dynamic considerations introduced by current account imbalance. Up to this point we have neglected the fact that current account imbalance involves changes in net foreign assets, in wealth, in asset demands, and in aggregate spending. These considerations are introduced in the last two chapters. Chapter 13 shows that the current account implies changes in wealth that affect real-money demand, equilibrium prices, and the exchange rate. It explores the adjustment process under rational expectations to anticipated and unanticipated disturbances. The important point involved is the way in which expectations affect the real equilibrium.

Chapter 14 illustrates a small general equilibrium model that brings together external asset accumulation through the current account with investment and physical capital accumulation. The framework illustrates the portfolio approach to exchange-rate determination.

A number of topics in international monetary economics are not covered in this book. The social cost of foreign exchange, the demand for international reserves, Euro-dollars, or optimal external borrowing—to name only a few issues—and the much broader range of topics dealing with the international monetary system are never addressed. Space, comparative advantage, and homogeneity were among the main reasons for excluding these topics. Our aim has been to unify a good part of the field rather than to write an operating manual.

REFERENCES AND SUGGESTED READING

Black, S. 1973. *International money markets under flexible exchange rates.* Studies in international finance. Princeton: Princeton University Press.

Caves, R. and Johnson, H.G., eds. 1968. *Readings in international economics.* Illinois: Richard D. Irwin.

Haberler, G. 1961. *A Survey of international trade theory.* Special papers in international economics. Princeton: Princeton University Press.

Laursen, S. and Metzler, L.A. 1950. Flexible exchange rates and the theory of employment. *Review of economics and statistics.* 32:251-299.

Meade, J.E. 1951. *The balance of payments.* Oxford: Oxford University Press.

Metzler, L.A. 1972. *Collected papers.* Cambridge: Harvard University Press.

Mundell, R.A. 1968. *International economics.* New York: Macmillan Publishing Co.

Mundell, R.A. 1971. *Monetary theory.* Santa Monica: Goodyear Publishing Co., Pacific Palisades.

Some Basic Relations

In this chapter we introduce the subject of macroeconomics in the open economy by investigating a few key relations and concepts. We begin with a sketch of the balance of payments accounts. Next we turn to national income accounting in the open economy. The chapter concludes with the relation among the balance of payments, credit creation by the banking system, and the budget. The topics are chosen because they provide us with a basic set of identities that serves as a frame of reference for subsequent models. They also bring up some of the interesting issues of policy and analysis with which this book is concerned.

I. BALANCE OF PAYMENTS ACCOUNTS

The balance of payments records economic transactions between residents of the home country and the rest of the world. The relevant transactions include trade in goods and services, transfer payments, and transactions in assets. They include private as well as official transactions.

Some Basic Relations

Table 2-1 shows the typical presentation of the balance of payments accounts. A distinction is made between transactions on *current account*—transactions arising from the sale or purchase of goods and services as well as unilateral payments—and asset transactions or transactions on *capital account*. Among the latter a distinction is frequently made between long- and short-term capital transactions, depending on whether the maturity of the assets exceeds or falls short of a year. An alternative distinction on capital account is between portfolio investment and direct investment. For the present the distinctions are inconsequential, and we retain simply the concept of capital account transactions arising from trade in assets.

Table 2-1 shows only three balances—the current account, the capital account, and the *official settlements balance.* Official settlements balance denotes the monetary authorities' (central bank, treasury, or exchange

TABLE 2-1

U.S. Balance of Payments
(billions of U.S. dollars)

	1975	1976	1977	1978
Current account	$ 22.3	$ 9.0	$ −9.9	$ −9.2
Capital account	−26.7	−19.5	−25.1	−22.4
Official settlements	4.5	10.5	35.0	31.7

SOURCE: IMF *Annual Report*, 1979.

equalization account) *financing* of the external imbalance. If on current and capital account combined there is a deficit, we have an excess demand for foreign currency to effect payments of the *net* purchases of goods, services, and assets. Under fixed exchange rates or dirty floating, as we shall see later, the central bank will intervene in the foreign exchange market in order to prevent a currency depreciation in response to the excess demand. Conversely, if on current and capital account combined we have a surplus, the central bank intervenes to buy foreign exchange to avoid the appreciation of the home currency.

The official settlements balance shows the extent of the intervention by the exchange authorities. Table 2-1 shows us that official settlements precisely match the imbalance on current and capital account. The balance of payments, including official settlements, thus sums to zero. Equivalently, if on current and capital account there is a *net* purchase of foreign goods, services, and assets, how do we pay for it? The exchange authorities must *finance* the imbalance through use of exchange reserves—the central bank's holdings of foreign currency—or through official borrowing abroad.

The accounts in Table 2-1 show a curent-account surplus in 1975 and 1976 and deficits in the ensuing years. The capital account is in deficit all four years, showing a net rate of purchases of foreign assets. All four years show an overall deficit, leading to official financing of the deficit. A positive official settlements balance is thus the counterpart of a deficit on current and capital account.

In order to understand the role of official settlements, we take the example of 1978. Here the United States had a deficit on current account of $9 billion. The capital account showed a deficit of $22 billion. Hence, net purchases of goods, services, and assets led to an overall deficit of $32 billion, or *net* liabilities in foreign currency of $32 billion. How was that excess demand for foreign currency accommodated? It was accommodated through "official settlements." Foreign central banks acquired claims on the United States equal to $32 billion, purchasing these claims by issuing in return the foreign exchange that was in excess demand.

With this interpretation we can look at the sum of the current account and the capital account, including errors and omissions, as the balance of payments surplus or deficit. In practical terms that means the domestic or foreign central banks intervene in the foreign exchange market. If the home country has a deficit, which would tend to depreciate the domestic currency, intervention would amount to buying dollars and selling foreign exchange. The central banks that buy the dollars and sell foreign exchange thus acquire claims on the United States, thereby increasing our "liabilities to foreign official holders." If there were no such intervention, then current-account and capital-account transactions would have to balance.

Table 2-2 presents a more disaggregated view of the external balance, introducing distinctions within each of the broad accounts. Within the current account we distinguish between the merchandise trade balance and the category services and private transfers. An export of goods or services or the receipt of a transfer is treated as a credit item; the converse is true for an import of goods or services or a transfer payment. Services here include not only such items as tourist receipts and receipts of royalties, but also the income on net foreign assets owned by domestic residents and the net service payments on external debt. On capital account we show as main categories long-term capital, including official transfers, and a residual category including short-term capital flows and statistical errors.

Within the official settlements balance we distinguish two ways of financing the imbalance: the use of reserve holdings and increases in liabilities to foreign official agencies, including the International Monetary Fund (IMF). How do we account financial transactions? A net purchase of foreign assets

TABLE 2-2

U.S. Balance of Payments
(billions of U.S. dollars)

	1975	1976	1977	1978
Current Account				
Trade balance	$ 9.1	$ −9.3	$−30.9	$−34.2
Services and private transfers	13.3	18.3	20.9	25.0
Capital Account				
Long-term capital	−23.7	−19.5	−17.6	−22.4
Other	−3.0	0.2	−7.5	−6.3
Official Settlements				
Increase in liabilities to				
foreign official agencies	5.3	13.1	35.4	30.9
Change in reserve assets	0.8	2.6	0.4	−0.8

NOTE: Long-term capital flows include official transfers; other capital accounts include statistical errors and omissions.
SOURCE: IMF *Annual Report,* 1979.

or a *capital outflow* is treated as a debit item on capital account. Conversely, net purchases of domestic assets by the rest of the world are a capital inflow or a credit item. Within official settlements we treat an increase in our liabilities to foreign official holders—their buying claims on us—like a capital inflow and record it as a credit item. Conversely, our adding to reserves is an increase in our claims on the rest of the world or a capital outflow and is therefore treated as a debit item.

There has been considerable debate in the postwar period over the proper definition of balance of payments *deficits* and the presentation of the balance of payments accounts. The discussion centers on the following question. Which transactions should be viewed as autonomous and which should be thought of as accommodating?* Clearly there is no question that central bank changes in reserves are transactions designed to finance a deficit. The same effect, however, might be achieved through an interest rate policy that causes commercial banks to borrow abroad, leading to a private capital inflow. In the latter case our presentation in Table 2-2 would be misleading, as it implicitly counts *all* transactions other than changes in reserves and changes in liabilities to official holders as autonomous or "above the line." Pursuing this line of reasoning, it has been argued that short-term private capital flows respond largely to the state of the balance of payments. This

*For a discussion of these issues, see Department of Commerce (1976) and Stern *et al.* (1977).

type of transaction might be set apart from other transactions, to be included along with official settlements as a financing item. It is immediately clear that the same argument can be made for long-term borrowing abroad by the public sector, or, indeed, for certain current-account transactions. There is no satisfactory dividing line between autonomous and accommodating transactions, and we therefore stay with the (unsatisfactory) classification of Table 2-2.

In Table 2-3 we pursue the question of balance of payments imbalance or changes in net external asset positions. Table 2-3 shows how the United

TABLE 2-3

International Investment Position
of the United States
(billions of U.S. dollars)

	1970	1975	1977
Net Position of the U.S.	$ 58.6	$ 73.9	$ 70.0
U.S. Assets Abroad	165.5	295.1	381.3
U.S. official assets	46.6	58.0	68.3
U.S. private assets	118.8	237.1	312.4
Direct investment	75.5	124.1	148.8
Securities and claims	43.3	113.0	163.7
Foreign Assets in the U.S.	106.8	221.2	311.3
Foreign official assets	26.1	87.6	143.1
Foreign private assets	80.7	133.6	168.2
Direct investment	13.3	27.7	34.1
Securities and claims	67.4	106.5	134.1

NOTE: Direct investment is reported at book value. Securities and claims include bonds, corporate stock holdings as well as claims by banks and nonbank lenders.
SOURCE: *Economic Report of the President*, 1979.

States asset position has evolved over time; as well as the distribution of assets and liabilities between private and official agencies and among types of securities. At first glance, we see from·the top line that the United States remains a net creditor, but that the net creditor position has been declining. The U.S. private sector is a net external creditor vis à vis the foreign private sector, while the U.S. official sector is a net debtor vis à vis the foreign official sector. We note that the rapidly increasing foreign official assets reflect U. S. deficits. It is also worth noting that the U. S. private sector is a net direct investor by a substantial margin, while for portfolio investment the accounts are more nearly balanced.

II. WORLD PAYMENT PATTERNS

In this section we show an application of the balance of payments accounts in studying world payments patterns. Table 2-4 reports the current-account balance and its components for several groups of countries. We distinguish here the OECD countries, which have the common characteristic of being industrialized and developed, from OPEC countries (the Organization of Petroleum Exporting Countries) and non-oil-producing developing countries. Table 2-4 supports two sets of observations. The first concerns the structure of the external balance between rich and poor countries, or developed and developing countries, while the other relates to the impact of the oil shock on the external balance.

Consider first the external balance of non-oil-producing developing countries. Throughout the 1970s there were deficits on trade account, on services including private transfers, and on current account. Official transfers in the form of aid were insufficient to cover the net imports of goods and services by this group of countries. Accordingly, they were running a current-account deficit (including official transfers) financed by external borrowing. The continuing deficit of the developing countries has a counterpart in the current-account surpluses of OPEC and the OECD countries combined. OPEC countries invariably run surpluses, as their oil export revenue currently more than compensates for imports of goods and services. OECD countries run current-account surpluses some of the time, but the oil shock has introduced a tendency for deficits. Statistical problems apart, however, the sum of deficits must be zero.

An interesting fact brought out in Table 2-4 is that although the trade and current balance of OECD countries varies between deficits and surpluses, the service balance always shows a surplus. This reflects the fact that service income, particularly income from foreign assets, is relatively stable throughout the business cycle compared with merchandise trade. On service account the OECD countries ran a surplus, because they are net creditors to the rest of the world. They are also, of course, relatively specialized in the production of such services as transport, insurance, and technology.

We turn next to the impact of the oil shock on the external balance position of different groups. It is immediately apparent from Table 2-4 that in 1973-1974 the OPEC surplus increased substantially in response to the higher oil prices, given inelastic world demand. The trade surplus of OPEC rose from $10 billion in 1972 to $77 billion in 1974. The counterpart of the

TABLE 2-4

World Payment Patterns
(billions of U.S. dollars)

	1972	1973	1974	1975	1976	1977	1978	1979
Trade balance								
OECD	$ 9.2	$ 8.2	$−26.2	$ 5.5	$−17.6	$−23.1	$ 5.1	$−34.5
OPEC	10.0	21.5	77.1	49.4	65.0	61.5	43.0	104.0
Non-oil-producing developing countries	−6.5	−7.5	−23.5	−38.5	−25.0	−23.5	−36.5	−47.0
Services and private transfers, net								
OECD	6.0	10.0	9.4	6.8	11.5	11.5	19.7	27.5
OPEC	−8.3	−12.5	−15.1	−19.3	−25.9	−30.1	−35.1	−35.0
Non-oil-producing developing countries	−3.7	−4.7	−8.2	−9.0	−9.5	−9.0	−10.5	−16.0
Current balance								
OECD	7.8	9.9	−27.5	−0.3	−19.1	−26.3	6.4	−31.5
OPEC	1.3	7.7	59.5	27.1	36.6	29.1	5.9	75.5
Non-oil-producing developing countries	−5.2	−6.2	−23.3	−37.5	−25.5	−23.0	−35.0	−60.0

SOURCE: OECD *Economic Outlook*, July 1979 and December 1979.

OPEC surplus in 1974 was a large trade deficit for the OECD and developing countries. Taking into account transfers, we find that the OECD current balance turned by almost $37 billion from 1973 to 1974. The deficit of the developing countries rose by nearly $15 billion. The oil shock clearly exerted a major impact on the pattern of net trade receipts.

In Table 2-5 we pursue that question further by asking how the developing countires financed their current-account deficit. In passing, we note the difference in accounting conventions of the OECD and the IMF, which give a discrepancy in the current-account balances between Tables 2-4 and 2-5. Table 2-5 shows the current-account deficit excluding official transfers.

We distinguish here four sources of finance: (1) official aid or transfers, (2) direct investment, (3) reserve use, and (4) borrowing. The first is self-explanatory, and the extent of these transfers has been substantial. The second source of finance is foreign direct investment in developing countries. Table 2-5 shows that this source has been stable in dollar terms and is relatively insignificant, on the order of $6 billion. Next we look at external borrowing to finance the current account. Table 2-5 shows the substantial flows through official loans and loans from banks or suppliers. Finally, we note reserve use as a way of financing the current balance deficit. Here the striking

TABLE 2-5

Non-Oil-Producing Developing Countries: Current Account Financing, 1973-1978
(billions of U.S. dollars)

	1973	1974	1975	1976	1977	1978
Current account deficit	$11.3	$30.4	$38.0	$25.5	$21.2	$31.3
Financing through transactions that do not affect net debt positions	8.4	10.9	11.2	10.6	11.9	13.0
Net unrequited transfers received	4.2	6.2	6.2	5.8	6.7	7.0
Direct investment flows, net	4.2	4.7	4.9	4.8	5.2	6.0
Net borrowing and use of reserves	2.9	19.5	26.8	14.9	9.3	18.3
Reduction of reserve assets (accumulation, −)	−7.7	−2.9	−0.7	−11.3	−11.7	−12.5
Net external borrowing	10.6	22.4	27.5	26.2	21.0	30.8

SOURCE: IMF, *Annual Report*, 1979.

fact is that rather than draw down their reserves to finance their deficits, the developing countries have borrowed abroad to add to their reserves at a rate of nearly $12 billion over 1976-1978.

III. NATIONAL INCOME ACCOUNTING IN THE OPEN ECONOMY

We turn now from the balance of payments accounts to national income accounting in the open economy. Three important points are to be developed. The first concerns an extension of the national income accounting identity

$$Y \equiv C + I + G \tag{1}$$

to recognize the openness of the economy. The second point concerns the distinction between GNP and GDP—gross national product and gross domestic product, respectively. The third point, and by far the most important, deals with sectoral balances, or the relation that governs the current account, the government budget, and the private sector saving-investment balance. This relation is the cornerstone of modern balance of payments theory.

1. National Income Identity

In (1) the *national income identity* states that in a closed economy the value of output produced is equal to the disposition of output in terms of consumption, investment and government absorption of goods. The statement is an identity because it includes actual consumption, investment, and government absorption, rather than the planned values. Thus if there were an excess supply we would reckon it as an involuntary inventory accumulation. In terms of actual magnitudes, the identity merely states that all output is allocated to one or the other type of absorption.

In the open economy we must recognize that consumption, investment, and government spending are the spending on *all* goods, not only domestically produced goods. Accordingly, we are obliged to change the identity by subtracting the import component from $C+I+G$ to arrive at the absorption of *domestic* goods by domestic residents. There is also an additional source of demand for domestic output—exports. Exports have to be added as a source of demand. Hence we have

$$Y \equiv C + I + G + (X - M) \tag{2}$$

This is our revised form of the national income identity and includes *net exports X − M* as a component of demand for domestic goods.

We can restate the identity in (2) by emphasizing not the components of demand, but rather their sum, *aggregate spending by domestic residents*. For that purpose, total spending or absorption by domestic residents E is defined as

$$E \equiv C + I + G \tag{3}$$

and thus, using (3) in (2):

$$Y \equiv E + (X - M) \tag{2a}$$

In the form of (2a) the identity states that income is equal to aggregate spending by domestic residents E plus net exports. The notion of aggregate spending by domestic residents will be a convenient concept whenever we are not concerned about the composition of demand. We shall in most of this book use this concept rather than the components of demand.

To recapitulate the lesson of this section: we have a revised statement of the national income identity. Income in an open economy is equal to aggregate spending by domestic residents plus net exports. Aggregate spending and net exports in this context are understood to be actual magnitudes; hence we have an identity.

2. GNP and GDP

We briefly introduce here the distinction between gross national and gross domestic product. The distinction corresponds to that between the income received for productive activity by domestic residents (GNP) and the value of output domestically produced (GDP). The difference between the two magnitudes arises from net factor payments from abroad. Net factor payments from abroad correspond primarily to income from capital (interest and dividends) and to labor income accruing to domestic residents from abroad.

With this distinction in mind we can look back at identity (2a) and interpret it as an identity pertaining to GDP, provided that net exports $X - M$ represent only goods and services other than factor payments. Alternatively, with the interpretation of GNP on the left-hand side we treat net exports as inclusive of net factor receipts from abroad, so that it is equal to the balance on goods and services in terms of the balance of payments accounts.

How important is the distinction between GNP and GDP in practice? The distinction is important in all those cases where a significant part of output is produced with the help of external factors, that is where either capital or labor services from abroad are used on an extensive scale. Table 2-6 shows the ratio of net factor receipts to GNP for a number of countries.

TABLE 2-6

Net Factor Receipts from Abroad as a Percentage of GNP
(percent)

Borrowing or Lending Country	1970	1976	1978
Germany	0.0	0.2	0.3
United States	0.5	0.8	1.0
Portugal	0.5	−0.1	−1.8
Switzerland	3.5	3.4	3.8
Brazil	−0.9	−1.4	−1.9
Israel	−1.7	−3.5	−3.3
Pakistan	0.0	2.2	6.2

SOURCE: IMF *International Financial Statistics,* September 1979.

Table 2-6 shows the diversity of borrowing countries such as Brazil or Israel, which have a substantial external debt service liability, and lending countries, Germany or Switzerland, which have an important external source of income. The United States, as a net external creditor, shows positive net factor receipts from abroad, although the magnitude of these receipts is not substantial. An interesting case is that of Germany, whose net external credit position gives rise to factor receipts for capital, but whose extensive use of *Gastarbeiter* leads to a roughly offsetting payment of external labor services. Portugal represents the mirror image, an exporter of labor services with a growing external debt service. Pakistan has become a major exporter of labor services to the oil producing countries.

In much of this book we will ignore the distinction between GNP and GDP. Only when we come to questions of external asset accumulation will that distinction again be central. Meantime, we use the terms GNP and GDP interchangeably as if there were no net external factor receipts.

3. Sectoral Balances

We return now to equation (2a) to present the national income identity in terms of sectoral balances.

$$Y - E \equiv X - M \tag{2b}$$

In this first presentation net exports appear as *identically* equal to the excess of national income over aggregate spending by domestic residents, including the government. This is a very important statement because it directs our attention to the macroeconomic nature of external imbalance; namely, that net exports imply that spending falls short of income, whereas an excess of imports over exports implies that spending exceeds income. This perspective is important because it suggests that external balance problems *must* have a macroeconomic aspect and that their cure *must* include means whereby the balance between income and spending can be restored.

Consider next an alternative statement of (2) which we derive by subtracting net taxes T (taxes less domestic transfers) from both sides and adding net international transfer receipts R to both sides:

$$Y + R - T \equiv C + I + (G - T) + (X + R - M) \tag{4}$$

The left-hand term now measures disposable income of domestic residents.*

*Throughout, we are aggregating the household and corporate sector.

Some Basic Relations

On the right-hand side we find in addition to consumption and investment the government budget deficit $G - T$ and the current-account surplus $X + R - M$. Using the definition of saving, $S \equiv Y + R - T - C$, we arrive at our central identity:

$$X + R - M \equiv S - I + (T - G) \tag{4a}$$

In (4a) the current-account surplus is *identically* equal to the excess of private sector savings over investment plus the budget surplus. Whereas (2b) showed that an external surplus implies an excess of income over spending for the economy in the aggregate, the same statement is disaggregated in (4a) into the sector saving-investment balances. An external surplus requires that either the private sector saves more than it invests or that the government collects more in net taxes than it spends. In this perspective a deficit on current account implies insufficient saving relative to investment and government spending.

Table 2-7 shows the sectoral balances for the United States for selected years. The term *net foreign investment* is conceptually equivalent to the current-account surplus although differences between balance of payments accounting practices and those applying to national income accounting leave the actual values to differ. Table 2-7 shows that the private sector saving-investment balance, as well as the budget surplus, show substantial cyclical variation. Thus in 1975, for example, the sharp recession implies a low level of investments without a corresponding decline in saving. The public sector has a large deficit, but the net is still an external surplus. By contrast, although investment in 1978 is high relative to saving and the consolidated budget of the public sector is nearly in balance, a substantial external deficit remains.

TABLE 2-7

Sectoral Balances
(billions of U.S. dollars)

Year	$S - I$	$T - G$	Net Foreign Investment	Statistical Discrepancy
1969	$ −9.4	$ 10.7	$ −2.0	$−3.3
1973	−9.5	6.3	−0.6	1.7
1975	68.9	−64.4	11.9	4.2
1977	−7.0	−18.6	−20.9	4.7
1978	−24.1	−1.5	−24.8	0.9

SOURCE: *Economic Report of the President,* 1979.

23

Equation (4a) and Table 2-7 suggest a further point: there is no sense in which we can single out any one of the sectoral balances, say the current account, as being determined by the other two. The fact that they add to zero imposes consistency requirements and provides information convenience, but generally the three balances are all simultaneously determined by the general equilibrium of income and price determination.

The term net foreign investment in Table 2-7 points to an important aspect of the current account—we shall use these terms interchangeably from now on—that we have not yet mentioned: the current account indicates the rate at which the economy in the aggregate is adding to its net external assets. If we spend less than our income, we are building up claims on the rest of the world. In terms of balance of payments concepts, the current-account surplus equals the overall surplus less the capital-account surplus. Equivalently, it equals the increase in net official assets plus the rate of capital outflow or the rate of increase of private claims on the rest of the world:*

$$CA \equiv \Delta NFA \qquad (5)$$

where CA denotes the current-account surplus and ΔNFA denotes the change in our *net foreign assets*. Substituting now from (4a) and noting the equivalence of net foreign investment (the term used in national income accounts) and the current-account surplus (the term used in balance of payments terminology), we have

$$S - I + T - G \equiv \Delta NFA \qquad (6)$$

Identity (6) links net saving to asset acquisition. We now have the statement that the private sector net saving $S - I$ plus public sector saving, $T - G$ equals our acquisition of claims on the rest of the world. Suppose, for example, that saving equals investment for the private sector. The budget surplus is externally financed through an increase in net claims on the rest of the world.

What form could this increase in claims take? One possibility is a reduction in the external public debt. Another would be an increase in official reserves. We might also have the case where net private foreign assets increase—although saving equals investment—with no change in official net foreign assets. On the domestic scene that would imply a reduction in public sector debt held by the private sector, as we shall see in the following section.

*For the purposes of this discussion, we neglect changes in the value of existing holdings of net foreign assets. Even if the current account were in balance, we could increase our external holdings if the prices of our existing assets rose.

IV. MONEY ACCOUNTING

We shall wind up our discussion of accounting relations by looking at the relation between the balance of payments and the financial system. We start off with a simple model that focuses on both the central bank's balance sheet and the relation between the stock of high-powered money and the balance of payments. We then extend the analysis to cover the entire banking system, public sector financing, and private sector indebtedness.

In identity (6) we have introduced the change in net foreign assets of the entire country ΔNFA. There we aggregate all sectors, the central bank, commercial banks, the treasury, and the nonbank private sector. Our focus shifts now to questions of money, credit, and deficit finance. For that purpose we have to disaggregate. We first introduce the change in the central bank's (cb) net foreign assets ΔNFA^{cb}, as a particular component of the total change in the net foreign assets.

1. The Balance of Payments and the Monetary Base

Table 2-8 shows the balance sheet of the monetary authorities. For our purposes we consolidate the central bank and the exchange stabilization

TABLE 2-8

Monetary Authorities' Balance Sheet

Assets	Liabilities
Net foreign assets	–
Domestic credit	High-powered money

authorities. The assets are net foreign assets NFA^{cb} and domestic credit DC. The former includes reserves less liabilities to foreign official holders. The latter includes loans to the government and to commercial banks. (In the United States, domestic credit on the Federal Reserve balance sheet is called Federal Reserve Credit Outstanding.) The liability side of the balance sheet shows high-powered money, H.

Using the balance sheet identity:

$$NFA^{cb} + DC \equiv H \tag{7}$$

we have a relation between the official settlements balance, domestic credit creation, and high-powered money creation:

$$\Delta NFA^{cb} \equiv \Delta H - \Delta DC \tag{7a}$$

The identity in (7a) shows that the change in net reserves of the monetary authorities is equal to the excess of money creation over domestic credit creation. The framework, although still rather simple, does suggest approaches whereby external deficits or reserve losses can be controlled. To avoid a deficit, domestic credit creation has to be held in line with the growth in high-powered money. A framework such as (7a) or its more extended version presented below underlies the balance of payments stabilization programs conducted by the IMF.

In a setting of external imbalance a first question would be how much external financing ΔNFA is available for a given period. A second step is to predict from inflation and real growth the growth in demand for nominal high-powered money ΔH. The residual then is the expansion in domestic credit ΔDC compatible with these constraints and projections. To make the program come through the typical procedure is to impose *domestic credit ceilings* that will ensure that the central bank does not prejudice the external balance targets by "excessive" financing of government deficits or by loans to the domestic banking system. An exercise, such as the one we just sketched, is referred to as *financial programming* and serves to highlight the central role of accounting identities as tools for consistent macroeconomic planning.*

A second point in our identities deserves immediate recognition. If the central bank intervenes in the foreign exchange market buying or selling foreign exchange, there will be a change in the net foreign asset position and a corresponding change in high-powered money. Suppose there were a tendency for the currency to depreciate and that the central bank steps into the market buying domestic currency and selling foreign exchange that is in excess demand. There will be a reduction in net foreign assets as the central bank draws down foreign exchange reserves, as well as a corresponding reduction in high-powered money, because the central bank sells foreign exchange in return for high-powered money. Accordingly, foreign exchange sales *automatically* reduce the stock of high-powered money outstanding and conversely for purchases of foreign exchange. This point is essential because it indicates an automatic adjustment process for the external balance.

Not entirely "automatic."

*See E.W. Robichek (1967).

Some Basic Relations

In deficit countries the money supply will be contracting, while in surplus countries it expands. [by Eq. (7a).]

Sterilization

There is one way to frustrate this automatic adjustment process—*sterilization*. We observe from (7a) that if the central bank offsets changes in net foreign assets by changes in domestic credit, high-powered money can be held constant even in the face of changes in reserves. Practically speaking, this means that in a deficit country the central bank will sell foreign exchange, thereby reducing domestic high-powered money. The next step is to have an expansionary open market operation or an increase in domestic credit that restores the money stock to its initial level. The net effect, therefore, is an unchanged money stock, reduced net foreign assets, and an increase in domestic credit or central bank lending. This sterilization policy predominates in countries that pursue interest rate or money stock-oriented monetary policies.

2. The Current Account, Credit Creation, and Deficit Finance

In this section we expand our use of balance sheet identities to establish a link between the external balance, the financial sector, and the government budget. A first point is to introduce the *consolidated banking system*—commercial banks and the central bank combined. This is a useful aggregation for monetary questions because the money stock — say M_2 — is the liability of the consolidated banking system. For the combined banking system we write the balance sheet identity:

$$\Delta NFA^b \equiv \Delta M_2 - \Delta DC \tag{8}$$

where NFA^b, M_2, and DC denote the net foreign assets, the M_2 money stock and *total* domestic credit of the banking system to the government, and the nonbank private sector.

This perspective focuses on the banking system's acquisition of external assets as the balance between money expansion and credit expansion. The higher the increase in money relative to the credit expansion, the larger the net foreign asset expansion.

An alternative presentation is particularly useful for countries with underdeveloped capital markets and where the government budget is primarily financed by the banking system. We can write the consolidated banking system's increase in credit as the sum of credit to the government (g) ΔDC^g and the nonbank (nb) public ΔDC^{nb}:

$$\Delta DC \equiv \Delta DG^g + \Delta DC^{nb} \tag{9}$$

27

Using the fact that the government budget deficit is financed by government borrowing from the banking system or abroad, we have

$$G - T \equiv \Delta DC^g - \Delta NFA^g \tag{10}$$

Now using (8) and (10) gives us a particularly useful relation between the banking system's external asset changes and the government deficit finance:

$$\Delta NFA^b \equiv (T - G - \Delta NFA^g) + (\Delta M_2 - \Delta DC^{nb}) \tag{11}$$

Changes in the banking system's net external asset position have as their counterpart either an increased *net* indebtedness of the nonbank public toward the banking system—an increase in credit to the public in excess of a rise in money—or a budget deficit that is financed by the domestic banking system.

There is a very short step from (11) to financial programming. The financial programming would focus on a ceiling on domestic credit expansion to the government and the nonbank public, or equivalently, a reduction in the government budget deficit.

Table 2-9 illustrates identity (11). Here we look at Peru, where by 1978 the deficit in the budget was close to 5 percent of GNP, inflation was upward

TABLE 2-9

Peru – Budget and Net Foreign Assets
(billion soles)

Relations	1976	1977	1978
ΔNFA^b	−57.0	−79.9	−76.3
$T - G$	−48.4	−79.1	−82.6
$T - G - \Delta NFA^g$	−32.8	−44.5	−67.7

SOURCE: IMF *International Financial Statistics*, September 1979.

of 50 percent, the currency was depreciating rapidly, and the economy was responding to financial stabilization with a sharp decline in economic activity. We observe declining net foreign assets or external borrowing of the consolidated banking system. The counterpart is, in substantial measure, a budget deficit that is domestically financed by the banking system. Because the loss in net foreign assets exceeds the domestically financed deficit, it is apparent that the public also increased its net indebtedness to the banking system. This increased indebtedness represented largely increased credit to government enterprises whose deficit was not included in the budget.

V. CONCLUDING REMARKS

This chapter has integrated the openness of the economy into the accounting and balance sheet framework of the economy. Openness makes a difference to income determination because net exports are a component of demand. It makes a difference to sectoral balances because net exports are equal to the budget surplus plus the excess of saving over investment. Finally, looking at assets accumulation, openness enters the picture because the current account is equal to our aggregate acquisition of net foreign assets.

Important links between the monetary sector and the external balance arise from the exchange market functions of the central bank. In this regard we found that the balance of payments equals the excess of high-powered money creation over central bank credit expansion. For the consolidated banking system we found a link that ties deficit finance of the budget, private sector borrowing, and the banking system's change in net foreign assets.

Each of these relationships is an identity. As yet none tells us what determines what. The next step is to fill in this gap by looking at theoretical models of income determination, relative prices, and financial structure. These complete models, together with the accounting relations developed here, will permit us to interpret economic events and think about policy choices.

REFERENCES AND SUGGESTED READINGS

Dornbusch, R., and Fischer, S. 1978. *Macroeconomics,* New York: McGraw-Hill Book Co.

Robichek, E. W. 1967. Financial programming exercises of the international monetary fund in Latin America. International Monetary Fund.

Stern, R. M., Schwartz, C. F., Triffin, R., Bernstein, E. M., and Lederer, W. 1977. *The presentation of the U.S. balance of payments: a symposium.* Essays in international finance, no. 123. Princeton.

U.S. Department of Commerce. 1976. Report of the advisory committee on the presentation of balance of payments statistics. Survey of current business: 18-27.

Part 2

Employment,

the Trade Balance,

and Relative Prices

Income Determination and the Trade Balance

In this chapter we develop an initial approach to income determination and the trade balance in an open economy. Our framework of analysis will be highly simplified. We assume a country that is small in the sense that its import prices are given in world markets and independent of the level of imports. With a fixed exchange rate, domestic prices of imports are fixed as well. The second simplifying assumption is that, because of unemployment, prices of our goods are given. Output is a function of demand. The merit of making these assumptions is that we analyze income determination first, and then go on to examine how relative prices are determined.

The third assumption concerns world demand for our exports, which we take as given. Export demand in general depends on the relative price of our goods compared to competing goods in the rest of the world and on foreign income. Here we first assume that changes in the home country, particularly in the level of our imports, are sufficiently negligible with respect to the level of foreign income so that repercussion effects can be ignored. (These repercussion effects are considered later in this chapter.) By assumption, relative prices are given. Finally, we abstract from assets market considerations and assume that our level of spending depends only on income.

In summary, our model will assume given prices, domestic output to be determined by demand, and a given level of world demand for our exports. In section I we will show the determination of equilibrium output and the associated trade balance. In section II we proceed to some comparative static exercises. The problem of repercussion effects is addressed in section III. The chapter concludes with a discussion of interdependence.

I. EQUILIBRIUM OUTPUT AND THE TRADE BALANCE

Output in our small open economy is demand determined. The demand for our output arises from domestic private spending on domestic goods D, government spending G, and world imports or our exports M^*. (We use the letter M to denote imports and an asterisk to denote a foreign variable. Thus M^* denotes foreign imports or our exports.) In equilibrium, output supplied Y is equal to demand. Thus,

$$Y = D(Y, p) + G + M^*(Y^*, p) \qquad (1)$$

Equation (1) differs, of course, from the identities developed in chapter 2. It differs because here we have behavioral functions on the right-hand side. Specifically, domestic demand D is assumed to depend on income and the given relative price of our goods p. Exports are dependent both on foreign income Y^*, which we take as given and on the relative price. To determine the equilibrium level of income we use the standard 45° diagram of Keynesian income determination in Figure 3-1. The components of demand for domestic output are added (vertically) at each level of income to give us the demand schedule $D + G + M^*$. Demand is an increasing function of the level of domestic output, as higher output and income increase the level

Income Determination and the Trade Balance

FIGURE 3-1

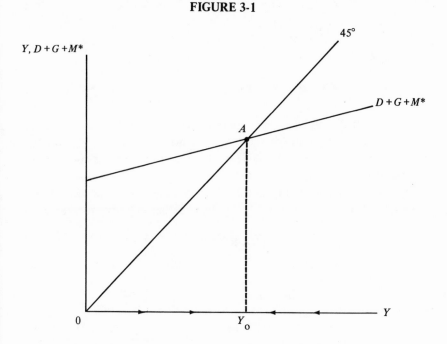

of spending, part of which falls on domestic goods. The slope of the demand schedule is $d \equiv \delta D/\delta Y$, which is positive and less than unity.

The equilibrium level of income is shown by point A, where income equals the amount of spending on domestic goods. At a higher level of output, output will exceed demand and there will be involuntary inventory accumulation. Conversely, at a lower level of output there is excess demand and inventories are run down. With output adjusting to excess demand the economy will converge to point A.

An alternative derivation of the equilibrium level of income emphasizes not the *components* of demand for domestic output, but rather the *level* of spending by domestic residents and net exports or the trade balance. We already defined aggregate spending by domestic residents in chapter 2 as

$$E \equiv C+I+G \equiv D+G+M \qquad (2)$$

In (2) we write the definition of total spending by domestic residents alternatively as the sum of the components of total spending $(C+I+G)$ by sectors, or as the sum of spending on domestic goods $(D+G)$ and imports M. Adding and subtracting imports in (1) allows us to write

35

$$Y = D(Y,p) + M(Y,p) + G + M^*(Y^*,p) - M(Y,p) \qquad (3)$$

$$= E(Y,p,G) + T(Y,Y^*,p)$$

where

$$T = M^* - M = T(Y,Y^*,p) \qquad (4)$$

denotes our trade surplus or net exports.* Equation (3) states that in goods, market equilibrium output is equal to total planned spending by domestic residents plus net exports. Spending by domestic residents E is also referred to as *absorption.*

We can return now to Figure 3-1 to reinterpret the demand schedule for domestic output as total spending adjusted for net exports. An alternative

FIGURE 3-2

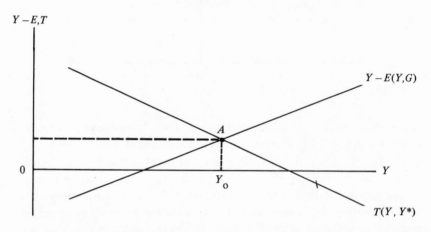

depiction is offered in Figure 3-2. The upward-sloping schedule shows income or output less absorption $Y - E(Y,G)$. With a marginal propensity to spend $1 - s \equiv \delta E/\delta Y$, that is positive and less than unity, an increase in income leads

*In later chapters we will introduce flexibility of relative prices, but we should now pay attention to units of measurment. With imports M measured in terms of physical units of foreign output and M^* measured in units of domestic output we would be adding apples and blankets. So either M must be interpreted as expenditure on imports, measured in terms of domestic output, or we would have to write

$$T = M^* - pM \qquad (4a)$$

where p is the relative price of imports in terms of domestic goods. For the present these points remain innocuous, but they are of substance in later chapters. Here we assume that $p = 1$ by convention and choice of units.

to increased net saving (or net foreign investment, as it is sometimes called). The slope of this schedule thus reflects the marginal propensity to save s.

The negatively sloped schedule in Figure 3-2 shows the trade balance as a function of the level of income. It is drawn for a given level of exports. Increasing income raises imports and worsens the trade balance. The slope of the schedule is given by the negative of the marginal propensity to import: $\delta T/\delta Y \equiv -m$.

Equilibrium income is determined at point A, where the excess of income over spending is equal to the trade surplus. Alternatively, using national income accounting terminology, at point A net foreign investment $Y - E$ is equal to net exports $M^* - M$. The advantage of the latter perspective, as we shall amply see below, is to separate out the total *level* of spending from the *composition* of spending between domestic and foreign goods. Such a separation is helpful when we consider the anatomy and cure of trade and employment problems.

II. COMPARATIVE STATICS

Here we shall draw on the model of income determination to study how various disturbances affect the level of equilibrium output and the balance of trade. In particular we will consider changes in world demand, shifts in domestic expenditure patterns, and changes in domestic saving.

1. An Increase in World Demand

Suppose world demand for our goods increased either because of a shift in foreign expenditure patterns or because of an increase in foreign income. What is the effect on our income and our net exports? In Figure 3-3 we show the increase in exports as an upward shift of the trade balance schedule. At each level of income net exports rise by the increase in world demand. Thus at the initial equilibrium level of income Y_0 we now have an excess demand for goods. Accordingly output expands until we reach point A', where we again have balance between income and spending.

In the new equilibrium at point A' we have an increase in equilibrium income and an improvement in the external balance. Because the vertical shift of the trade balance schedule is equal to the increase in exports ΔM^*, it is apparent that the change in the trade balance at A' is less than the increase in exports. This is so because the induced income expansion raises import spending thereby offsetting, to some extent, the trade balance improvement. The important point, however, is that there is an increase in equilibrium net exports or a trade balance improvement.

Equations (3) and (4) provide us with the system to derive algebraically the relation between export disturbances and the resulting changes in equilibrium income and the trade balance. Differentiating (3) totally and using the definitions of the marginal propensities to save s and import m we have

$$dY/dM^* = 1/(m + s) \tag{5}$$

Equation (5) shows the effect of increased exports on the equilibrium level of income. This is the simple open-economy multiplier. Increased exports will raise equilibrium income more, the larger is the induced spending on domestic goods $d = 1 - s - m$ or the smaller is the marginal propensities to save and import. With high induced spending it takes a larger change in output to generate the excess supply with which to meet increased export demand.

To determine the effect of increased exports on the trade balance we differentiate (4) to obtain

$$dT = dM^* - m\,dY \tag{6}$$

or, using (5)

$$dT/dM^* = 1 - m/(m+s) = s/(s+m) \tag{6a}$$

Increased exports thus improve the trade balance as we saw in Figure 3-3. The extent of the improvement depends on the propensities to save and import. A larger propensity to save—in terms of Figure 3-3 a steeper $Y - E$ schedule—will imply a larger trade balance improvement. A larger propensity to import, on the contrary, implies higher induced import spending, hence a lower trade surplus. This would be shown in Figure 3-3 by a steeper T schedule.

Why does the trade balance improve at all? Is it not possible that the income expansion is sufficiently large to raise import spending beyond the increase in exports leaving us with a net deficit? This is impossible because income will rise only when there is an increase in demand for domestic goods.

FIGURE 3-3

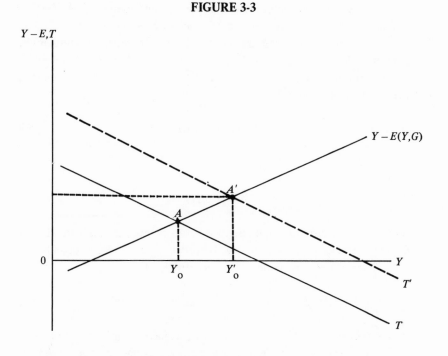

Aggregate spending by domestic residents rises only in response to induced increases in income. Therefore we *must* have an improvement in net exports if we are to sustain the higher level of income.

This gives us our first, firm result. Increased world demand raises equilibrium income and improves the balance of trade. The result is intuitive and simple and remains one of the central facts of open economy macroeconomics, the simplicity of our model notwithstanding.

2. Shifts in Expenditure Patterns

The next disturbance we consider is a shift in demand from imports to domestic goods. We assume that demand shifts so that at each income level import spending will be lower and that the demand, as well as the excess demand, for domestic goods will be correspondingly higher. This case is, of course, also represented by Figure 3-3, in which we now have to interpret the upward shift of the T schedule as arising from reduced import demand. Clearly, just as in the case of increased exports, we have an increase in equilibrium income and an improvement in the external balance. It is important to recognize that a shift in the pattern of spending or in the *composition* of spending between domestic goods and imports has no impact on the *level* of spending. It is for this reason that the $Y - E$ schedule is unaffected.

To determine algebraically the effect of demand shifts on equilibrium income we differentiate the equilibrium condition in (3), noting that we now have an exogenous change in imports $d\overline{M}$ plus induced import changes, depending on changes in income:

$$dY = (1 - s)dY - d\overline{M} - mdY \qquad (7)$$

or

$$dY/d\overline{M} = -1/(s + m) \qquad (7a)$$

Equation (7a) confirms that an autonomous increase in imports, with an offsetting reduction in demand for domestic goods, reduces equilibrium income. The effect on the trade balance is derived in (8):

$$dT/d\overline{M} = -1 - m \, dY/d\overline{M} = -s/(s + m) \qquad (8)$$

The trade-balance adjustment is again dampened by induced changes in income and imports. A shift in demand toward domestic goods improves the trade balance, but by less than the reduction in autonomous imports. Conversely, increased import spending, because it leads to a contraction in domestic income as demand shifts away from our goods, leads to a worsening in the trade balance that falls short of the initial shift.

3. A Reduction in Saving

The third disturbance to be considered is a reduction in saving or increase in aggregate spending. At each level of income absorption now increases. This is shown in Figure 3-4 as a downward shift of the $Y - E$ schedule. But we also have to ask whether this increase in aggregate spending falls on domestic goods or imports, or both.

In Figure 3-4 we show the case where all the spending increase falls on domestic goods. (There is no autonomous change in imports and accordingly no shift of the T schedule.) We see that increased spending raises the equilibrium level of income. Furthermore, as income rises in response to increased spending, this induces more import spending and accordingly worsens the trade balance.

FIGURE 3-4

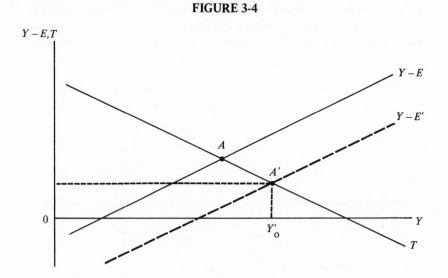

Algebraically we derive the effect on income and the trade balance of an increase in autonomous spending by differentiating (3), where $d\bar{M}/d\bar{E}$ denotes the share of increased autonomous spending that falls on imports

$$dY/d\bar{E} \ = \ [1 - d\bar{M}/d\bar{E}]\,/(s + m) \tag{9}$$

and

$$dT/d\bar{E} \ = \ - \ [s/(s + m)]\ d\bar{M}/d\bar{E} \ - \ m/(s + m) \tag{10}$$

It is apparent from (9) that income will be unaffected if all increased spending falls on imports $(d\bar{M}/d\bar{E} = 1)$ and that in this case the trade balance worsens by the full increase in spending. At the other extreme, if all spending falls on domestic goods, output rises by the normal multiplier and the worsening in the trade balance is only a fraction, $m/(s+m)$, of the increased spending. This is the case shown in Figure 3-4.

4. Internal and External Balance

We briefly introduce in this section the policy issue of internal and external balance that will occupy much of our later analysis. Suppose there is an income level $\bar{Y}$ at which we have full employment, or *internal balance*.

In Figure 3-5 the income level is shown as a vertical line. We also pinpoint an initial situation of underemployment equilibrium A, where the goods market clears and the trade balance is in deficit, giving us an external trade imbalance. The policy issue is how to achieve both internal and external balance simultaneously.

FIGURE 3-5

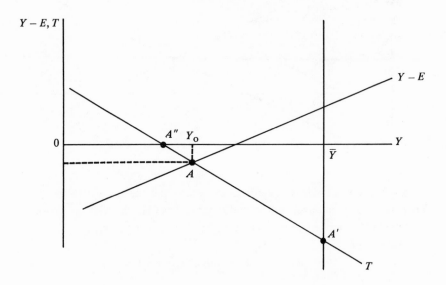

It is apparent that a situation such as the one represented by point A constitutes a dilemma. Suppose we expand the *level* of aggregate demand through an increase in government spending or a cut in taxes, shifting the $Y - E$ schedule down to point A'. Such a policy would clearly move us toward internal balance, because the demand expansion raises income and employment. At the same time, however, the expansion in income will raise imports and worsen the external balance. Conversely, a contraction in demand to point A'' will achieve external balance because income and import spending are reduced, but of course we are also moving further away from full employment.

The situation depicted in Figure 3-5 requires two instruments—one to achieve internal balance by raising demand for domestic goods, and another to prevent the external balance from getting worse. In chapter 4 we will discuss devaluation and tariffs as possible instruments for these purposes.

The issue of a *policy dilemma* does not necessarily arise. We have four possible constellations of internal and external balance problems. Of these four only the cases of deficit/unemployment and the surplus/overemployment present conflicts. The remaining two situations can be handled by general expansion or contraction of demand.

The idea of this section is that external balance considerations place an important constraint on macroeconomic stabilization. Certainly the case of a deficit and unemployment is a common situation where an inadequacy of reserves or financing forces a country to maintain slack in the economy until a gain in competitiveness through deflation has restored external balance. An alternative would be to *finance* the deficit arising from an expansion if, for example, only a transitory decline in exports prevailed.

Dilemmas such as those we have discussed have had an important place in international policy discussions. Deficit countries that find themselves in unemployment situations have urged an expansion on the part of surplus countries so as to have the benefit of increased exports to remedy both the internal and external balance problems. These are the issues we will address in the following sections.

III. REPERCUSSION EFFECTS

In the previous analysis we have dealt with a country that is "small" in the sense that repercussion effects associated with income and import expansion or contraction in that country can be neglected. We expand our framework of analysis now to incorporate these repercussion effects and to look at the simultaneous determination of income in a two-country setting. We will maintain throughout the assumption that relative prices are given and that expenditure levels depend only on income.

1. Determining Equilibrium Incomes

Our model must be expanded now to encompass equilibrium conditions in both countries' goods markets. Equation (3) is repeated here for convenience as the condition of equilibrium in the domestic goods market. Equation (11) is the equilibrium condition in the foreign goods market:

$$Y = E(Y,G) + T(Y,Y^*) \qquad (3)$$

$$Y^* = E^*(Y^*,G^*) - T(Y,Y^*) \qquad (11)$$

Note, opposite signs.

where it is to be remembered that T represents the home country's trade surplus, so that $-T$ in equation (11) is the foreign surplus.

An illustration of our model for determining equilibrium incomes is given in Figure 3-6. The schedule YY shows equilibrium in the domestic goods market and the schedule $Y*Y*$ shows equilibrium in the foreign goods market. It is readily verified that the YY schedule is flatter than the $Y*Y*$ schedule, because

$$\left.\frac{dY}{dY*}\right|_{YY} = \frac{m*}{s+m} < \frac{s*+m*}{m} = \left.\frac{dY}{dY*}\right|_{Y*Y*} \tag{12}$$

where the slopes are derived from (3) and (11), respectively. We next look at the trade balance also shown in Figure 3-6.

Repeating the trade balance shown in equation (4):

$$T = M*(Y*) - M(Y) \tag{4}$$

FIGURE 3-6

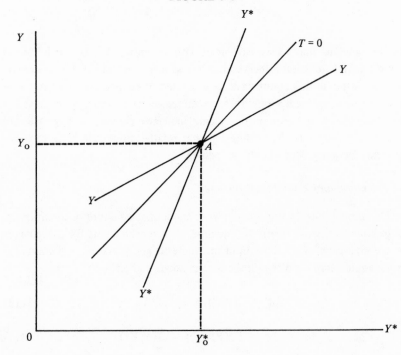

Income Determination and the Trade Balance

the slope of the trade balance equilibrium schedule is given by

$$\frac{dY}{dY^*}\bigg|_{T=0} = m^*/m \tag{13}$$

and is thus intermediate between the YY and Y^*Y^* schedules. Initial equilibrium is assumed to obtain at point A with balanced trade.

2. An Increase in Domestic Spending

We return now to our earlier comparative static questions to assess the limitation of the "small-country assumption." How much difference does it make, and for what questions, to assume away repercussion effects? To study that question we look again at a reduction in saving that falls entirely on domestic goods. In the same way, we can think of it as an increase in government spending on domestic output.

In Figure 3-7 we show that at the initial equilibrium point A the increased

FIGURE 3-7

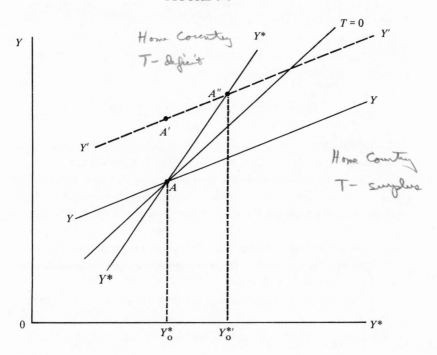

spending implies an excess demand. Our output will have to rise in order to restore equilibrium or foreign output, and therefore foreign demand for our goods, would have to decline to make room for our increased spending. Accordingly, the *YY* schedule shifts up and to the left. (Remember our assumption that the increased spending falls on domestic goods. There is no change in autonomous import spending, and thus neither the $T = 0$ nor the $Y*Y*$ schedule is affected.)

Neglecting repercussion effects amounts to moving from *A* to *A'*, where equilibrium in the domestic goods market is restored, but where foreign output is held constant. Of course *A'* is not an equilibrium point. Our income expansion has raised our demand for foreign goods and there is excess demand leading to a foreign income expansion. The income expansion abroad, in turn, feeds increased demand for our exports and thus a further domestic expansion. These repercussion effects lead to a new equilibrium at point *A"*. Here output in both countries has fully adjusted to world demand.

The importance of repercussion effects can easily be recognized by comparing points *A'* and *A"*. Repercussion effects add to the income expansion. To the small country increased imports appear as a "leakage" from the income flow. The analysis of interdependent income determination developed here shows that in part these increased import expenditures reappear as increased foreign demand for our goods.

We can study these points formally with the help of equations (3) and (11). (See Appendix.) Differentiating the system and assuming an exogenous increase in domestic spending $d\bar{E}$ we have

$$dY/d\bar{E} = 1/[(s+m) - mm*/(s*+m*)] \qquad (14)$$

It is apparent that the multiplier in (14) is larger than that for the small economy. An adjustment term appearing in the denominator arises from the induced import spending per dollar increase in our income *m* times the increase in foreign income that originates as our imports expand $1/(s*+m*)$ times the marginal propensity abroad to spend on our goods as their income rises $m*$. The adjustment term thus reflects that part of induced imports which is recaptured through increased foreign income and spending on our goods. This fact is responsible for increasing our income expansion when repercussion effects are recognized.

The foreign income expansion can be calculated from (3) and (11) to be

$$dY*/d\bar{E} = m/[(s*+m*)(s+m) - mm*] = [m/(m* + s*)] \, dY/d\bar{E} \quad (15)$$

and thus the trade balance worsens by

$$dT/d\overline{E} = -m \ [1 - m^*/(s^*+m^*)]/[(s+m) - mm^*/(s^*+m^*)] \quad (16)$$

which is to be compared with (10) (for $d\overline{M}/d\overline{E} = 0$). It is apparent from (16) and Figure 3-7 that the trade balance must worsen as a consequence of our expansion. But will the foreign induced expansion and increased imports dampen or worsen the deterioration of the balance of trade? It is readily shown that the process of deterioration will be diminished in intensity once repercussion effects are taken into account because the additional income expansion leads to increased saving at home.

The role of repercussion effects can also be directly incorporated in our analysis of either Figure 3-3 or 3-4. All we require is the recognition that foreign demand for our exports depends, indirectly, on *our* income. Our income expansion raises our imports, their income, and consequently their demand for our goods. This positive relation between our income and their import demand implies that the trade balance schedule will be flatter: now a rise in our income not only raises our imports but induces also an export expansion.* Accordingly, a shift in aggregate spending will raise income by more and will worsen the trade balance by less than in the absence of repercussion effects.

3. A Shift in Demand

Let us consider now a shift in spending from domestic goods to imports in the home country. We study that question with a slightly modified presentation of our equilibrium conditions. Rather than using (3) and (11), let us use (3) and the condition that world income equals world spending; or

$$Y + Y^* = E(Y,G) + E^*(Y^*,G^*) \quad (17)$$

which, of course, is equal to the sum of (3) and (11). Equation (17) is shown in Figure 3-8 as the downward-sloping schedule *WW*. Along that schedule world income equals world spending. Points above correspond to a world excess supply of goods, and points below to a world excess demand. Along *YY*, as before, demand is equal to supply for domestic goods. At the equilibrium point *A* both the level and composition of world spending are in equilibrium. We also assume an initially balanced level of trade.

*You will want to show that a rise in our income raises exports by a fraction $m^*m/(s^*+m^*)$ and that the trade balance schedule, whose slope equals $m[m^*/(s^*+m^*)-1]$, is still negatively sloped.

FIGURE 3-8

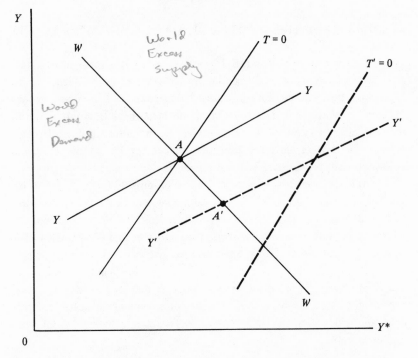

Suppose now a shift in demand from domestic goods to imports. With no change in the world *level* of spending the *WW* schedule is unaffected. But at *A* there is an excess supply of domestic goods and a deficit. To restore domestic goods market equilibrium output would have to decline. The *YY* schedule shifts down by $1/(s+m)$ times the shift in demand. To restore trade balance, given foreign income, our income would have to fall by $1/m$ times the demand shift.

The trade balance schedule also shifts down, but by more than the *YY* schedule. The new equilibrium is shown at point A'. Our income falls and income abroad rises. This is a first, perhaps not surprising, implication of the demand shift. It is worth noting that the foreign income expansion dampens, but does not reverse, the decline in our income.

The second point to note from Figure 3-8 is that our trade balance must worsen. Even though our income falls and the foreign level of income rises, the increased autonomous import spending dominates, leaving us with a net deficit.*

---

*In terms of Figure 3-8 we note that the horizontal shift of the *YY* and *T* = 0 schedules is equal and amounts to $d\overline{M}/m^*$. Accordingly, point A' must be a deficit point.

Income Determination and the Trade Balance

The two-country model thus confirms the predictions already derived in the small-country example. A demand shift toward imports reduces income and worsens the trade balance. What we also learn about here is the dampening effect caused by the foreign income expansion. This dampening effect means that our income will fall less and that the trade balance will worsen by less than in the absence of repercussion effects.

4. The Transfer Problem

The transfer problem will reappear frequently in this book. It makes a first appearance here as the question: Will a transfer from one country to the other leave the current account in balance once the induced changes in incomes are allowed for, or will there be a deficit or surplus for the paying country? The question is of interest because, as we shall soon see, a deficit would imply the need to have a deterioration in the terms of trade and thus a further burden over and above the initial transfer payment. Now suppose that the home country pays an international transfer in the amount K, raised at home through taxes and redistributed abroad through tax cuts. Because spending depends on disposable income, a contraction in total spending will ensue at home in contrast to an increase in total spending abroad. Our demand for all goods—domestic and foreign—will decline, and foreign spending on all goods will rise.

Are there conditions under which equilibrium output will remain unchanged? Yes, if the foreign increased spending precisely offsets our spending reductions. In particular, increased spending abroad must match our spending reduction in amount—that means the same saving propensities out of disposable income—and in proportions. The latter requirement means that their propensity to spend on our goods is equal to our own, and similarly for our propensity to spend on their goods. This is clearly the benchmark case, wherein world demand for each country's output is unchanged and outputs therefore remain unaffected.

In this case of no distribution effects, what would happen to our current account? The account worsens as a direct function of the amount of the transfer; however, it improves when we cut our disposable income (hence imports) while disposable income is increased abroad, with the consequent rise in our exports. The net effect is thus:

$$dCA/dK = -1 + m + m^*$$

(18a)

where CA denotes the current account and K the transfer.

Thus the current account improves or deteriorates as the sum of the marginal propensities to import exceeds or falls short of unity. The transfer is said to be *overeffected* if the payment of a transfer leads to a current account surplus. Conversely it is *undereffected* if net exports increase by less than the transfer, leaving us with a deficit in the current account.

We return now to (18a) to recognize that the condition was derived for the case of no distribution effects. Specifically it was derived on the assumption that the foreign propensity to spend on our goods equals our own. That means $m^* = d$, or

$$dCA/dK = -1 + m + d = -s \qquad (18b)$$

Thus it is apparent that in the case for which there are no distribution effects the transfer *must* be undereffected. The reason? Part of the taxes at home are financed by a reduction in savings, rather than by decreased consumption. Accordingly, our net exports do not increase by the full amount of the transfer, giving us a current balance deficit.

Generally, where saving propensities or spending proportions differ between countries, we have a less clear-cut pattern. From our equilibrium conditions we derive the following comparative static results (see appendix):

$$dY/dK = (m^*s - s^*d)/\Delta \qquad dY^*/dK = (sd^* - s^*m)/\Delta \qquad (19)$$

where

$$\Delta = (s+m)(s^*+m^*) - mm^* > 0$$

Conditions leading to an expansion in our output are those for which there is an excess demand at the initial level of output. That means either a rise in world spending with unchanged marginal spending patterns ($s > s^*$, $m^* = d$) or unchanged world spending despite a redistribution of demand in favor of the home country ($s = s^*; m^* - d > 0$).

Even if distribution effects work favorably so as to create an excess demand for our goods, the output expansion will be insufficient to compensate for the transfer. Disposable income $Y - K$ must fall. This outcome is readily established from the definition of disposable income and equation (19):

$$d(Y-K)/dK \equiv dY/dK - 1 = -s^*/\Delta \qquad d(Y^*+K)/dK = s/\Delta \qquad (20)$$

Our disposable income falls, but spending falls by less, because part of the transfer is financed by dissaving. It is immediately apparent, therefore, that the home country will experience a deficit in the current account, while the receiving country enjoys a surplus.

IV. INTERDEPENDENCE

In this part we look at some empirical evidence of international interdependence. Such evidence is provided by econometric models of the world economy, such as project LINK or the recent OECD International Linkage Model.* We follow here the OECD model.

We start by looking at Table 3-1, which shows the impact of a 1 percent

TABLE 3-1

Interdependence and Repercussion Effects on Growth and the Current Account

Country	United States %	$	Germany %	$	Canada %	$	Japan %	$	OECD %	$
United States	1.5	(−3.4)	0.2	(0.4)	0.7	(0.4)	0.3	(0.9)	0.7	(−0.7)
Germany	0.1	(0.5)	1.3	(−2.4)	0.1	(0.2)	0.1	(0.3)	0.2	(−0.4)
Canada	0.1	(0.6)	0.0	(0.1)	1.3	(−1.0)	0.0	(0.1)	0.1	(−0.1)
Japan	0.0	(0.4)	0.1	(0.1)	0.1	(0.0)	1.3	(−1.2)	0.2	(−0.3)
OECD	1.8	(−1.1)	2.4	(−0.1)	2.3	(0.0)	1.8	(0.7)	2.0	(−1.7)

Numbers in parentheses represent billions of dollars.
SOURCE: OECD (1979).

change in autonomous spending in selected countries listed in the left-hand column on income of the countries listed across the top row.

For each country we show two numbers. The first number represents the percentage increase in growth induced by the domestic or foreign autonomous demand expansion. The numbers in parentheses represent the current-account impact of the expansion measured in U.S. $ billion. Thus, for example, a 1 percent increase in U.S. autonomous spending raises U.S. real growth by 1.5 percent and worsens the U.S. current account by $3.4 billion.

Consider now a U.S. expansion. We already noted that income in the United States will rise. But we also see spillover effects of the U.S. expansion.

*See OECD (1979) Ando et al. (1976) and Fair (1979). Early work on interdependence is reported in Modigliani and Neisser (1953).

In Germany income will rise by 0.2 percent, in Japan by 0.3 percent, and in Canada by as much as 0.7 percent. This is evidence of international interdependence through induced changes in imports. For OECD countries as a group, growth would rise by 0.7 percent, reflecting both the importance of spillover effects and the fact that the United States is one of the largest countries in that group.

Consider by contrast expansion in Japan. The direct impact on Japan is a multiplier effect. The side effects on other countries such as the United States or the major OECD countries are substantially smaller than in the case of the United States. U.S. growth would increase by 1/20th of 1 percent, and growth for the major OECD countries would rise by only one-fifth of 1 percent.

Consider next the row appropriate to a *joint* expansion by the OECD countries. If each of the OECD countries raised their spending by 1 percent U.S. growth would rise by 1.8 percent or one-third of 1 percent more than if the United States expanded alone. There are thus substantial side effects from a joint expansion. These side effects are even more substantial for the other major countries. For Japan the extra expansion would be nearly one-half of 1 percentage point (1.8 rather than 1.3), and for Canada it is a whole percentage point.

Table 3-1 also shows the effects of expenditure increases on the goods and service balances. The diagonal shows again the effects of an isolated expansion on the expanding country's balance. Consider first the United States. A 1 percent increase in autonomous spending leads to an increase in the trade deficit of more than $3 billion.

The impact of expansion on the current account differs substantially across countries. German expansion yields a very large deficit, whereas Japanese expansion (despite the same growth effect) yields a deficit that is only one-half that of Germany. These large differences in the trade-balance effect arise to some extent from differences in import propensities. For Germany and the United States the model assumes large import elasticities with respect to an income expansion. By comparison, for Japan the elasticity is only 1.5 percent. The comparison between the German and Japanese trade effects demonstrates that German expansion has a bigger effect on OECD growth than does a Japanese expansion, notwithstanding the fact that Germany is a smaller country (as a share of OECD GNP) than is Japan. Why the difference? German expansion spills over much more substantially into increased growth abroad because of higher induced imports.

Suppose next that all OECD countries expand together. We observe from Table 3-1 that the combined effect is a trade deficit for the group of $1.7

billion. How is the deficit shared among the major countries? Canada would stay in balance, despite the expansion of domestic demand. Japan would enjoy a surplus of nearly $0.7 billion. The United States, however, would show large deficits. These important differences in the trade effects of a *joint* expansion are puzzling. They arise because of differences in import propensities and multipliers and because of marginal export shares. Thus Japan, for example, not only has low import elasticities but also enjoys an above-average share in the expansion of world trade. Accordingly her trade balance improves despite her own expansion.

V. CONCLUDING REMARKS

Our first approach to open-economy macroeconomics has focused on output determination for the small economy and on the interdependence between economies. The results we have derived will stand up to the more complex models that we will examine shortly. But as yet our model is incomplete. The next step is to focus on relative prices and to study their role in changing the composition of aggregate spending. Combined with the present analysis, we will then have a basic model to work with.

APPENDIX

Figure 3-6 showed the determination of equilibrium income. Here we extend the analysis to ask whether that equilibrium will in fact be reached or, to put it another way, whether the system is dynamically stable. For that purpose we make a simple assumption about output adjustment: Output in each country adjusts in proportion to excess demand, or

$$\dot{Y} = k_1 [E(Y,G) + T(Y,Y^*) - Y] \qquad \text{(A-1)}$$
$$\dot{Y}^* = k_2 [E^*(Y^*,G^*) - T(Y,Y^*) - Y^*]$$

where an overdot on a variable designates the time derivative $d(\ )/dt$ and k_i are speeds of adjustment.

FIGURE A-1

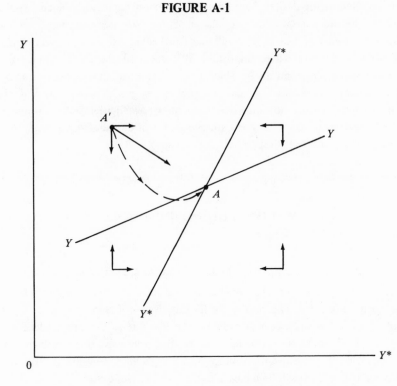

To investigate the stability we linearize the system around equilibrium and, for the sake of simplicity, assume equal unitary speeds of adjustment $k_i = 1$:

$$\dot{Y} = -k_1(s + m)(Y - \overline{Y}) + k_1 m^*(Y^* - \overline{Y}^*) \qquad \text{(A-2)}$$
$$\dot{Y}^* = k_2 m(Y - \overline{Y}) - k_2(s^* + m^*)(Y^* - \overline{Y}^*)$$

where $\overline{Y}$ and $\overline{Y}^*$ denote the long-run equilibrium levels of income. Defining the operator $\lambda = d(\ )/dt$ and noting that $\lambda(Y - \overline{Y}) = \dot{Y}$, since by definition long-run equilibrium $\overline{Y}$ is a constant, we can write (A-2) as follows:

$$\begin{bmatrix} -(s+m) - \lambda & m^* \\ m & -(s^* + m^*) - \lambda \end{bmatrix} \begin{bmatrix} Y - \overline{Y} \\ Y^* - \overline{Y}^* \end{bmatrix} = 0 \qquad \text{(A-3)}$$

To determine stability, we evaluate the characteristic equation or the determinant of the matrix in (A-3):

Income Determination and the Trade Balance

$$\lambda^2 + \lambda(s+m+s^*+m^*) + (s+m)(s^*+m^*) - mm^* = 0 \qquad \text{(A-4)}$$

Stability requires that both the coefficient of λ and the determinant be positive. With positive savings and import propensities, stability is ensured.

The dynamics are shown in Figure A-1, where we have drawn arrows to indicate the adjustment process formulated in (A-1). At a point A' we have an excess supply of domestic goods and an excess demand for foreign goods. Thus our income will fall and foreign income will rise. The adjustment paths are either direct or a half-cycle, as indicated in Figure A-1.

We next come to comparative statics. First we look at the effects of an increase in aggregate demand, then at a transfer. Our model is shown in equations (A-5) to (A-7):

$$Y = E(Y) + M^*(Y^*) - M(Y) \qquad \text{(A-5)}$$
$$Y^* = E^*(Y^*) - M^*(Y^*) + M(Y) \qquad \text{(A-6)}$$
$$T = M^*(Y^*) - M(Y) \qquad \text{(A-7)}$$

Differentiating the system totally and taking $d\overline{E}$ as the increase in autonomous spending we obtain

$$\begin{bmatrix} 0 & s+m & -m^* \\ 0 & -m & s^*+m^* \\ 1 & m & -m^* \end{bmatrix} \begin{bmatrix} dT \\ dY \\ dY^* \end{bmatrix} = \begin{bmatrix} d\overline{E} \\ 0 \\ 0 \end{bmatrix} \qquad \text{(A-8)}$$

Using Cramer's rule, we solve for the changes in output and trade balance:

$$dY/d\overline{E} = (s^*+m^*)/\Delta \qquad dY^*/d\overline{E} = m/\Delta \qquad dT/d\overline{E} = -m^*s^*/\Delta \quad \text{(A-9)}$$

where

$$\Delta = (s+m)(s^*+m^*) - mm^* > 0$$

For the case of a transfer we note that spending will depend on disposable income $Y - K$ at home and on $Y^* + K$ abroad. Making that substitution in (A-5) through (A-7) we obtain the following equations:

$$\begin{bmatrix} 0 & s+m & -m^* \\ 0 & -m & s^*+m^* \\ 1 & m & -m^* \end{bmatrix} \begin{bmatrix} dT \\ dY \\ dY^* \end{bmatrix} = \begin{bmatrix} (m^*-d)dK \\ (d^*-m)dK \\ (m^*+m)dK \end{bmatrix} \qquad \text{(A-10)}$$

Solving these equations for output and the trade balance we have

$$dY/dK = (m^*s - ds^*)/\Delta \qquad dY^*/dK = (sd^* - s^*m)/\Delta$$
$$dT/dK = (m^*s + ms^*)/\Delta \tag{A-11}$$

REFERENCES AND SUGGESTED READINGS

Ando, A., Herring, R., and Marston, R., eds. 1976. *International aspects of stabilization policies.* Boston Federal Reserve Conference Series, no. 12.

Fair, R. 1979. On modeling the economic linkages amount countries. *International economic policy: theory and evidence.* eds. R. Dornbusch and J. Frenkel. Baltimore Md.: Johns Hopkins University Press.

Modigliani, F., and Neisser, H. 1953. *National incomes and international trade.* Urbana: University of Illinois Press.

Organization for Economic Cooperation and Development. January, 1979. *Economic outlook, occasional studies.* Paris: (OECD) 3-33.

Robinson, R. 1952. A graphical analysis of the foreign trade multiplier. *Economic journal* LXII: 546-564.

C H A P T E R

4

Relative Prices, Equilibrium Output, and the Trade Balance

Chapter 3 introduced output determination and the trade balance on the assumption of given relative prices. The only policy instrument we considered were variations in the level of aggregate demand induced by general fiscal policy. That model is a useful first approximation, but it does leave out important instruments of policy and adjustment. In particular, tariffs, devaluation, and export subsidies cannot be discussed unless we explicitly focus on relative prices as an integral part of our macro model. The same is true for adjustments to changes in demand through the classic process of wage and price adjustment. The topic of this chapter, then, is to round out our analysis by introducing relative prices. In section I we lay down the general model.

Section II shows how commercial policies and devaluation affect equilibrium output and the balance of trade. In section III we introduce the classic adjustment process through wages and prices. In that context we discuss the problem of real-wage resistance.

I. THE MODEL

The economy we consider here is completely specialized in the production of exportables. Importables are available in the world market in perfectly elastic supply at a foreign currency price P^*. Let e denote the domestic currency price of foreign exchange. Then import prices in home currency are eP^*. The domestic currency price of the goods we produce is P. With these definitions we introduce the $\boxed{terms\ of\ trade}$ or the $\boxed{relative\ price}$ of domestic goods in terms of importables as

$$\text{Relative price of M-ables} \equiv\ p \equiv eP^*/P\ =\ \frac{\text{Units dom. good}}{\text{Units for. good}} \tag{1}$$

The terms of trade as defined in (1) have the dimension of units of domestic output per unit of foreign output. A rise in p implies that domestic goods have become relatively cheaper or that we have to give up more units of domestic output to secure a unit of foreign goods. We refer to a rise in p as a terms of trade deterioration. The most striking example of a terms of trade deterioration is the oil price increase, which reduced the purchasing power of the industrialized nations' output in terms of oil.

The relative price, or terms of trade, play a key role in the determination of output and the trade balance. For a given level of income and spending the relative price determines the *composition* of domestic spending between imports and domestic goods. The relative price also affects the world demand for our goods. Specifically we assume that a rise in the relative price of imports, a rise in p, will reduce imports and raise exports. This assumption is shown in (2), where foreign demand for our goods is a function of the relative price, as is the home import demand:

$$M^* = M^*(p) \qquad M = M(p,Y) \tag{2}$$

The trade balance, measured in terms of domestic output, is equal to the

Relative Prices, Equilibrium Output, and the Trade Balance

excess of exports over the *value* of imports:

$$T = M^*(p) - pM(p, Y) \tag{3}$$

From (3) we see that the trade balance depends on income and relative prices. The important point to note, however, is that an increase in the relative price of imports need not necessarily improve the trade balance. Although it is true that exports rise as we are now more competitive and that imports in physical terms decline, it is also true that we pay more per unit of imports. This cost effect dominates unless exports and imports in physical terms are sufficiently price elastic. This point is formalized in the *Marshall-Lerner condition* which we now derive.

We define the price elasticity of foreign demand for our exports and domestic import demand as follows:

$$\alpha^* \equiv (\delta M^*/\delta p)\, p/M^* > 0 \qquad \alpha \equiv - (\delta M/\delta p)\, p/M > 0$$

Differentiating (3) with respect to the terms of trade we obtain

$$\delta T/\delta p = \delta M^*/\delta p - M - p\, \delta M/\delta p = M(\alpha^* + \alpha - 1) \tag{4}$$

where we assumed initial trade balance, so that $M^* = pM$.

Equation (4) states that a terms-of-trade deterioration, or a rise in the relative price of imports, will improve the trade balance provided the sum of export and import elasticities exceeds unity. The condition thus insures sufficient quantity response to offset the increased cost of imports brought about by a worsening of the terms of trade. We assume that this condition is satisfied.

We turn next to the goods market. Here the equilibrium condition is that aggregate spending by domestic residents E plus net exports T equal output:*

$$Y = E(Y) + T(p, Y) \tag{5}$$

Figure 4-1 shows the schedule YY that represents equilibrium in the domestic goods market. The schedule is positively sloped provided the Marshall-Lerner condition in (4) is satisfied. A rise in output raises income and spending, but spending on domestic goods rises less than output because

---

*We assume that spending depends only on output and not on relative prices. A more general formulation is introduced in the Appendix, where we discuss the *Laursen-Metzler effect*. (See Laursen and Metzler, 1950.)

FIGURE 4-1

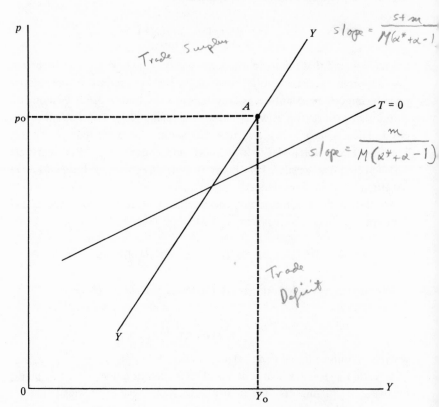

part of the increased income is saved or spent on imports. Accordingly there is an excess supply that has to be eliminated by a worsening in the terms of trade or a fall in the price of domestic goods. Such a fall in the relative price of domestic goods creates demand for home output since it raises exports and reduces import spending thereby shifting demand toward our goods. A rise in the relative price of imports thus exerts an *expenditure-switching effect* in favor of domestic goods. The slope of the YY schedule is given by .

$$\frac{dp}{dY}\bigg|_{YY} = \frac{s+m}{M(\alpha^*+\alpha-1)} \qquad (6)$$

A movement up and along the schedule corresponds to an increase in output that is sustained on the demand side by a growing trade surplus. The schedule is flatter the higher the price responsiveness of exports and imports and the higher the propensity to spend on domestic goods, $d = 1 - s - m$. The schedule is drawn for a given fiscal policy.

Figure 4-1 also shows the schedule $T=0$ along which trade is balanced. The schedule is positively sloped for the following reason: a rise in the relative price of imports, given the Marshall-Lerner condition, improves the trade balance. To restore equilibrium the level of income and hence import spending must rise. Points above and to the left of the $T=0$ schedule correspond to a surplus and points below to a deficit. The $T=0$ schedule is drawn flatter than the YY schedule. This reflects the fact that moving up and along the YY schedule we require a growing trade surplus to sustain increasing output levels. The slope of the $T=0$ schedule is $dp/dY = m/M(\alpha^* + \alpha - 1)$.

Suppose now that we have a given relative price p_0. In Figure 4-1 we show that for that relative price the equilibrium output level is determined at point A where the goods market clears. Corresponding to the relative price p_0 and the associated equilibrium level of output Y_0 there is a trade surplus at point A.

We return now to the discussion of internal and external balance and the question whether general aggregate demand policy is sufficient to attain simultaneously both targets. Figure 4-2 shows the trade balance equilibrium

FIGURE 4-2

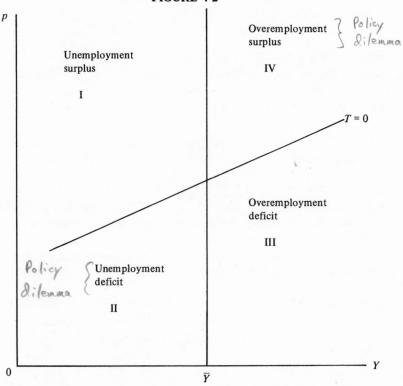

schedule $T=0$ and the full employment output level $\overline{Y}$. Points to the left of $\overline{Y}$ correspond to unemployment and points to the right to overemployment. Suppose we are in region I with unemployment and a trade surplus. Clearly, a demand expansion will reduce the surplus and improve the employment position. Similarly in region III, with overemployment and a deficit, a demand contraction will point in the right direction with respect to both targets. This is not the case, however, in regions II and IV. In these regions there is a dilemma for policy. In region II the deficit requires a contraction in demand, but the employment position calls for an expansion in demand. The converse is true for region IV. Regions II and IV make for our interest in additional policy instruments that can be used to simultaneously attain internal and external balance. The policy instruments we discuss here all have in common the feature that, by changing relative prices, they induce expenditure-switching effects. In combination with the expenditure-raising or -reducing effects of general aggregate demand policies, they provide a *policy mix* that will simultaneously achieve internal and external balance.

II. DEVALUATION AND COMMERCIAL POLICIES

Here we will discuss the effects on output and the trade balance of policy-induced changes in relative prices. At the same time we will study the relationship between three common policy interventions: devaluation, tariffs, and subsidies. We will show that a devaluation is equivalent to an import tariff plus an export subsidy.

1. Devaluation

Our analysis begins with a devaluation. Suppose that world prices of importables are given and that the price of domestic goods is given. Then the terms of trade depend only on the exchange rate. A currency depreciation raises the domestic currency price of imports or worsens the terms of trade. Under our assumptions there is one-to-one correspondence between exchange depreciation and terms of trade worsening:

$$\hat{p} = \hat{e} \tag{7}$$

where a caret or hat denotes a percentage change, that is, $\hat{p} \equiv dp/p$.

where $e = \dfrac{\#}{\#}$

Relative Prices, Equilibrium Output, and the Trade Balance

In Figure 4-3 we start with an initial equilibrium at point A and now introduce an exchange depreciation that raises the relative price of imports from p_0 to p'. The equilibrium moves to point A', with output rising and with an improvement in the trade balance. Specifically from (5) we can calculate the change in equilibrium income as

$$dY = [M^*(\alpha^* + \alpha - 1)/(s+m)]\,\hat{e} \qquad (8)$$

because, $M^* = p_0 \cdot M$

The assumption that the Marshall-Lerner condition is satisfied thus insures that an exchange depreciation or a terms of trade deterioration will raise equilibrium income.

The trade effect of the depreciation can be calculated from (3) using (8) as

$$dT = M^*(\alpha^* + \alpha - 1)\,\hat{e} - mdY = [s/(m+s)]\,M^*(\alpha^* + \alpha - 1)\,\hat{e} \qquad (9)$$

FIGURE 4-3

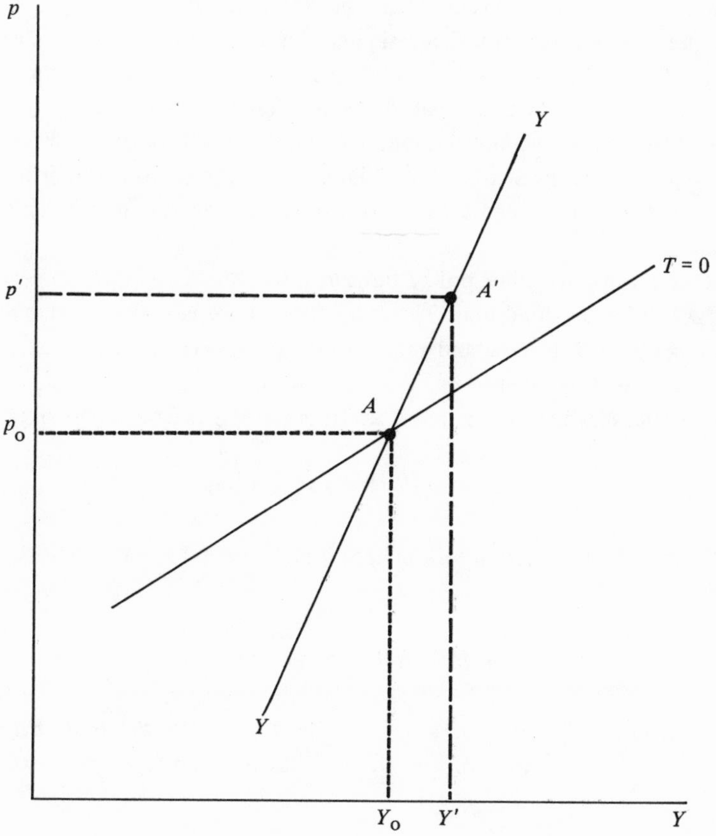

63

With the Marshall-Lerner condition satisfied, an exchange depreciation will improve the trade balance. An interesting feature of the result in (9) is the term $s/(s+m)$. The income expansion induced by the shift in demand toward domestic goods leads to increased imports, partly offsetting the initial improvement of the trade balance due to the depreciation. The term $s/(s+m)$ reflects this dampening effect.

To summarize the effects of an exchange depreciation we can state the following: at the initial level of output a depreciation lowers the relative price of domestic goods. As a consequence, given the elasticity condition, demand shifts toward domestic goods and the trade balance improves. The shift in demand leads to an income expansion that dampens, but does not offset, the initial trade improvement.

One cannot overemphasize the strategic assumption we have made, namely that domestic prices are entirely unaffected by the depreciation. It is only under these conditions that a nominal exchange rate change translates one for one into a *real* exchange rate or terms of trade change. If the depreciation and income expansion leads to offsetting domestic price increases, relative prices and competitiveness will remain unchanged and depreciation will exert no real effect. We return to these issues in discussing real wage resistance. We already note here, however, that the expansion in output and the trade improvement do not come without tears. They are brought about by a worsening in the terms of trade or a reduction in the purchasing power of our goods. That *does* represent a real cost, namely, a reduction in the standard of living.

Before turning to other policy measures, we should comment briefly on the Marshall-Lerner condition. The point to be made is that a relative price change exerts both income and substitution effects. The demand elasticities in (4) can therefore be split up into these two effects by defining the compensated price elasticities or pure substitution elasticities $\bar{\alpha}^*$ and $\bar{\alpha}$ to obtain

$$\alpha^* = \bar{\alpha}^* + m^* \qquad \alpha = \bar{\alpha} + m \qquad (10)$$

Substituting this decomposition into the Marshall-Lerner condition we obtain

$$M(\bar{\alpha}^* + \bar{\alpha} + m^* + m - 1) \qquad (4a)$$

A condition sufficient for a depreciation to improve the trade balance is therefore that the sum of the propensities to import, $m + m^*$, exceeds unity.

Relative Prices, Equilibrium Output, and the Trade Balance

2. A Tariff

A tariff is a tax on imports. It raises the *domestic* relative price of imports, but it leaves the prices faced by the rest of the world unchanged. A tariff differs from a devaluation in the important respect that we ourselves collect the tariff revenue that corresponds to the price increase. Our external terms of trade do not worsen. Since we collect the tariff revenue at the initial level of output a tariff will lead to a budget surplus.

Consider now the effect of an import tariff at the rate t. The domestic relative price of importables is $\bar{p} = p(1+t)$, while the rest of the world continues to face the relative price p. Tariff collection is equal to tpM. To derive the effect of the tariff on income we have to rewrite (5), recognizing the difference between domestic and world prices:

$$Y = D + M^* = D + \bar{p}M + (M^* - pM) + (p - \bar{p})M = E + T - tpM \quad (5a)$$

$$= E + M^* - pM \qquad \qquad \text{where} \quad D = E - M$$

where D is the domestic demand for domestic goods. The equilibrium condition in the home goods market thus is that spending by domestic residents, at domestic prices, plus the trade balance, at world prices, less the tariff collection equal output. From (5a), taking the initial tariff to be zero, we readily find the impact on income as

$$dY/dt = M^*(\alpha - 1)/(s + m) \quad (11)$$

A tariff thus leads to an expansion in output provided the elasticity of demand of our imports is larger than one. The explanation of this result is the following. The imposition of the tariff raises the relative price faced by importers and therefore reduces imports in physical terms. But what happens to import spending? Only if the price elasticity is high enough does import spending at domestic prices actually decline and demand for domestic goods increase. The fact that a tariff does not necessarily lead to a demand expansion is explained by the fact that it is a combination of substitution, owing to the change in relative prices, and deflationary fiscal policy, because the government collects the tariff revenue and thus reduces the purchasing power of a given level of spending. Only if the demand elasticity exceeds unity do the substitution effects outweigh the income effect and an output expansion takes place.

The trade balance effect of the tariff, however, is unambiguous:

$$dT/dt = M^*\alpha - mdY/dt = [(\alpha s + m)/(s + m)] M^* \quad (12)$$

Suppose, in looking at (12), we take the borderline case of $\alpha = 1$ so that output remains unchanged. In that event the trade balance improvement is exactly equal to the increase in tariff revenue: $dT = pMdt$. There is a trade surplus that matches the increased budget surplus or public sector saving. If the demand elasticity exceeds unity, the trade balance improves by more, the income expansion notwithstanding.

From the perspective of internal and external balance policies a tariff thus represents some uncertainties. Without a redistribution of the tariff revenue we are certain of a trade improvement but we do not know whether output will expand. The conditions for output to expand are more stringent than the Marshall-Lerner condition.

3. An Export Subsidy

An export subsidy leaves the domestic relative price of goods unchanged but it lowers the real cost of our exportable to the rest of the world. The price faced by foreigners can be written as $p^* = p/(1-v)$, where v is the subsidy rate. Thus from the perspective of the rest of the world our export subsidy lowers the relative price of our goods and leads to increased foreign demand or increased exports.

The increase in exports that is induced by the subsidy unambiguously raises output and employment. Output rises by

$$dY/dv = M^*\alpha^*/(s+m) \tag{13}$$

How about the trade effects? It is true that exports rise, but at the same time we receive less per unit of exports because of our subsidy. Imports expand because of the increase in income. The trade effects therefore are ambiguous. The trade balance will improve only if foreign demand is sufficiently elastic. Using the trade balance equation $T = (1-v)M^* - pM$ we derive the following result:

$$dT/dv = M^* [\alpha^*s/(s+m) - 1] \tag{14}$$

4. A Balanced Budget Export Subsidy

How do budgetary policies affect our results? Suppose that instead of deficit financing of the export subsidy we had a balanced budget. Increased income taxes, in this case, would finance the subsidies. With spending depending on disposable income, $Y - vM^*$, the effect on output of increased subsidies is equal to:*

$$dY/dv = M^*(\alpha^* - d)/(s + m) = M^*(\bar{\alpha}^* + m^* - d)/(s + m) \qquad (15)$$

This result has a very simple and attractive interpretation. A balanced budget subsidy has two aspects. On one hand it changes the relative price faced by foreigners and therefore induces substitution effects on their part. The substitution effect, captured by the term $\bar{\alpha}^*$, unambiguously raises the demand for domestic goods. The other aspect of the subsidy is the implicit real income transfer—at-home taxes are raised to pay for the subsidy that reduces the price charged abroad. The effect of the transfer on the demand for our goods is ambiguous. Foreign demand rises by m^*, but domestic demand, because of reduced real disposable income, declines by d. The net effect then depends on the term $m^* - d$. If both countries have the same spending propensities, a balanced budget subsidy *must* raise output because there are only substitution effects and no distribution effects.

The balanced budget export subsidy is more likely to lead to a trade improvement since now we avoid the budget deficit or public sector dissaving. The trade effect is readily calculated as

$$dT/dv = M^*[(\alpha^*s + m)/(s + m) - 1] \qquad (16)$$

Accordingly a sufficient condition for the trade balance to improve is an elasticity of foreign demand in excess of unity.

5. Equivalence of Devaluation and Commercial Policies

We extend our analysis of commercial policies to demonstrate that an equal rate tariff and export subsidy are equivalent to a devaluation. For that demonstration we simply add (12) and (14) setting $dv = dt$ and assuming initially $M^* = pM$, to obtain

$$dT/dt = M^*(\alpha s + m + \alpha^*s - m - s)/(s + m) \qquad (17)$$
$$= [s/(s + m)](\alpha^* + \alpha - 1)M^*$$

It is apparent from (17) that the combination of policies replicates the effect of a devaluation. This is the case because, just as in the case of a devaluation, we have the combination of a rise in the relative price of foreign goods faced by both the home country and the rest of the world.

*The result is derived from the equilibrium condition $Y = E(Y - vM^*) + M^*(p^*) - pM(p, Y - vM^*)$, noting that $1 - s - m = d$. Real disposable income $Y - vM^*$ rises only if $\alpha^* - 1 > 0$.

The policy combination can be thought of as generating substitution effects and a transfer. In both countries the relative price of domestic goods falls as a result of the tariff—subsidy combination thus inducing substitution toward our goods. There is also an implicit income transfer. At-home tariff revenue is collected and it is redistributed abroad through the export subsidy. Thus the policy combination implies a balanced budget income transfer toward the foreign country.

6. Quotas

We complete our analysis of commercial policies by looking at quotas. Here we have to make quite a few adjustments in the basic model. (See Figure 4-4.) The home country sets a maximum level of imports $\bar{M}$ and rights to these quotas are auctioned off with the proceeds giving rise to a budget surplus. An effective quota implies that the domestic price of importables is entirely divorced from the world price since at the margin, unlike in the case of tariffs, there is no opportunity for price arbitrage. We call the domestic

FIGURE 4-4

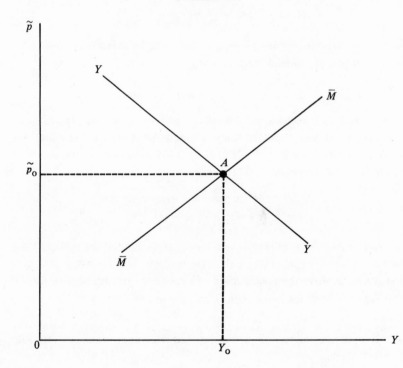

Relative Prices, Equilibrium Output, and the Trade Balance

relative price of importables $\tilde{p}$. The world relative price remains p and is unchanged in our analysis.

One further assumption that we need to restate is that spending depends only on output. Accordingly, we have as the goods market equilibrium condition:

$$Y = D + M^* = (D + \tilde{p}\overline{M}) + M^* - \tilde{p}\overline{M} = E(Y) + M^*(p) - \tilde{p}\overline{M} \quad (18)$$

Equilibrium in the home goods market is shown in Figure 4-4 by the downward-sloping schedule YY. Given the quota level of imports $\overline{M}$, the higher the domestic relative price of imports, and therefore auction proceeds accruing to the government, the lower is spending on domestic goods.

We also show the positively sloped schedule $\overline{MM}$ along which the demand for imports is equal to the quota level:

$$\overline{M} = M(\tilde{p}, Y) \quad (19)$$

The schedule is positively sloped, since an increase in the relative price reduces imports below the quota level. To restore the quota to effectiveness income must rise. The equilibrium domestic relative price and income level, given the world price p and the quota level $\overline{M}$, are determined at point A.

A change in the quota induces both expenditure switching and expenditure reducing effects. With a reduction in the quota, demand shifts toward domestic goods. At the same time, however, the domestic relative price of imports rises and that price increase is collected by the fiscal authorities thereby reducing the purchasing power of income. Which effect will dominate? If import demand is highly price elastic, a restriction in the quota will only lead to a relatively small price increase and quota fee collection. Conversely, if demand is inelastic import spending inclusive of the quota fees rises and demand for domestic goods declines. Once more we recognize the importance of the budgetary effects in assessing the impact of commercial policies. We also observe that the quota must improve the trade balance since we purchase less imports at unchanged world prices, but that the effect on income and employment is uncertain. Therefore a quota is primarily a balance of payments policy, unless we are assured of high demand elasticities or balanced budget fiscal policies.

III. REAL WAGES AND COMPETITIVENESS

The analysis of devaluation and commercial policies has shown means of adjustment to internal-external balance problems that supplement broad fiscal policy. In this part we ask whether departures from internal balance or full employment do not, by themselves, lead to adjustment in costs, prices, and competitiveness that are self-correcting. Specifically we explore the link between wages and the terms of trade on one side and wages and unemployment on the other. The analysis shows that changes in relative prices imply changes in real wages or the standard of living. Real-wage resistance is shown to be an obstacle to complete adjustment.

1. Wages, Costs, and Prices

Our model of the pricing process assumes that firms set prices with a markup on unit labor cost:

$$P = aW(1+x) \tag{20}$$

In (20) P is the domestic price set by firms, a is the unit labor requirement or the inverse of the constant average product of labor, and x and W are the profit markup and the money wage rate, respectively. Unit labor cost thus are aW which are increased by the profit markup to arrive at price. The higher the level of labor productivity, the lower the unit labor requirement; hence, the lower are prices relative to wages.

Labor, in setting money wages, looks at the consumption bundle of domestic goods and importables. The cost of living or price level labor considers is a function of both prices:

$$Q = P^\beta (P^*e)^{1-\beta} \tag{21}$$

where Q is the price index and β is the expenditure share of domestic goods.

Labor is assumed to fix the *real* wage w in terms of the price index defined in (21). To obtain a real wage w at the price level Q the required money wage is given in (22) as

$$W = wQ \tag{22}$$

Using (21) and (22) in (20) and collecting terms we obtain the following relation:

Relative Prices, Equilibrium Output, and the Trade Balance

$$\bar{p} = [aw(1+x)]^{-1/(1-\beta)} \qquad (23)$$

Equation (23) defines unique terms of trade $\bar{p}$ consistent with the real wage required by labor, the pricing policy of firms, and prevailing productivity. The lower productivity and the higher the markup, the lower the relative price of imports consistent with labor's objectives and firms' pricing. The reason is that with low productivity, the real wage in terms of domestic output is low. To secure a given real wage in terms of the consumption bundle there has to be a correspondingly high real wage in terms of imports. Thus the relative price of imports must be low. We refer to $\bar{p}$ as the "required" terms of trade as distinguished from the terms of trade that actually prevail.

2. Real-Wage Resistance

Is the real-wage demand w that is the basis of our required terms of trade $\bar{p}$, entirely exogenous, or does it depend on the rate of employment? Our simplifying assumption here is that the real-wage demand is an increasing function of the ratio of actual to full employment output:

$$w = \bar{w}(Y/\bar{Y})^\phi \qquad (24)$$

where $\bar{w}$ is a constant and ϕ measures the elasticity of the required real wage with respect to the level of output and employment. Substituting this real wage expression in (23) yields the final formula for the required terms of trade:

$$\bar{p} = [(1+x)a\bar{w}(Y/\bar{Y})^\phi]^{-1/(1-\beta)} \qquad (25)$$

What are the properties of the required terms of trade $\bar{p}$? Figure 4-5 shows $\bar{p}$ for given productivity and profit margins. The higher the level of output, the higher the real-wage demands, and accordingly the more favorable are the required terms of trade. The figure also makes the point that real-wage resistance is an additional dimension of the internal-external balance problem. There is a unique term of trade, shown by point A, at which we have full employment consistent with labor's required real wage. This serves as an additional constraint on stabilization policy because a point like A', where we have internal balance, is not sustainable. In fact, only a point like A'' is sustainable. Let us turn to this issue in more detail.

At any point in time we have a given wage rate and productivity, and therefore, from (20) and the given import prices there are actual terms of trade p. These actual terms of trade determine the level of output along

FIGURE 4-5

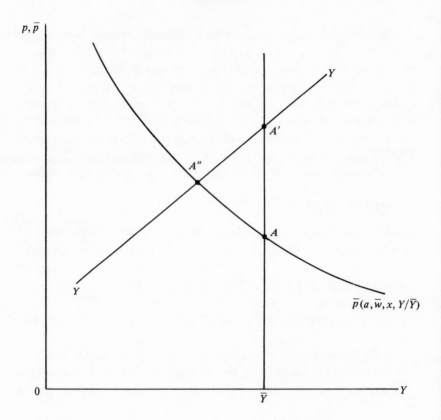

the YY schedule. Thus suppose in Figure 4-6 we have actual terms of trade p_0 and a corresponding output level Y_0. The actual terms of trade imply a real wage lower than the required real wage for that level of employment, as evidenced by the vertical gap $p - \bar{p}$ at Y_0.

Since actual real wages are below the required level, we expect money wages to be raised and therefore the actual terms of trade to be improving. We write this adjustment process of wages and the terms of trade to the real-wage gap as follows:

$$\dot{p} = - \rho(p/\bar{p}) \qquad \rho' > 0 \qquad \rho(1) = 0 \qquad (26)$$

where $\bar{p}$ is evaluated at the output level determined by p. It is apparent then from Figure 4-6 that anywhere along YY to the right of point A'' the terms of trade are improving because labor responds to low real wages by raising

$(p \downarrow)$

FIGURE 4-6

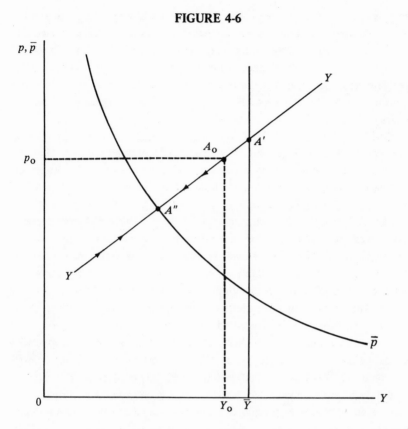

wages, thus leading to higher costs and prices of domestic goods. Conversely, to the left of point A'', real wages are high and so is unemployment. Accordingly, wages are cut and the terms of trade are deteriorating. The system will converge to an underemployment equilibrium at point A''. The required real wage is inconsistent with a level of competitiveness in world trade that ensures full employment, given fiscal and commercial policies.

Can a devaluation solve the problem? Not if there is *real*-wage resistance as we have argued. Suppose policymakers, because of the unemployment, and perhaps an external deficit, at point A'' depreciate the exchange rate. The exchange depreciation, given wages and domestic prices will, of course, immediately worsen the terms of trade and make the home country more competitive. Suppose in fact that the devaluation is sufficient to take us to full employment at point A'. Is that the end? Clearly, at A' the devaluation, by raising import prices has reduced the actual real wage while raising

73

employment. For both reasons there is now a real-wage gap. High employment and low real wages make labor call for money wage increases. The process continues until we return to the initial real equilibrium at point A''.

Over the long run devaluation cannot solve a structural unemployment problem that has real-wage resistance at its roots. Devaluation has only transitory benefits, and even these rely on a slow adjustment of domestic wages.

Real-wage rigidity clearly implies an additional constraint on internal-external balance policies. But how serious is real-wage rigidity? How can we tell the difference between a downward stickiness of money wages and real-wage resistance? Furthermore, how do we know that the schedule $\bar{p}$ will stay put, even in the face of a very long period of unemployment? Perhaps it is possible that with unemployment persisting real-wage demands themselves get scaled down so that in the longest run there is no real-wage resistance at all. No single answer is likely to characterize each situation. But the right view now is likely to concede to real-wage resistance an important role in the short and medium terms that are relevant for stabilization policy. That implies, in turn, that we must look for policies that help reconcile internal and external balance with real-wage requirements.

What are candidates for such structural policies? Increasing productivity would be one way to overcome a real-wage requirement inconsistent with a level of competitiveness that guarantees full employment. But gains in productivity are rarely at the policymaker's command. A different possibility is an employment subsidy or a cut in required profit margins though a reduction in employment or excise taxes or social security charges. Such subsidies or tax cuts would introduce a difference between the wages received by labor W and the cost of labor to firms W'. Let the subsidy be at the rate v then $W' = W(1 - v)$ and substituting this expression in (20) leads to

$$\bar{p} = [aw(1+x)(1-v)]^{-1/(1-\beta)} \qquad (23a)$$

Subsidies introduce a wedge between labor costs and wages and make it possible to achieve consistency and competitiveness at the same time. Of course, we should not be fooled by the solution. While achieving price competitiveness through the subsidy, we are simultaneously opening up a budget deficit to finance the subsidies. What we are doing comes down to substituting a budgetary problem for the real-wage problem.

Relative Prices, Equilibrium Output, and the Trade Balance

3. The Adjustment Process

We conclude this chapter with a dynamic exercise that demonstrates the interaction of macroeconomic policies and real-wage adjustments. We assume that the adjustment process for real wages and the terms of trade is as described in (26). With respect to aggregate demand we assume that government spending is raised in response to unemployment and a trade surplus. Whenever output falls short of the full employment level there is a tendency to raise spending and conversely when there is overemployment. That policy, however, is also affected by external constraints. A deficit dampens the expansionary tendency associated with unemployment while a surplus leads to a more forceful expansion. This behavior is described in (27):

$$\dot{G} = h(\overline{Y} - Y) + kT(Y, p) = \dot{G}(G, p) \qquad (27)$$

where G denotes government spending and h and k are adjustment coefficients. Note that in terms of Figure 4-6 an increase in government spending amounts to a rightward shift of the YY schedule, thereby raising at each terms of trade the equilibrium level of output and worsening the external balance. By contrast, a rise in the terms of trade raises equilibrium output and improves the external balance.

In Figure 4-7 we show the schedule $\overline{Y}\overline{Y}$, along which we have full employment and TT, along which trade is balanced. Higher government spending raises equilibrium output. To maintain full employment there has to be an offsetting loss in competitiveness. Thus $\overline{Y}\overline{Y}$ is negatively sloped. TT is positively sloped, since higher government spending raises output and thus worsens the trade balance so that a compensating gain in competitiveness is required to restore balance. Above and to the right of $\overline{Y}\overline{Y}$ there is overemployment, leading to cuts in government spending, while above and to the left of TT there is a surplus, leading to increased spending. There will be a locus of points such as $\dot{G} = 0$, where government spending remains constant with employment and external balance considerations precisely offsetting each other. We assume the schedule is positively sloped.*

We also show in Figure 4-7 the $\dot{p} = 0$ schedule. It is easily verified that it is flatter than the $\overline{Y}\overline{Y}$ schedule since along it output can deviate from the full employment level. Points below the $\overline{Y}\overline{Y}$ schedule on $\dot{p} = 0$ correspond to unemployment levels, where the consistent terms of trade prevail. Also

---

*The more important the external balance considerations the more clearly the $\dot{G} = 0$ schedule coincides with the TT schedule. Conversely, the more important employment considerations the more nearly it coincides with the $\overline{Y}\overline{Y}$ schedule.

FIGURE 4-7

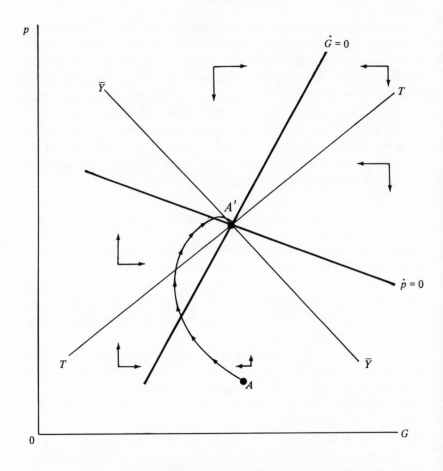

shown in Figure 4-7 are arrows indicating the direction in which the terms of trade and government spending adjust at each point. Finally we assume that, fortuitously, a full equilibrium exists at point A'.

Suppose we start at point A with unemployment and an external deficit, plus a real wage above the required level. Cuts in wages lead to an improvement in competitiveness and thus to employment gains. At the same time, because the deficit dominates policy concern, government spending is being reduced thereby dampening the employment gains, and improving the external balance. The process continues with an improving external balance and possibly a deteriorating employment position, until we reach $\dot{G}=0$, where spending policies are reversed. From now on the unemployment concern dominates, the trade balance having improved. Still, competitiveness is improving. The next phase is a reversal in the external balance where the gain in competitiveness leads to a surplus thus motivating the government to pursue a more expansionary fiscal policy. Employment rises and the terms of trade reach the consistent level, although still in the unemployment region. Government continues to expand demand, encouraged by the external surplus and unemployment, but failing to recognize that the consistent wage has already been reached. From here on we have terms of trade improvements as labor raises real wages in response to employment gains, while the fiscal expansion provides the demand. In the final adjustment a loss in competitiveness and a loss of the trade surplus are compensated by fiscal expansion of home demand.

The example shows the interaction of the wage-price adjustments and fiscal policy to attain internal and external balance. The adjustment process is stable, although time consuming. It is immediately apparent that exchange rate or commercial policies can reinforce or speed up the process. In particular an exchange depreciation could rapidly bring about much of the adjustment from A to A'. Moreover, if at A' we did not have a simultaneously internal and external balance, we would want to add commercial policies to reconcile the various objectives.

IV. SUMMARY

This chapter has introduced relative prices, exchange rate, and commercial policies, as well as the wage-price process. We have found that commercial policies and *real* depreciation affect the composition of spending, the trade balance and equilibrium output. They accordingly can supplement general aggregate demand policy in achieving internal and external balance.

The wage-price process described here relates the rate of change of the terms of trade to the output gap $Y/\bar{Y}$. When output is high relative to normal, wages rise and our terms of trade improve, thereby reducing demand for domestic goods. This aspect integrates well with the objective of achieving internal balance, as it provides an automatic adjustment process that can take place even in the absence of macroeconomic adjustment policies. But the problem is that real-wage adjustment and terms of trade changes may stop short of full employment. There may be real-wage resistance which stops employment short of the full employment level because the real wage required for full employment might be lower than what labor is prepared to accept. If this is the case, structural policies to achieve internal and external balance—tariffs, subsidies, quotas, supply management—must supplement broad monetary and fiscal policies.

APPENDIX: REAL INCOME, EXPENDITURE, AND RELATIVE PRICES

In the text we made a simplifying assumption that is far from innocuous. In assuming that spending depends only on the level of output, $E = E(Y)$, we slipped under the rug the entire issue of the response of the level of spending to a change in relative prices. The issue is as follows. Suppose output Y declines. Expenditure E would then fall as well in response to the reduced real income. Now suppose, on the contrary, that output remains constant but that the relative price of imports rises. The purchasing power of our income clearly has fallen because of the terms of trade worsening. Should we not also here expect an adjustment in spending?

To get a handle on these issues, we begin with the definition of real income—as opposed to output Y:

$$Z \equiv PY/Q \tag{A-1}$$

where Z is real income and equals the nominal value of output deflated by the consumer price index Q defined in (21). Consider Figure A-1 which shows indifference curves and initial terms of trade p_o, the slope of the budget line tangent at point A. Spending measured in terms of domestic goods is E. Suppose next that the terms of trade worsen to p', but that spending in terms of domestic goods is unchanged. [This is the assumption made when writing $E = E(Y)$.] Our new equilibrium will be at A' with reduced consumption of imports and a change in demand for domestic goods that depends on the offsetting income and substitution effects. The substitution effect of a worsened terms of trade is to raise demand for domestic goods, but the reduced purchasing power of the spending level E works in the opposite direction.

Now we ask by how much spending would have to rise to attain the initial consumption basket at A. It is easily verified that if spending increased by

FIGURE A-1

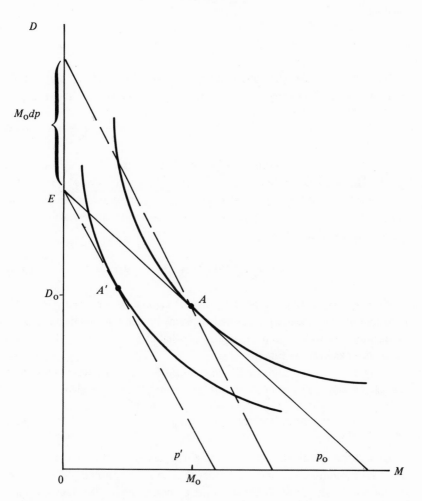

$M_o dp$—the increased cost of the initial level of imports—then we would be able to purchase exactly the bundle at point A. Thus an increase in spending that shifts the budget line outward from A' to pass through A, but with slope p' implies a constant *real* expenditure level.

How, then, do we expect people to react to a loss in real income? One extreme is point A', where real expenditure falls by the full amount of the terms of trade deterioration. The other extreme is an increase in nominal spending so as to maintain the initial purchasing power at A.

Now define the real value of expenditure, measured in terms of the price index, as V. We assume that *real* spending is an increasing function of real income:

$$V = V(Z) \qquad V' > 0 \qquad\qquad \text{(A-2)}$$

Next we establish the link between real spending and the level of expenditure measured in terms of domestic output, which we still denote E:

$$PE/Q \equiv V \qquad\qquad \text{(A-3)}$$

In (A-3) we show the definition of expenditure measured in terms of home goods. The real price of home goods in terms of the price level P/Q multiplies expenditure E to translate it into units of the consumption basket. Now substituting (A-2) into (A-3) permits us to solve for E as a behavioral equation or expenditure function:

$$E = (Q/P)V(Z) = E(p,Y) \qquad\qquad \text{(A-4)}$$

With real expenditure depending on real income, as we assume in (A-2), it turns out that spending measured in terms of home goods depends both on output Y as well as on relative prices.* What can we say about the properties of this expenditure function?

Using the formula indicated in the footnote, we can readily show that the elasticity of expenditure E, with respect to the terms of trade is

$$(\delta E/\delta p)(p/E) = (1-\beta)(1-\epsilon) \qquad \epsilon \equiv V'Z/V \qquad \text{(A-5)}$$

where ϵ is the elasticity of real spending with respect to real income. Thus if the real expenditure elasticity is smaller than unity a worsening in the terms of trade will raise expenditure in terms of home goods. But does spending rise enough to leave initial real expenditure unchanged in the sense of point A of Figure A-1? Clearly not. Because real income has fallen, real expenditure falls too, and we are somewhere between—below the initial indifference curve, yet above point A'.

What are the implications of this revised expenditure equation for our analysis in the main text? We have shown here that our earlier assumption $E = E(Y)$ is only a special case that arises if the expenditure elasticity is unity. If the elasticity is less than unity than a devaluation, for example, will bring

*From $Q/PV(Z)$ using (21) and (A-1), we have $p^{1-\beta}/V(Yp^{-(1-\beta)}) = E(p, Y)$.

about a more expansionary effect on home demand because expenditure increases to partly offset the reduction in the purchasing power of the initial spending level. At the same time, this implies that the trade improvement will be less. We will not rework our analysis but rather set an exercise for ourselves. Using the expenditure equation developed here we will seek to demonstrate that an import tariff, with full rebate of the tariff revenue, *must* raise income and improve the external balance. Try!

REFERENCES AND SUGGESTED READINGS

Cardoso, E. 1979. *Inflation, growth and the real exchange rate: essays on economic history in Brazil.* Unpublished Ph.D. dissertation, Massachusetts Institute of Technology, Cambridge, Mass.

Harberger, A. 1950. Currency depreciation, income and the balance of trade. *Journal of political economy* no. 1, 58: 47-60.

Hicks, J. 1975. What is wrong with monetarism? *Lloyds bank review* October, no. 18: 1-3.

Johnson, H. G. 1956. The transfer problem and exchange stability. *Journal of political economy* no. 3, 64:212-25.

Johnson, H. G. 1962. *Money, trade and economic growth* [Chapter 1]. London: Unwin University Books.

Kemp, M. 1964. *The pure theory of international trade.* [Part V]. Englewood Cliffs, N.J.: Prentice-Hall.

Laursen, S. and Metzler, L. 1950. Flexible exchange rates and the theory of employment. *Review of Economics and Statistics* 32:281-99.

5

Intermediate Goods and Nontraded Goods

In the preceding chapters we developed an integrated and complete model of the goods markets of an open economy. This brief chapter rounds out the analysis by introducing two important extensions. Two categories of goods are introduced—intermediate goods and nontraded goods—that so far had no place in our model.

The extension brings more realism to our model, as nontraded and intermediate goods are important in practice. We will find that the introduction of these complications brings with it some interesting qualifications of our earlier results.

Section I sets out a very simple model of an economy in which money wages are fixed and where labor is the only primary factor of production. In section II we study a real depreciation. Section III introduces an exogenous increase in intermediate goods prices.

Intermediate Goods and Nontraded Goods

I. THE MODEL

The home country produces two commodities—an exportable and a non-traded good. The commodity that is nontraded can best be thought of as services—haircuts, and so forth—or as a tradeable good that is not, in fact, traded because of transport costs, quotas or prohibitive tariffs. Both commodities are produced by labor and an imported intermediate good. In both industries technology is one of constant returns with fixed co-efficients.

1. The Basic Structure

With competition and constant returns, prices of goods are equal to their marginal and average costs. Letting a_i and b_i denote the unit labor and intermediate goods requirements W and P_m, the wage and the intermediate goods price we have

$$P_x = a_x W + b_x P_m \qquad P_n = a_n W + b_n P_m \qquad (1)$$

where P_x and P_n denote the price of exportables and home goods (or non-traded goods) and where the subscripts x and n denote those two sectors, respectively. We also introduce the domestic currency price of foreign goods competing with our exportables in world markets P^*. Next we look at relative prices. The relative price of exportables in terms of home goods and in terms of foreign goods are derived from (1) as

$$p \equiv P_x/P_n = (a_x w + b_x)/(a_n w + b_n) \qquad w \equiv W/P_m \qquad (2)$$

and

$$TOT \quad = p^* \equiv P_x/P^* = (a_x w + b_x)/\lambda \qquad \lambda \equiv P^*/P_m \qquad (3)$$

where w denotes the real wage in terms of intermediate goods and λ is the exogenous relative price of intermediate goods and export competing goods given in the rest of the world. $\left\} w = \dfrac{W}{P_m} \right.$

To complete our model we specify the demand side, employment, and the trade balance. We start with demand. Domestic demand for exportables and nontraded goods depends on relative prices and real income:

$$D_x = D_x(p, Y) \qquad D_n = D_n(p, Y) \tag{4}$$

where real income is equal to labor income WL, deflated by the consumer price level:

$$Y \equiv WL/Q(P_x, P_n) \tag{5}$$

The deflator Q is once again a linear homogeneous function of the market prices of the consumption bundle with elasticities equal to the budget shares. Foreign demand for our exportable depends only on the relative price:

$$M^* = M^*(p^*) \tag{6}$$

Employment is demand determined. Given the unit labor requirements a_x and a_n the levels of demand determine employment:

$$L = a_x(D_x + M^*) + a_n D_n \tag{7}$$

The trade balance, finally, is equal to exports less intermediate goods imports:

$$T = P_x M^* - P_m b_x(D_x + M^*) - P_m b_n D_n \tag{8}$$

2. Relative Prices and Employment

We can now solve for equilibrium output and employment as well as for the relative price structure in terms of the exogenous real wage w. We start with the effect of a change in w on relative prices. An increase in the wage in terms of intermediate goods, using (2), yields the following elasticities of relative prices:

$$d\ln p/d\ln w = (\beta_x - \beta_n) \qquad d\ln p^*/d\ln w = \beta_x \qquad \beta_i \equiv a_i W/P_i \tag{9}$$

where β_i is labor's share in the ith sector. The effect of a change in the real wage on relative prices is a straightforward application of the *Stolper-Samuelson theorem*—a rise in the real wage raises the relative price of the commodity that uses labor intensively. Thus if exportables are labor intensive, the relative price of exportables will rise in terms of home goods.

Two points are important to recognize in relation to (9). First, domestic relative prices need not change as a consequence of changes in relative factor

Intermediate Goods and Nontraded Goods

prices. If distributive shares, or factor intensities, are the same, there will not be any differential cost effects, and hence no relative price change. Furthermore, with small differences in shares—10 or even 20 percentage point differences—we still have relatively small price changes. Suppose real wages rise by 10 percent, then we would obtain only at most a 2 percent relative price change. Consequently there is a substantial dampening effect. The second point concerns the fact that a devaluation—a fall in wages relative to import prices—may raise the relative price of home goods in terms of exportables. This must happen if home goods are intensive in materials. The circumstance may well prevail in many developing countries where the home goods sector includes substantial manufacturing activity that is sheltered from imports by prohibitive tariffs but which nevertheless have substantial import requirements in terms of intermediate goods.

With regard to p^*, the relative price of exportables, unambiguously rises in terms of foreign goods. The increase in price is proportionally less than the real wage increase because labor costs are only a fraction or total cost and price. In fact, the elasticity is equal to labor's share or value added as a fraction of price. This point is of interest because it suggests that wage increases do not translate one for one into a loss of competitiveness.

Consider next the determinants of changes in real income. Log-differentiating (5) we obtain

$$\hat{Y} = \hat{W} + \hat{L} - \alpha_x \hat{P}_x - \alpha_n \hat{P}_n \tag{5a}$$

where α_i is the budget share of the ith commodity. Adding and subtracting $\hat{P}_m$ on the right-hand side yields

$$\hat{Y} = \hat{w} + \hat{L} - \alpha_x(\hat{P}_x - \hat{P}_m) - \alpha_n(\hat{P}_n - \hat{P}_m) \tag{5b}$$

which in turn, using (1) reduces to

$$\hat{Y} = \sigma \hat{w} + \hat{L} \qquad \sigma \equiv 1 - \alpha_x \beta_x - \alpha_n \beta_n > 0 \tag{10}$$

Accordingly, a rise in our real wages raises real income, as does a rise in employment. Higher real wages, in terms of intermediates, raise real income only by a fraction of the real wage increase. That fraction is in fact equal to the part of labor income derived from the production of exports. With unchanged productivity we can raise our real income only by having more favorable terms of trade.

We now have done all the preliminary work needed to discuss the effect of a change in real wages on employment. Before going on to the algebra, let us look at the effects that are to be isolated:

1. A rise in real wages, by (9) raises the relative price of our exportable therefore reducing foreign demand and hence employment.

2. A rise in the real wage raises the domestic relative price of the labor intensive goods, thereby inviting substitution away from that commodity. Interestingly, we can show that this effect *must* reduce employment.

3. A rise in real wages by (10) raises real income, real expenditure, and hence employment.

4. There is a multiplier effect associated with induced changes in employment, as these [by (10)] raise real income, spending, and hence employment.

We now derive and progressively simplify an equation describing the change in employment. Differentiating (7) we have

$$dL = a_x dM^* + [a_x(\delta D_x/\delta p) + a_n(\delta D_n/\delta p)] dp +$$
$$[a_x(\delta D_x/\delta Y) + a_n(\delta D_n/\delta Y)] dY \qquad (11)$$

To simplify the expression, we define the domestic marginal propensities and the foreign price elasticity of demand:

$$\gamma_i \equiv (p_i/Q)(\delta D_i/\delta Y) \qquad \eta^* \equiv - (dM^*/dp^*) p^*/M^* \qquad (12)$$

With the help of (10), these definitions, and the distributive share expressions in (9) we have

$$dL = [1/(1 - \phi)] [-\eta^* M^* a_x \hat{p}^* +$$
$$(a_x \delta D_x \delta p + a_n/\delta D_n/\delta p) dp + \phi \sigma \hat{w}] \qquad (13)$$

where $\phi \equiv \beta_x \gamma_x + \beta_n \gamma_n$

The remaining term to be simplified is that describing the employment effect of domestic substitution between exportables and home goods. The expressions $\delta D_x/\delta p$ and $\delta D_n/\delta p$ describe real income constant changes in demand or changes along an indifference curve. Maximization then implies that

$$p\delta D_x/\delta p = - \delta D_n/\delta p \qquad (14)$$

Substitution affects employment only to the extent that sectoral unit labor requirements differ. Using (14) in (13) and substituting from (9) for the relative price changes yields the final equation:

Intermediate Goods and Nontraded Goods

$$\hat{L} = [1/(1-\phi)] [-\sigma\eta^*\beta_x - (\beta_x - \beta_n)^2 \alpha_x \bar{\eta} + \phi\sigma] \hat{w} \qquad (15)$$

where σ is again the fraction of our labor force employed in the production of exports and $\bar{\eta} \equiv -(\delta D_x/\delta p)p/D_x$.

Equation (15) shows that a rise in our real wage will reduce employment in the production of exports. This reduction is larger, the larger the fraction of the labor force is employed in the production of exports and the higher the foreign elasticity and labor's share in exportables. The latter determinant comes in because a rise in the real wage $\hat{w}$ raises the relative price only by a fraction equal to labor's share. Next we look at the domestic substitution effect. Substitution must unambiguously lower employment. The reason is that a rise in real wages raises the relative price of labor-intensive goods, leading to substitution away from the commodity that is labor intensive and thus reducing employment. Finally, we have the income effect of a rise in real wages. This leads to an expansion in demand and employment. The net effect, all channels considered, is ambiguous. Without the income effect employment must fall but the income effect potentially offsets the result.

There is a slightly different way of looking at the employment results, emphasizing that the rise in our real wages redistributes real income from abroad to the home country. Using the result $\eta^* = \bar{\eta}^* + \gamma_x^*$ and breaking up the term ϕ we obtain

$$\hat{L} = [1/(1-\phi)] [\sigma\beta_x(\gamma_x - \gamma_x^*) - \sigma(\beta_x\bar{\eta}^* - \beta_n\gamma_n) - \alpha_x\bar{\eta}(\beta_x - \beta_n)^2] \hat{w} \qquad (15a)$$

The term $(\gamma_x - \gamma_x^*)$ reflects the effect of income redistribution on employment. Our real income rises, raising demand for exportables, while the converse occurs abroad. The net effect depends on differences in marginal spending patterns. Even assuming identical spending patterns we retain the ambiguity in the employment effect because the home country spends part of the real income gain on nontraded goods, where foreigners have a zero propensity by definition. This is one of the features that nontraded goods introduce into the analysis.

II. A DEVALUATION

We now apply the model to the question of devaluation. Assume that money wages are constant and that the exchange rate is depreciated. This raises import prices for intermediate goods or it lowers the real wage $\hat{w}$. At the same time domestic goods become cheaper abroad in proportion $\beta_x \hat{w}$ owing to the reduced real cost of our labor. What are the effects of such a depreciation on real income Y and the trade balance?

We already studied the employment effect of a real wage change. Now we look at the change in real income, using (10) and (15a) to obtain

$$\hat{Y} = [1/(1-\phi)] [1 - \eta^*\beta_x\sigma - \alpha_x(\beta_x - \beta_n)^2\bar{\eta}] \, \hat{w} \qquad (16)$$

The effect of a change in the real exchange rate on real income is ambiguous. If elasticities are sufficiently high, it is possible for the adverse employment effect to more than offset the higher real wage.

The trade balance effect of a change in the real wage can be obtained most simply from the recognition that with goods market equilibrium the trade balance is equal to the excess of income over spending:

$$T = P_x M^* - b_x P_m M^* - P_m(b_n D_n + b_x D_x) = WL - (P_n D_n + P_x D_x) = Q[Y - A(Y)] \qquad (17)$$

where $A(Y)$ is real expenditure measured in terms of the consumer basket. Using (17) the trade balance effect is given by

$$dT/WL = (1-\rho)\hat{Y} \qquad (18)$$

where ρ is the marginal propensity to spend.

The trade balance improves if the depreciation raises real income. The trade balance *must* improve, then, if employment remains unchanged or rises, for in that case real income increases unambiguously. More generally, the factors making for an improvement in the trade balance are the same as those making for a rise in employment in response to a depreciation. They are high foreign elasticities and a high labor share in exportables. A high domestic substitutability and large differences in sectoral labor shares, likewise, serve to enhance the employment and trade balance effects of a depreciation.

Comparing these results with the Marshall-Lerner condition studied in the previous chapter, we see the effect of a depreciation on the trade balance in both cases, but find that the channels and certainly some of the details are quite different. Here we emphasize on the export side a devaluation as a way of reducing the real price of domestic value added—labor—in terms of foreign goods.

On the import side the response to devaluation appears quite different from the model of the previous chapter since we do not have at all a demand for final import goods. The response to depreciation here is one of *derived* demand for intermediate goods. The substitution toward the labor-intensive commodity noted in discussing employment has as its counterpart a substitution away from the commodity intensive in intermediate goods. The derived demand for intermediate goods therefore unambiguously declines. The only question is whether the elasticity is sufficiently large to offset the higher real cost of intermediate goods.

With this interpretation, then, we are back to the proposition that a devaluation improves the trade balance, provided the export and import elasticities are sufficiently large to offset the worsening in the terms of trade. The important point that is being made is that we can always write our trade balance, measured in terms of exportables:

$$T = M^* - (P_m/P_x)M \qquad M \equiv b_x(M^* + D_x) + b_n D_n \qquad (17a)$$

and derive the Marshall-Lerner condition. But in so doing we lose a lot of the extra information we may discern from our knowledge about the structure of the economy, which is being used in (16) and (18).

III. AN INTERMEDIATE GOODS PRICE INCREASE

Here we pursue the analysis of intermediate goods to see the impact on employment and the trade balance of an exogenous increase in the real price of intermediate goods in the world. In terms of our equations this exercise corresponds to a constant exchange rate, money wage, and price of export competing goods abroad. Only P_m the price of intermediate goods rises. How does this exercise differ from a devaluation? In the devaluation case we kept the external terms of trade constant thus changing the wage in terms of both materials and export competing goods. Now we change only material prices. The difference is essential for the following reason: We saw in the last chapter that a devaluation is equivalent to an export subsidy and an import tax. Now that symmetry is lost, because we have only a material price increase and therefore an increase in costs in the exportable sector and thus a net tax on exports.

Formally we retain the change in the domestic relative price due to a change in the real wage w, but now for the relative price of exportables we have a different expression:

$$d1np/d1nP_m = -(\beta_x - \beta_n) \qquad d1np^*/d1nP_m = (1 - \beta_x) \qquad (9a)$$

Thus an increase in intermediate goods prices raises the relative price of the commodity using intermediates intensively, and it unambiguously raises the relative price of our exportables in terms of foreign, competing goods. The latter result reflects simply the fact that our exportable uses intermediates and that an increase in their price raises costs by their share in costs $1 - \beta_x$.

The employment effects are straightforwardly obtained from (13) by substituting $\hat{w} = -\hat{P}_m$ and by using (9a) for p^*:

$$\hat{L} = [1/(1 - \phi)] [-\eta^*(1 - \beta_x)\sigma + (\beta_x - \beta_n)^2 \alpha_x \bar{\eta} - \phi\sigma] \hat{P}_m \qquad (19)$$

Three points are worth noting. First, as in the devaluation case, the income effect associated with the deterioration in the terms of trade is to lower spending, demand, and employment. This is the term $\phi\sigma$. Second, domestic substitution toward the labor intensive good, just as in the case of a devaluation, works to raise employment. Third, unlike the case of devaluation, exports will fall and therefore will work to reduce employment. The latter effect arises because the intermediate goods price increase raises export costs and thus makes us lose competitiveness. It is apparent from (19) that the net effect is ambiguous. Compared with a devaluation, an expansion in employment now is *less* likely because exports move in the direction of less employment. Indeed, the only force for an expansion in employment is domestic substitution toward the labor-intensive good.

Suppose we had a situation in which a devaluation raises employment but where an intermediate goods price increase reduces employment. How can we offset with exchange rate policy the adverse employment effects of an intermediate goods price increase? We would have to depreciate the exchange rate thus raising intermediate goods prices even further; this part, as we already have seen has a net adverse employment effect. But the implicit subsidy to exports implied by a devaluation more than offsets, by assumption, these adverse effects, thereby bringing about a net expansion in employment.

IV. CONCLUDING REMARKS

This chapter has introduced the complications of intermediate goods and nontraded goods to round out our analysis of relative prices and employment determination in the open economy. What are the important points of difference or similarity with our earlier analysis?

First, the introduction of imported intermediate goods makes it essential to distinguish output and value added, relative prices of goods and relative prices of factors. It is still true that a devaluation tends to create employment through the effects of substitution and tends to reduce employment by means of its adverse income effects. The presence of nontraded goods makes the income effect more than a simple international redistribution effect.

An exercise that we could not conduct before, an exogenous increase in material prices, shows interesting results. Higher prices of imported materials have adverse employment effects because they are an implicit tax on our exportables and because they imply a reduction in real income and therefore in spending. But there is a favorable effect as well. The decline in the domestic relative price of labor intensive goods tends to make for an expansion in employment.

A final point worth emphasizing concerns the Marshall-Lerner condition. Here we have an example where all imports are intermediate goods. Still, we can think of the elasticity of import demand and we find that it is the elasticity of *derived* demand for intermediates reflecting as much the elasticity of foreign demand for our exports as purely domestic intersectoral substitution. The point to be recognized is that across models what appears as the same Marshall-Lerner condition reflects very different economic structures and channels through which relative prices affect demand.

REFERENCES AND SUGGESTED READINGS

Berglas, E., and Razin, A. 1973. Real exchange rate and devaluation. *Journal of international economics.* 179-91.

Corden, M., and Jones, R. 1976. Devaluation, nonflexible prices, and the trade balance for a small country. *Canadian journal of economics.*

Dornbusch, R. 1973. Real and monetary aspects of the effects of exchange rate changes.

National monetary policy and the international financial system, ed. R.A. Aliber. Chicago: University of Chicago Press.

Findlay, R., and Rodriguez, C. 1977. Intermediate imports and macroeconomic policy under flexible exchange rates. *Canadian journal of economics.*

Jones, R. 1965. The structure of simple general equilibrium models. *Journal of political economy.*

Kemp, M. 1969. *The pure theory of international trade.* Englewood Cliffs: Prentice-Hall.

Schmid, M. 1976. A model of trade in money, goods and factors. *Journal of international economics.*

C H A P T E R

6

Home Goods and Traded Goods: the Dependent Economy Model

Our discussion of models can now be extended to include nontraded goods. Nontraded goods were introduced in the preceding chapter in the context of intermediate goods and employment determination. Here we shift the focus to a model with full employment. The main question we address is how adjustments in the relative price of nontraded goods help achieve internal-external balance. To simplify our analysis we will initially assume a small country with given terms of trade. The only relative price we are concerned with is the relative price of home goods in terms of traded goods.

In section I we motivate our model of nontraded goods. First, we show reasons for the existence of nontraded goods, then we distinguish two basic models that have been used extensively in the literature. These are, respectively, the Australian model and the Scandinavian model. In the remainder of the chapter we develop and use the Australian model. The analysis shows that this is a very useful analytical framework for the discussion of internal-external balance problems in small countries. Section IV extends the model to endogenous terms of trade.

I. MODELS WITH NONTRADED GOODS

In this part we develop a rationale for the existence of nontraded goods and then proceed to sketch alternative models of the supply side of the economy.

1. A Motivation for Nontraded Goods

We introduce our discussion here with a brief motivation of nontraded goods, *sheltered goods*, or *home goods* as they are interchangeably called. There are several reasons why particular commodities may be nontraded. The most important reasons are transport costs and commercial policy obstacles. Transport costs provide a particularly intuitive explanation and we use them here as an example.

Suppose a given commodity has a world market price P^* and suppose the commodity is consumed and produced at home. Under what conditions will the good be imported, exported, or nontraded? Let the transport cost, in any direction, be a fixed percentage charge per unit. In Figure 6-1 we show the domestic and foreign price on the axes as well as a cone that defines the region of nontraded goods, which we now derive.

For the commodity we are discussing to be exported, domestic price inclusive of transport costs $P(1+\phi)$ would have to be smaller than or equal to foreign price. Using that relation with equality defines the price $\underline{P}$ for which the commodity is at the margin between being nontraded and exportable: $\underline{P}(1+\phi) = P^*$. For the commodity to be imported, the foreign price inclusive of transport charges $P^*(1+\phi)$ would have to be smaller than or equal to the domestic price. This defines the maximum price for which the good is nontraded before it becomes an importable: $\overline{P} = P^*(1+\phi)$.

We show in Figure 6-1 the world price P_0^* and the corresponding maximum and minimum prices that can prevail in the home country. The horizontal distance between the two prices $\underline{P}$ and $\overline{P}$ defines the range of prices for

FIGURE 6-1

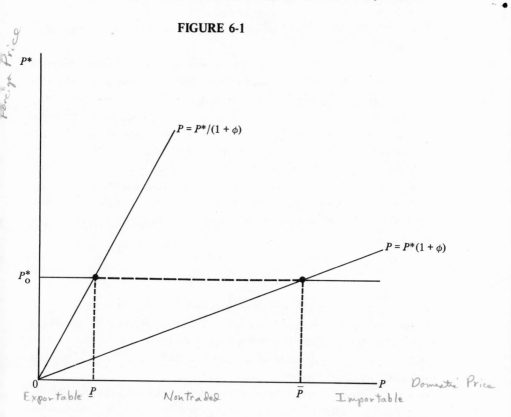

which the commodity is nontraded. It is sheltered from world market competition by transport costs. If domestic price comes to the border line, the commodity becomes tradeable at the transport cost adjusted world price.

The analysis immediately suggests that an expansion in demand that raises domestic prices will push some goods to the margin of becoming importables. Conversely a fall in demand and prices will make some nontraded goods exportable.* In this chapter we assume away this endogeneity of nontraded goods and assume, instead, that there is a group of commodities that is sufficiently sheltered to remain nontraded at all relevant prices. A frequently cited example is services, such as housing or haircuts.

2. The Scandinavian and the Australian Models

The role of nontraded goods in open economy macroeconomics has long been emphasized, beginning with Cairnes (1874) and the important contri-

---

*We leave it to the reader to develop the analysis for the case of an import tariff in the home country at rate t.

butions by Hawtrey (1931), Wilson (1931), and Iversen (1935) in the interwar period.

Nontraded goods have since been analyzed in the Australian model by Meade (1951), Salter (1959), Swan (1960, 1963), and Pearce (1961), in the Latin American tradition by Diaz Alejandro (1964) and Harberger (1966) and in the Scandinavian model by Aukrust (1977) and others. The broad popularity of the model suggests that it captures essential aspects of the price adjustment mechanism in relation to external balance problems.

The Scandinavian variant is a Ricardian model, in which labor is the only factor of production and where home goods and traded goods are produced with constant returns, fixed coefficients production functions. With a given labor force L, maximum output of home goods and traded goods, respectively, equals

$$L/a_N \text{ and } L/a_T \tag{1}$$

where a_N and a_T are the unit labor requirements in the production of nontraded and traded goods, respectively. Moreover, because of fixed unit labor requirements, there is a constant marginal rate of substitution between traded and nontraded goods. The transformation curve for this model is accordingly a straight line.

The equation for the transformation schedule is easily derived from the equations for output levels Y_T and Y_N and the aggregate labor market equilibrium condition:

$$L_N = a_N Y_N \qquad L_T = a_T Y_T \qquad L = L_N + L_T \tag{2}$$

and hence, using (2):

$$Y_N = L_N/a_N = (L - L_T)/a_N = L/a_N - (a_T/a_N)Y_T \tag{3}$$

Equation (3) shows the level of output of nontraded goods as a function of the available labor force and the level of traded goods production. The marginal rate of substitution dY_N/dY_T is given by the ratio of unit labor requirements a_T/a_N. The marginal rate of substitution sets the relative price of the two commodities. Thus in the Scandinavian model the relative price is given by technology alone and is constant and independent of the composition of output between home goods and traded goods.

Figure 6-2 below shows the Australian model. Here the production side, with labor mobile between sectors but with diminishing returns, gives rise to a bowed out transformation curve. The relative price of home goods in terms of traded goods is given by the slope of the transformation curve. Clearly, the relative price depends on the composition of output. If we produce relatively few home goods there is a low relative price of home goods. Conversely, with a larger share of output being home goods, their relative cost and price is high.

In chapter 5 we looked at an unemployment version of the Scandinavian model, complicated by the presence of intermediate goods. Here we concentrate entirely on the Australian model.

II. THE DEPENDENT ECONOMY MODEL*

The model we are developing in this part has its origin in the writings of Wilson, Swan, and Salter in the Australian trade literature. It is called the "dependent economy model" to emphasize the fact that the country is assumed to be a price taker in the world market for importables and exportables alike. The terms of trade are thus exogenously given, and a distinction between importables and exportables becomes immaterial for most questions. The model differs sharply from those studied in chapters 4 and 5, in which the terms of trade and the world demand for the home country's exportable were assumed to be endogenous. With no need to distinguish between exportables and importables we can aggregate them into a composite commodity called traded goods. (A composite commodity is a group of goods whose relative prices are given.) Traded goods as a group are then distinguished from nontraded goods or home goods.

To the assumption of given terms of trade we add the further assumption of wage and price flexibility. Wage and price flexibility will ensure full employment. In section II(1) we develop the supply side of our model. Section II(2) introduces demand conditions; Sections II(3,4) deal with internal and external balance and the analysis of disequilibrium, respectively.

1. Factor Markets and Output Supplies

The two sectors—traded and nontraded goods—are assumed to have specific capital in a fixed amount that is immobile between sectors in the short run, which we are concerned with. The labor force is fixed in the

*This section draws on Dornbusch (1974).

aggregate but the allocation between sectors is endogenous. Given the fixed capital stock in each industry and the assumption that firms view themselves as operating in competitive markets, we can derive the demand for labor in each sector as a function of the given technology, the capital stock, and the product wage. Equilibrium in the labor market then requires that

$$L_T(W/P_T, K_T) + L_N(W/P_N, K_N) = L \qquad (4)$$

where W is the nominal wage, P_T and P_N denote traded and nontraded good prices, and K_i the capital stock in the ith sector. The aggregate labor force is equal to L. With fixed capital and hence diminishing returns, the demand for labor will be a decreasing function in each sector of the product wage. The product wage means here the wage measured in terms of the output of the respective sectors.

We can solve the labor market equilibrium condition for the equilibrium wage rate as a function of output prices and capital endowments:

$$W = W(P_N, P_T; K_i) \qquad (5)$$

We note that the equilibrium wage is a linear homogeneous function of the output prices. Specifically, for given capital stocks and productivity we have

$$\hat{W} = \gamma \hat{P}_N + (1 - \gamma)\hat{P}_T = \hat{P}_T - \gamma(\hat{P}_T - \hat{P}_N) \qquad 0 < \gamma < 1 \qquad (6)$$

where a caret ($\wedge$) denotes a percentage change.* Equation (6) is one of the key relations we are interested in. It states that the change in the equilibrium wage rate is equal to the change in the price of traded goods adjusted for changes in the relative price of traded goods in terms of home goods.

Alternatively, taking $\hat{P}_T$ or $\hat{P}_N$ to the left-hand side we derive a relation between product wages and relative prices:

$$\hat{W} - \hat{P}_T = -\gamma(\hat{P}_T - \hat{P}_N) \qquad \hat{W} - \hat{P}_N = (1 - \gamma)(\hat{P}_T - \hat{P}_N) \qquad (6a)$$

A rise in the relative price of traded goods lowers the equilibrium relative wage in terms of traded goods and raises the real wage in terms of home goods. Given the labor force, a higher real wage in terms of home goods implies a fall in employment in that industry, while the lower real wage in the traded goods sector encourages increased employment there.

---

*The term γ is defined as $\gamma \equiv \xi_N \alpha_N / (\xi_N \alpha_N + \xi_T \alpha_T)$ where ξ_i and α_i are the elasticities of labor demand and the share of the labor force in sector i. Equation (6) can be derived from (4) by log-differentiation.

Home Goods and Traded Goods: the Dependent Economy Model

Turning now to equilibrium supplies we introduce the shorthand notation v for the relative price of traded goods in terms of home goods:

$$v \equiv P_T/P_N \tag{7}$$

From (5) or (6a) and the demand functions for labor, we recognize that employment and output in each sector will be a function of relative prices:

$$Y_T = Y_T(v) \qquad Y_N = Y_N(v) \tag{8}$$

In (8) output of traded goods is an increasing function of the relative price of traded goods, while the output of home goods declines as the relative price rises. As these supply schedules are derived from the condition of equilibrium in the labor market they correspond to full employment supplies "along the transformation curve," as shown in Figure 6-2. Here we illustrate the transformation curve CC between home and traded goods and a relative price ratio with the associated levels of equilibrium output in each industry.

FIGURE 6-2

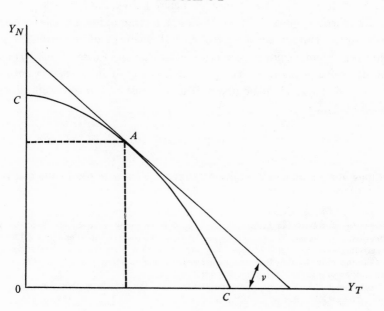

2. Demand Conditions

We write our demand functions for home goods and traded goods as a function of relative prices v, and real expenditure, where we measure the latter in terms of home goods:*

$$D_N = D_N(v, E) \qquad D_T = D_T(v, E) \qquad (9)$$

where E measures real spending in terms of home goods and where the D_i are the demand functions. A rise in the relative price of traded goods, given E, reduces demand for traded goods both on account of the income and substitution effect. A rise in the relative price of traded goods has an ambiguous effect on home goods demand. The substitution effect raises home goods demand, whereas the income effect reduces demand. A rise in real spending raises both demands. For subsequent reference we define real expenditure E as follows:

$$E \equiv D_N + vD_T \qquad (10)$$

3. Internal and External Balance

We combine now the demand and supply side of the economy to show the combinations of expenditure levels and relative prices that will, respectively, yield internal and external balance. In Figure 6-3 we show three schedules. The YY schedule shows the value of output in terms of home goods for each relative price, corresponding to the vertical intercept of the price line in Figure 6-2. From Figure 6-2 we can predict that an increase in the relative price of traded goods (a steeper price line) will yield an increase in output measured in terms of home goods. The schedule is formally defined by equation (11):†

$$Y \equiv Y_N + vY_T \qquad (11)$$

Along the BB schedule we have external balance. A rise in the relative

---

*We could follow the procedure given in chapter 5 and measure all quantities in terms of a price index. The procedure used here is entirely equivalent and only relies on the zero homogeneity in nominal spending and all prices of the real commodity demands. That homogeneity implies that we can use *any* nominal quantity as the numéraire—be it a price index or a particular commodity price.

†Remember that because of maximization along the transformation curve, $dY_n = -v \, dY_T$; thus $dY/dv = Y_T$.

FIGURE 6-3

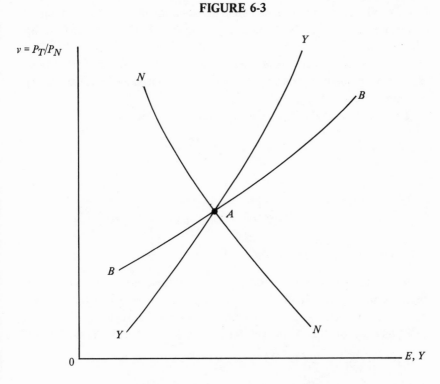

price of traded goods reduces demand but raises supply of traded goods and accordingly there is a trade surplus. To eliminate the trade surplus, real spending—and therefore demand for traded goods—must rise. Thus the *BB* schedule is positively sloped. Finally, along the *NN* schedule we have home goods market equilibrium. Assuming that substitution effects dominate the income effects of a relative price change, we draw the schedule with a negative sloped. A reduction in the relative price of traded goods creates an excess supply—reduced demand and increased supply—that has to be offset by an increased level of spending to maintain equilibrium in that market.

In passing we note that if it were positively sloped, the *NN* schedule would have to be steeper than the *YY* schedule. The reason is that along *YY*, at point *A*, expenditure equals income, and therefore changes in the relative price of traded goods generate no *net* income effect. As consumers we are worse off by the amount $D_T dv$, but as producers our incomes rise by $Y_T dv$. With balanced trade (at point *A*) the two cancel out, leaving us only substitution effects to reckon with. But the substitution effect of an increase in the relative price of traded goods unambiguously creates excess demand for home goods, thus requiring a reduction in spending *below* the value of output to restore equilibrium. By the same argument it is readily shown that the *BB* schedule must be flatter than the *YY* schedule. The point we are making here is very important: there are no net income effects in the economy from a change in the relative price of home goods. These income effects are reserved for terms of trade changes.*

The equations of the *BB* and *NN* schedules are, respectively:

$$Y_T(v) = D_T(v, E) \tag{12}$$

and

$$Y_N(v) = D_N(v, E) \tag{13}$$

4. Anatomy of Disequilibrium

In this section we characterize disequilibria in terms of overspending or underspending and in terms of an overvalued or undervalued *real exchange rate*. The real exchange rate here is the relative price of traded goods and the interpretation of that term will become apparent shortly. The excess of income over spending is equal to

$$Y - E = v(Y_T - D_T) + (Y_N - D_N) \tag{14}$$

or, writing the expression in terms of the trade balance $Y_T - D_T$

$$v(Y_T - D_T) = (D_N - Y_N) + (Y - E) \tag{14a}$$

Equation (14a) tells us that trade balance problems are either a reflection of imbalance between income and spending $Y - E$ or of a disequilibrium in the home goods market. A trade surplus either reflects an excess of income over spending or an excess demand for nontraded goods. When the home goods market clears, the trade surplus is equal to the excess of income over expenditure.

These relationships are illustrated in Figure 6-4, where we again show the external and internal balance schedules. Suppose the relative price is v_o. At

---

*Two important qualifications are in order here. Our categorical assertion that a change in the relative price of home goods does not generate net income effects is correct only with initially balanced trade and with no domestic distribution effects between capital and labor or between the private sector and the government. These issues are dealt with in Krugman and Taylor (1978).

FIGURE 6-4

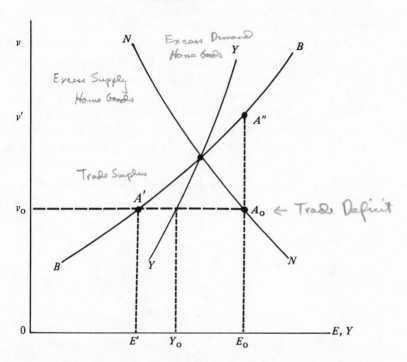

that relative price we have home goods market equilibrium at an expenditure level E_0. But at that level of spending there is a trade deficit. The size of the trade deficit is $E_0 - Y_0$. To have external balance at the relative price v_0, expenditure would have to be E', but at that level of spending there would be an excess supply of home goods. Conversely, if expenditure were at level E_0, external balance would require a much higher relative price of traded goods v'. Again at A'' there is disequilibrium in the home goods market reflecting the imbalance between income and spending.

III. ADJUSTMENT FOR INTERNAL AND EXTERNAL BALANCE

We now have understood the structure of the dependent economy model and can use it to study the adjustment to a number of disturbances. We depart from the spirit of analysis in earlier chapters in two quite fundamental respects. First, we assume *full* and *instantaneous* wage and price flexibility, thus ensuring full employment. Second, we assume that expenditure is *identically* equal to income. (In terms of Figure 4 we are always along the *YY* schedule.) What interesting questions are left once employment and trade balance problems are ruled out by assumption? The remaining question concerns the adjustment in the equilibrium real exchange rate required to accommodate a variety of disturbances.

Case (1) Suppose we find ourselves in a situation of disequilibrium because of a demand shift from home goods to traded goods. This situation is shown in Figure 6-5, where *A* is the initial equilibrium. The demand shift implies

FIGURE 6-5

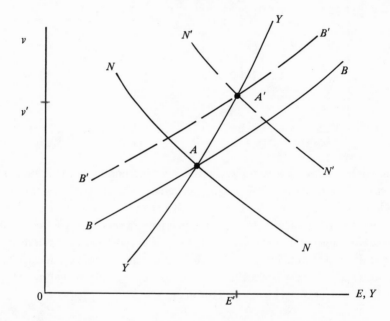

that at *A* there is an excess supply of home goods and a matching trade deficit. In order to restore internal and external balance we make adjustments in spending and in relative prices. The relative price of traded goods rises to *v'* and spending, measured in terms of home goods, rises to *E'*. (In terms of traded goods, we have a decline in income and spending, as can be verified from Figure 6-2.)

(2) Consider next the case of a transfer received by the home country. First we have to redefine external balance as current-account equilibrium and note

104

that the YY schedule shifts to the right by the transfer. The BB schedule shifts by $1/m$ times the transfer, where m denotes the propensity to spend on traded goods. As is shown in Figure 6-6, the equilibrium relative price of

FIGURE 6-6

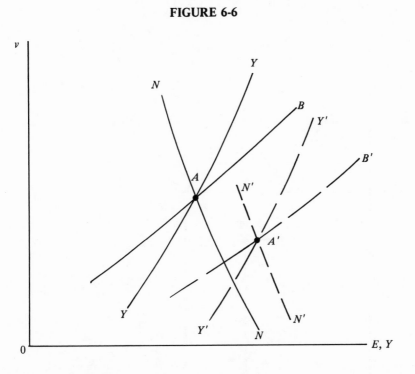

traded goods falls, and income and spending will rise in order to maintain internal and external balance.

The relative price adjustment is an important aspect of the transfer because of the following point: at the initial relative price, part of the transfer-induced spending falls on home goods, and *not* on traded goods. What then ensures that we return to current account balance with a trade deficit that matches the transfer exactly? The answer is that the equilibrium relative price of home goods will rise, thereby inducing substitution toward traded goods until the home goods market clears, or equivalently, until the trade deficit equals the transfer.

The analysis of a transfer can similarly be conducted in terms of demand and supply schedules in the home goods market. The analysis is useful because it shows the general equilibrium interpretation of these schedules. We showed in (8) that the supply of nontraded goods, given labor market equilibrium or along the transformation curve, is an increasing function of the relative price of home goods in terms of traded goods. This is the supply schedule shown in Figure 6-7. The increasing marginal cost of home goods

FIGURE 6-7

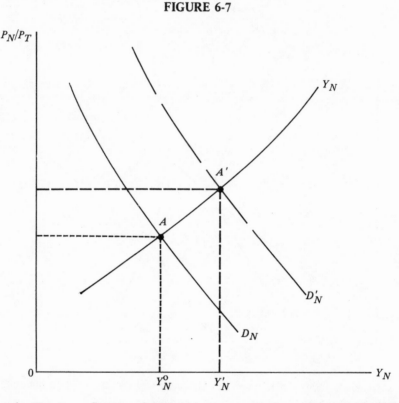

production is a reflection of diminishing returns in the two sectors. We also show the demand schedule. It is shown downward sloping and is drawn for a level of expenditure equal to income. Thus movements along the schedule reflect only substitution effects. A decline in the relative price of home goods leads to an increase in demand.

Consider again the receipt of a transfer. This raises disposable income and expenditure. Demand for home goods rises at each relative price, thereby shifting out the demand schedule by the marginal propensity to spend on home goods times the transfer. The equilibrium relative price of home goods rises, as does the level of home goods production. What factors are responsible for the correspondence between a worsening trade balance and the transfer? In part, the trade balance deteriorates because the increase in demand for traded goods increases as a direct function of rising disposable income. For the rest, the trade balance deteriorates because on the supply side, resources are withdrawn from traded goods production in order to supply increased quantities of home goods. On the demand side, the rise in the relative price of home goods leads to substitution toward traded goods and a consequent increase in the trade deficit.

(3)   We conclude our analysis with the case of increased productivity in the traded goods sector. Suppose we have improved technology and that it raises labor productivity in that sector at each level of employment. Figure 6-8 plots the growth in productivity as an outward shift in the transformation curve. Maximum home goods production remains unchanged because there is no productivity growth in that sector. But for each level of home goods production the level of traded goods output rises because of enhanced productivity.

Our initial equilibrium is at point A with a relative price given by the tangent to the transformation and indifference curves at that point. What will happen to relative supplies at the initial relative price? We would move to a point A', with reduced home goods production and increased supply of traded goods. Why? At initial prices growth in productivity implies that in the traded goods sector the marginal-value product of labor rises above the initial wage, causing labor demand to expand and wages to increase. But with higher wages and unchanged prices the real wage in terms of home goods rises, and employment and output in that sector fall. The redundant labor is absorbed in the traded goods sector that can afford the higher real wages because of increased productivity. With increased labor and increased productivity, output of traded goods must rise. This establishes that we move from A southeast to a point like A'.

It is apparent from Figure 6-8 that at A' we are in a state of disequilibrium. To restore internal and external balance we have to move to point A'', where the relative price of traded goods is lower than at A or A'. At A'' the home goods market clears, $D_N = Y_N$, and income equals expenditure. Thus we have restored full equilibrium.

We have now gone through a number of examples in which economic disturbances call for a change in the equilibrium relative price of nontraded goods. What justifies calling that relative price the real exchange rate? The link is very simple. Suppose that the *nominal* price of home goods were given. Then adjustments in the equilibrium relative price would have to come through changes in the nominal price of traded goods. Given world prices, that means the exchange rate would have to adjust. A rise in productivity in the traded goods sector that requires a rise in the equilibrium relative

FIGURE 6-8

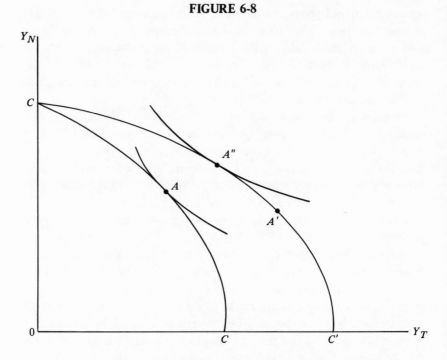

price of home goods would call for an appreciation of the exchange rate. Similarly, a transfer receipt would call for an appreciation so as to raise the relative price of home goods or the *real* exchange rate. With nominal home goods prices given, changes in the exchange rate will bring about a change in relative prices.

IV. THE MODEL WITH ENDOGENOUS TERMS OF TRADE

Here we depart from the small-country assumption by making the terms of trade endogenous. This process completes our model and permits us to discuss disturbances that affect both the terms of trade and the equilibrium relative price of home goods. In section IV (1) we look at the case of an exogenous change in the terms of trade. In section IV (2) we introduce foreign demand to close the model.

Home Goods and Traded Goods: the Dependent Economy Model

1. An Exogenous Terms-of-Trade Change

The reintroduction of the terms of trade makes it necessary to distinguish between importables and exportables and to introduce their separate relative prices. We define the relative price of exportables in terms of home goods by the lowercase $p_X \equiv P_X/P_N$ and similarly for importables $p_M \equiv P_M/P_N$.

The demand for nontraded goods now depends on the two relative prices and on the value of output, having assumed that expenditure is equal to income. Thus

$$D_N = D_N(p_X, p_M, Y) \tag{15}$$

Income, measured in terms of home goods, is defined in (16):

$$Y \equiv p_X Y_X + p_M Y_M + Y_N \tag{16}$$

Similarly, the supply of home goods is a function of relative prices:

$$Y_N = Y_N(p_X, p_M) \tag{17}$$

The equilibrium condition in the home goods market is stated in (18) as the equality of demand and supply:

$$Y_N(p_X, p_M) = D_N(p_X, p_M, Y) \tag{18}$$

On the production side, a rise in home goods prices relative to either export or import prices raises the supply of home goods. On the demand side, care must be taken to distinguish substitution and income effects. A rise in the price of exportables in terms of home goods raises demand unambiguously because of both substitution and income effects. A rise in the relative price of imports, by contrast, induces income and substitution effects in opposite directions. We assume here that the substitution effect dominates. These assumptions are reflected in the downward-sloping home goods market equilibrium schedule *NN* shown in Figure 6-9. Above the schedule there is an excess demand for home goods, while below it there is an excess supply.*

---

*Movements up and along the ray OR keep the terms of trade constant, raising both traded goods prices in terms of home goods. For this experiment we can use once again the idea of traded goods as a composite commodity. As we move up and along OR traded goods rise in terms of home goods, consumers substitute toward home goods, and producers move away from home goods. Accordingly an excess demand develops.

We also show in Figure 6-9 the ray $0R$ whose slope represents the given terms of trade. For the initial terms of trade our equilibrium is at point A, where the home goods market clears. Suppose now that the terms of trade improve, as shown by the leftward rotation of the ray $0R$ to $0R'$. Our new equilibrium will be at point A'. The relative price of exportables in terms of home goods rises while the relative price of imports in terms of home goods declines.

What can we say about the adjustment process to the exogenous terms-of-trade change? It is convenient, once again, to introduce the notion of nominal and real exchange rates. Suppose, then, that the nominal price of

FIGURE 6-9

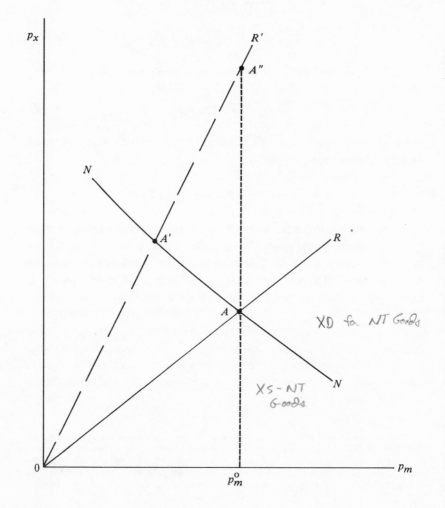

home goods is given and that, at the going exchange rate we experience an increase in the world nominal price of our exportable. From an initial position at A we thus move immediately to point A'', where import prices, absolutely and in terms of home goods, are unchanged, and where export prices have risen in terms of both goods. Clearly, at A'' there is an excess demand for home goods and a corresponding trade surplus. The trade surplus leads to currency appreciation, lowering the domestic currency prices of both exportables and importables along OR' until we reach point A'. The move from A'' to A' thus corresponds to a nominal *and* real appreciation. The adjustment process to a terms-of-trade improvement involves a real appreciation. In addition, there is an adjustment of production and demand. Exportable production unambiguously expands, while production of importables falls. Demand for all goods expands because the terms-of-trade improvement raises real income. The substitution effect favors importables and home goods versus exportables.

2. Foreign Demand and the Equilibrium Terms of Trade

So far we have taken the terms of trade to be exogenous. We now close the model by introducing foreign demand for domestic goods and the condition of trade balance equilibrium. This extension shifts our model from the small-country case to a model with endogenous terms of trade. For a given foreign demand function we will determine the equilibrium price structure that ensures internal and external balance.

We maintain the assumptions about the home goods market shown in (15)-(18) and in Figure 6-9. We add now the foreign demand for our exportable. Foreign demand is a function only of the terms of trade. An improvement in our terms of trade or a rise in the relative price of our exports will reduce foreign demand:

$$M^* = M^*(p_X/p_M) \qquad (19)$$

Our supply of exports X is equal to the excess of domestic production Y_X over domestic demand D_X. Export supply thus is a function of relative prices and income:

$$X \equiv Y_X(p_X,p_M) - D_X(p_X,p_M,Y) = X(p_X,p_M,Y) \qquad (20)$$

A rise in the relative price of exportables p_X raises exports both because of increased production and because of substitution away from exportables on the demand side. There is, however, an income effect as well. The rise in the relative price of exportables implies a terms-of-trade gain and therefore a rise in real income. The income effect leads to increased demand for exportables. The net effect is ambiguous. We assume that substitution effects dominate so that the net response is one of increased exports. A rise in the relative price of imports reduces exportable supply and raises demand through substitution. The adverse income effect, however, reduces demand. Once again, we assume that substitution effects dominate, so that a rise in import prices reduces exports.*

Equilibrium in the market for our exports requires that domestic export supply X equal foreign demand:

$$X(p_X, p_M, Y) = M^*(p_X/p_M) \tag{21}$$

Figure 6-10 shows the NN schedule introduced in the previous section. We also show now the schedule XX along which our export market is in equilibrium. The schedule is positively sloped and is flatter than a ray through the origin. Using an example, suppose we move along OR, raising traded goods prices in terms of home goods, but leaving the terms of trade unchanged. With unchanged terms of trade, foreign demand is constant, as is our real income. Accordingly, we only have substitution effects that lead to an excess supply of exports because of increased production and reduced domestic demand. In order to restore market equilibrium, import prices must rise, thereby raising foreign demand in response to the decline of the relative price of our exports, while lowering domestic supply, as argued earlier. Our initial equilibrium is at point A, where both markets clear.

Do *all* markets clear at point A? In particular, can we be sure that trade is, indeed, balanced? This point is easily established from the fact that income equals expenditure, by assumption, and that home goods and export markets clear. The demonstration uses the equality of income and spending, $Y = E$:

$$p_X Y_X + p_M Y_M + Y_N = p_X D_X + p_M D_M + D_N \tag{22}$$

Adding and subtracting the value of exports from the right-hand side, rearranging terms, and using import and export definitions yields

---

*Remember that because spending is equal to income the net income effect of a relative price change is equal to the initial level of exports (imports) times the change in export (import) prices. The elasticity condition implied by the dominance of substitution effects is related to the Robinson-Bickerdike-Metzler condition for a successful devaluation. For an analysis of this question in the present model, see Dornbusch (1975).

FIGURE 6-10

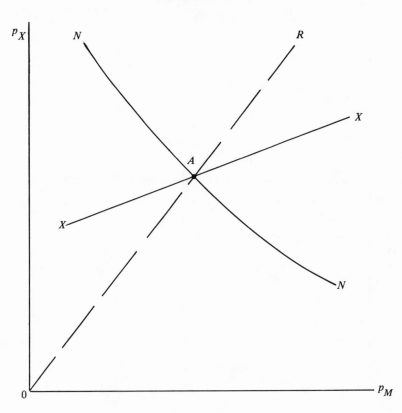

$$p_X(X - M^*) + (Y_N - D_N) = p_M M - p_X M^* \qquad (22a)$$

Equation (22a) shows that when the export and home goods markets are in equilibrium, trade is balanced. The counterpart of an excess supply of exportables or of home goods, given the equality of income and spending, would be a trade deficit.

Now let us suppose that starting from our initial equilibrium at point A in Figure 6-11 there is an increase in foreign demand for our exports. At A there is an excess demand for exportables and a corresponding trade surplus. The XX schedule shifts upward to $X'X'$, and our new equilibrium is at point A'. The increased demand for our exports leads to an improvement in the terms of trade p_X/p_M, a rise in the relative price of exportables in terms of home goods, and a fall in the relative price of importables. Production of exportables expands, while importable production falls.

FIGURE 6-11

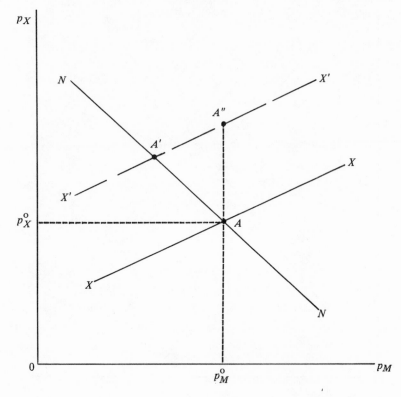

How does the change in equilibrium relative and absolute prices come about? We assume, once again, that home goods prices are given in nominal terms, as are world prices of our importable. The increase in foreign demand would, in the first place, raise the price of our exportable, moving from A to A'', where export market equilibrium again obtains. But clearly at A'' there is an excess demand for home goods and, from (22a), a matching trade surplus. Accordingly, the exchange rate will appreciate, lowering export and import prices absolutely and relative to home goods, until the new equilibrium at A' is reached. Once again, we have a real appreciation as part of the adjustment to a real disturbance.

3. Concluding Remark

We have now developed a first set of models that focus on spending and relative prices, internal and external balance. Throughout we have emphasized that to resolve trade balance problems requires adjustments both in relative prices and in the balance between income and spending. The key relative prices differ from model to model, and the diversity here serves to emphasize that in different circumstances one model will be more appropriate than another. What the models have in common is that they lend themselves to a uniform approach or analysis that centers on the macroeconomic balance of income and spending, as well as a "structural" analysis, which looks at relative prices and conditions of equilibrium in individual markets.

These approaches are already quite complex, but as yet they are not complete. In the next few chapters we complicate them first by the introduction of money, a link between money and spending, and a link between the external balance and the money supply. A further set of complications is added in part 5 of this book, where we focus on the interaction of goods and assets markets and devote our attention to dynamic questions.

REFERENCES AND SUGGESTED READINGS

Aukrust, O. 1977. Inflation in the open economy: The Norwegian model. *World wide inflation*, eds. L. Krause and W. Salant, Washington: Brookings Institution.

Cairnes, J. 1874. *Some principles of political economy newly expounded.* New York: Harper & Brothers.

Caves, R., and Jones, R. 1973. *World trade and payments.* Boston: Little, Brown.

Corden, M. 1960. The geometric representation of policies to attain internal and external balance. *Review of economic studies* 28:1-22.

Diaz Alejandro, C. 1964. *Devaluation in a semi-industrialized country: the case of Argentina.* Cambridge: Massachusetts Institute of Technology Press.

Dornbusch, R. 1974. Real and monetary aspects of the effects of exchange rate changes. in *National monetary policies and the international financial system.* ed. R. Z. Aliber. Chicago: University of Chicago Press.

Dornbusch, R. 1975. Exchange rates and fiscal policy in a popular model of international trade. *American economic review* 65:859-71.

Harberger, A. 1966. The case of the three numeraires. Unpublished manuscript, University of Chicago.

Hawtrey, R. 1931. *Trade depression and the way out.* London: Longmans Green & Co.

Iversen, C. 1935. *International capital movements.* Reprinted. 1967. New York: August M. Kelley.

Krueger, A. O. 1969. The role of home goods and money in exchange rate adjustment. *International trade and finance.* ed. W. Sellekaerts. White Plains: International Arts and Sciences Press.

Krugman, P., and Taylor, L. 1978. Contractionary effects of devaluation. *Journal of international economics* 8:445-56.

Meade, J. E. 1951. *The balance of payments.* Oxford: Oxford University Press.

Pearce, I. 1961. The problem of the balance of payments. *International economic review* 2:1-28.

Robinson, J. 1947. *Essays in the theory of employment*, Oxford: Blackwell.

Salter, W. 1959. Internal and external balance: the role of price and expenditure effects. *Economic record* 35:226-38.

Swan, T. 1960. Economic control in a dependent economy. *Economic record* 36:51-66.

Swan, T. 1963. Longer run problems of the balance of payments, *The Australian economy: a volume of readings*, eds. H. Arndt and M. Corden. Melbourne Australia: Cheshire Press.

Taylor, L. 1979. *Macro models for economic development.* New York: McGraw-Hill.

Wilson, R. 1931. *Capital imports and the terms of trade.* Melbourne Australia: Melbourne University Press.

Part 3

Money and Payments

Adjustment

CHAPTER

7

Money, Prices, and Payments Adjustment

This chapter introduces financial considerations in the open economy model of trade and price determination, concentrating on money as the only asset and assuming for the present that we have full employment and price flexibility.* Questions that arise from the interaction of the monetary adjustment mechanism and price rigidities are taken up in chapter 8. For the present we look at the automatic payments adjustment mechanism in a monetary fixed exchange rate economy.

Here we introduce money as a determinant of aggregate expenditure. Through its influence on aggregate spending, money has an effect on the level of prices, on relative prices and on the balance of payments. In the absence of sterilization the balance of payments in turn affects the money supply so that a dynamic system emerges that is referred to as the monetary adjustment process or *price specie-flow mechanism*.

*This chapter draws on Dornbusch (1973a,b, 1975a).

In this chapter we first introduce the relationship between money, spending, and the trade balance in a one-commodity world. We study first the short-term determination of prices and the trade balance as well as the longer-term adjustment through a redistribution of the world money stock. As an application of the model the effects of a devaluation are studied. In sections II and III we extend the analysis to relative prices. Section II introduces home goods in order to show that a monetary inflow, by raising spending raises the relative price of home goods, while a devaluation lowers their relative price. In section III we study the role of the terms of trade in a monetary model. The chapter concludes with a sketch of the world quantity theory of money.

I. THE MONETARY MODEL

This part abstracts from all possible complications to highlight the role of money in payments adjustment. We leave aside in particular two areas of complication: The first is price inflexibility and the resultant employment effects of changes in nominal money. The second area, considered later in this chapter, concerns relative prices. For the moment let us assume that relative prices are constant so that we can talk about goods as a composite commodity. Net trade in such a world is attributable to differences between income and spending. Those differences are highlighted here.

1. The Basic Model

At the center of our monetary model stands the relation between income and spending. We make the simplest possible assumption, namely that *nominal* spending E is proportional to nominal money holdings H:

$$E = VH \tag{1}$$

where V is the constant of proportionality that can be interpreted as the expenditure velocity.* We also define *nominal* income $\tilde{Y}$ as the product of the price level P and the given full employment output level Y:

---

*For a derivation of such an expenditure function in an intertemporal optimization setting, see Dornbusch and Mussa (1975b).

Money, Prices, and Payments Adjustment

$$\tilde{Y} = PY \qquad (2)$$

For the private sector, the rate of increase of money balances is equal to the excess of income over spending, or

$$\dot{H} \equiv \tilde{Y} - VH \qquad (3)$$

and this is a function of the level of money holdings relative to income.*

Now we assume that the foreign country is governed by the same behavioral equations:

$$E^* = V^*H^* \qquad (4)$$

where all foreign nominal quantities are measured in terms of foreign currency.

For the present we assume a one-good world, or equivalently, that relative prices are constant so that goods are aggregated into a composite commodity. In a one-good world spatial arbitrage assures that goods prices are the same at home and abroad, provided they are measured in the same currency:

$$P = P^*e \qquad (5)$$

where e is the domestic currency price of foreign exchange.

where $e = \#/£$

Equilibrium in the world goods market requires that world spending equal world income or that the demand for goods equal the available supply. Thus using the expenditure functions and the supplies in each country we can write

$$Y + Y^* = (1/P)(VH + V^*eH^*) \qquad (6)$$

We note that goods market equilibrium is stated here in terms of the

*Commenting briefly on alternative specifications of the expenditure function, two alternatives come to mind. The first starts with a money demand function $L = k\tilde{Y}$, proportional to nominal income. Expenditure is then equal to income less an adjustment for excess money demand: $E = \tilde{Y} - \alpha(k\tilde{Y} - H)$. Thus if there is a stock excess demand for money, $k\tilde{Y} - H > 0$, spending falls short of income and conversely when money holdings exceed the stock demand for money. With $\beta = 1 - \alpha k > 0$ the expenditure function is: $E = \beta\tilde{Y} + \alpha H$. We leave it to the reader to show that our analysis is substantially unaffected by this specification.

An alternative and more comprehensive change in specification brings interest rates and alternative assets into the model. Here money demand would depend on income and the interest rate: $L = k(i)\tilde{Y}$ and aggregate spending depends on income and interest rates $E = E(i,\tilde{Y})$. Such a model, once more, yields substantially the same conclusions as we derive here. See, for example, Dornbusch (1975a).

world market for the single commodity. The fact that we assume only a single good implies the coincidence of goods market equilibrium and the world income and spending balance.

The equilibrium condition in (6) can be solved for the equilibrium price level:

$$P = (VH + V^*eH^*)/(Y + Y^*) \tag{7}$$

The equilibrium price level depends on the level of world output and the distribution of the world money supply across countries. The world money supply here is defined as $\bar{H}$:

$$\bar{H} \equiv H + eH^* \tag{8}$$

Figure 7-1 shows a graphic interpretation of the goods market equilibrium. Here we focus not on world income and demand but rather on each country's rate of hoarding. *Hoarding* is defined as the excess of income over spending. For the home country we show the hoarding schedule as a positive function of the price level. The schedule is drawn for a given level of output and nominal money. Given the money stock, and hence spending, higher prices raise income relative to spending or increase hoarding.

FIGURE 7-1

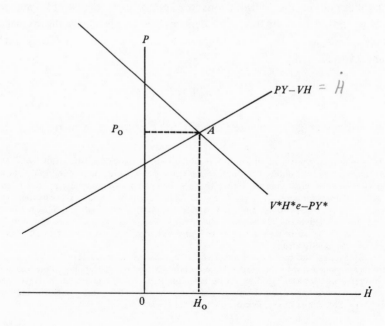

122

Money, Prices, and Payments Adjustment

For the foreign country we show the rate of *dis*hoarding or the excess of spending over income. At a lower price level the value of output is lower and hence spending, determined by money holdings, exceeds income and there is excess spending or dishoarding. The foreign schedule is drawn for given output, nominal money, and a given exchange rate.

Equilibrium in the world goods market obtains at point A, where world income equals world spending or our rate of hoarding equals the foreign rate of dishoarding. The equilibrium price level is P_0. At that price level the home country runs an excess of income over spending of $\dot{H}_0$. Note two important interpretations of the equilibrium rate of hoarding. First, because it is the excess of income over spending, we can look at the equilibrium rate of hoarding as our trade surplus. Second, and again because we are looking at the excess of income over spending, we can think of the equilibrium rate of hoarding as the rate at which we are accumulating assets. With money the only asset $\dot{H}_0$ measures the equilibrium rate of addition to our money holdings. Finally, because the same relationships obtain abroad, $\dot{H}_0 = -e\dot{H}^*$ measures the rate at which the foreign money stock is declining.

Unless there is sterilization, our one asset world implies that the trade balance is not only equal to the balance of payments but also to the rate at which the home country creates domestic money and absorbs foreign exchange in the process of maintaining the fixed exchange rate. In the next section we investigate the implications of these money flows.

FIGURE 7-2

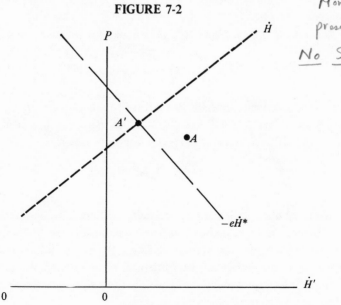

Monetary Approach presumes No Sterilization

2. The Adjustment Process

We turn now to the adjustment process that is induced through monetary flows. This adjustment process can be studied in terms of Figure 7-2. Beginning with our initial trade surplus at point A there is an inflow of money at home and an equal outflow abroad. Accordingly, our cash balances rise, as does our level of spending. Abroad money holdings fall as does spending. It follows that our hoarding schedule shifts up and to the left while the foreign dishoarding schedule shifts down and to the left. There will be a new equilibrium at a point like A'. At A' the equilibrium rate of our surplus has declined to $\dot{H}'$. The price level may have risen or fallen.

The dynamics can be formalized by using (3) together with the *equilibrium* price level in (7):

$$\dot{H} = PY - VH = \theta(VH + V^*eH^*) - VH \qquad \theta \equiv Y/(Y + Y^*) \quad (9)$$

From (9) the equilibrium balance of payments surplus, $\dot{H}$, is a function of the distribution of money holdings between countries. Using the definition of the world money stock in (8) we can rewrite (9) as

$$\dot{H} = \theta V^*\overline{H} - [(1-\theta)V + \theta V^*]H \qquad (10)$$

For a given world money stock $\overline{H}$ our deficit is larger, the larger are our cash balances.

Equation (10) is a differential equation with the following solution:

$$H_t = \lambda\overline{H} + (H_o - \lambda\overline{H})\exp(-\phi t) \qquad \lambda \equiv \theta V^*/[\theta V^* + (1-\theta)V] \quad (11)$$

where λ is our long-run share in the world money stock, H_o is our initial money stock and $\phi \equiv \theta V^* + (1-\theta)V$ is the speed of adjustment as can be noted from differentiation of (11) with respect to time:

$$\dot{H} = -\phi(H_t - \lambda\overline{H}) \qquad (11a)$$

Thus the equilibrium balance of payments deficit is proportional to *excess* cash balances. Excess cash balances here are defined as the difference between current and long-run equilibrium holdings. The speed of adjustment of the system to a disequilibrium distribution of money holdings is given by the term ϕ, the average velocity in the world. The weights in the average velocity are the income shares of the two countries.

Money, Prices, and Payments Adjustment

[margin note: 2 Key Points]

Our model highlights two important features of the monetary approach to the balance of payments. The first is the idea that balance of payments problems are essentially monetary problems. The second is the idea that the balance of payments is equal to the flow excess demand for money.

Consider next the behavior of the price level over time. Differentiating the equation for the equilibrium price level in (7) and using (11a) we have:

$$\dot{P} = -[(V - V^*)/(Y + Y^*)]\phi(H_t - \lambda\bar{H}) \tag{12}$$

The behavior of prices in the adjustment process depends on the difference between velocities. If velocities were identical then the redistribution of monies through the balance of payments would leave *world* nominal spending and thus the equilibrium price level unchanged. This is, of course, the transfer problem once more. If our velocity exceeds that abroad then a surplus on the part of the home country would lead to an increase in world spending, excess demand and therefore rising prices. Conversely, if foreigners have the higher velocity then their spending contraction would outweigh our increased spending and world spending and therefore equilibrium prices would fall.

In the long run, money flows will cease as income and spending equalize. In terms of Figure 7-2, the schedules will shift until they intersect on the vertical axis with a price level and a distribution of monies such that income equals spending in each country. The long-run price level would be

$$P = \lambda V\bar{H}/Y \tag{13}$$

In summary we have now shown that the world distribution of money stocks determines in the short run the price level and the balance of payments. Over the long term the distribution of money stocks is endogenous through the balance of payments. Money stocks are redistributed until income and spending are equal in each country. In the adjustment process the world price level rises or falls as the surplus country—whose spending rises—has a higher or lower velocity than does the deficit country. The redistribution of monies through the balance of payments thus acts like a transfer.

3. A Devaluation

In preceding chapters we have studied the effects of devaluation in circumstances where exchange rate changes move relative prices and thereby induce substitution, income and employment effects. We now have an entirely different framework of analysis, because we are assuming full employment and only one commodity. What then can a devaluation do?

In the present model a devaluation is a change in the relative price of two monies. (This is always true. Here it is the *only* aspect of a devaluation.) At initial prices in terms of domestic currency a devaluation would lower prices abroad in the same proportion. This follows from differentiation of (5), where the caret (‸) denotes a percentage change:

$$\hat{P}* = \hat{P} - \hat{e} \tag{5a}$$

Figure 7-3 explores the effects of a devaluation. With unchanged domestic prices, the domestic currency value of foreign income, PY^*, would be unchanged. Foreign spending in domestic currency, eV^*H^*, would rise, however, in proportion to our devaluation. Thus foreigners would be dishoarding. Starting from an initial equilibrium at A our devaluation would shift the foreign dishoarding schedule up and to the right. A new short-run equilibrium is established at point A'. Here the home country has a surplus equal to $\dot{H}_0$ and the domestic price level has risen by AB/OA while the exchange rate was devalued in the proportion AC/OA. The foreign price level, using (5a), thus falls in the proportion BC/OA.

Why does a devaluation improve the home country's trade balance? At a constant domestic price level a devaluation implies that foreign prices

FIGURE 7-3

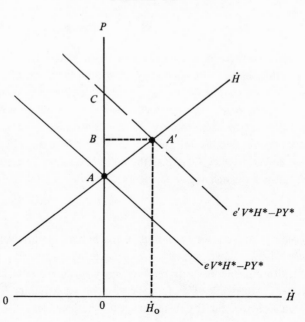

fall and the purchasing power of cash balances abroad increases. Excess real balances cause foreigners to increase their spending. Accordingly, there will be a world excess demand for goods and the price level in terms of either currency will rise. With increased prices, foreign real balances will have risen less than the impact effect and our real balances will actually be lower. At home spending falls below real income while abroad it exceeds real income. We have a trade surplus and foreigners have a matching deficit.

A devaluation is like a capital levy in that it reduces the real money stock, thereby leading to reduced absorption. It follows immediately that if devaluation was accompanied by an equiproportionate increase in money, the net effect on real variables would be zero.

The impact effect of a devaluation on the price level can be calculated from (7) as

$$\hat{P} = [eV^*H^*/P(Y+Y^*)]\hat{e} = (1-\theta)\hat{e} \qquad (14)$$

Thus the price level rises in proportion to the foreign share in world income. If the foreign country is "large" and we are "small" our price level rises roughly in proportion to the depreciation.

The change in our balance of payments, using (9), is proportional to our income:

$$d\dot{H} = PY\ \hat{P} = PY(1-\theta)\hat{e} \qquad (15)$$

Over time, the trade balance and balance of payments surplus imply a redistribution of money stocks. As a consequence, spending at home will rise and it will fall abroad. These adjustments in spending levels restore external balance over time. The effects of a devaluation are therefore entirely transitory.

II. MONEY, HOME GOODS, AND TRADED GOODS

The one good model of the preceding sections has highlighted the role of money in the adjustment process. We now make the analysis a bit more realistic by increasing the menu of goods. This section starts with nontraded goods to show how the balance of payments adjustment process systematically affects their absolute and relative prices. The framework of analysis is a small country that takes traded goods prices as given. It is obvious that we can broaden the model to take account of foreign repercussions but these are not of interest at present.

1. Market Equilibrium

The supply of traded and nontraded goods Y_T and Y_N, respectively, depend on relative prices:

$$Y_N = Y_N(P_N/P_T) \qquad Y_T = Y_T(P_T/P_N) \qquad (16)$$

The level of nominal spending depends, as before, on nominal money holdings. The composition of spending depends on relative prices. Specifically, we assume, without much loss of generality, constant expenditure shares γ and $1 - \gamma$ for home goods and traded goods. Thus expenditure on home goods and traded goods are respectively:

$$P_N D_N = \gamma\, VH \qquad P_T D_T = (1-\gamma)VH \qquad (17)$$

Equilibrium in the home goods market requires that demand equals supply:

$$Y_N(P_N/P_T) = \gamma VH/P_N \ = \ D_N \qquad (18)$$

or, solving for the equilibrium price of home goods:

$$\bar{P}_N = \bar{P}_N(H,P_T) \qquad (18a)$$

In Figure 7-4 we show the schedule NN along which the home goods market clears. The schedule is drawn for a given level of traded goods prices or a given exchange rate. An increase in nominal money raises home goods spending and creates an excess demand. To restore equilibrium home goods prices must rise, though less than proportionately. A rise in home goods prices restores equilibrium because it raises the relative price of home goods. Consequently supply is increased and the real value of spending is reduced, thus reducing demand. Accordingly, the NN schedule is flatter than a ray through the origin with a slope determined by the elasticity of supply. A high elasticity of supply implies a relatively flat NN schedule.

Consider next the trade balance equilibrium schedule TT. Along that schedule we have

$$Y_T(P_T/P_N) = (1-\gamma)VH/P_T \ = \ D_T \qquad (19)$$

FIGURE 7-4

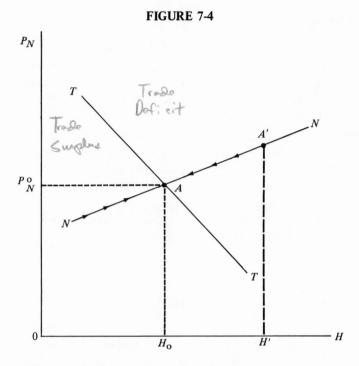

The schedule is negatively sloped, as an increase in home goods prices reduces supply and requires a decline in nominal money and hence demand to maintain balanced trade. Above the TT schedule we have deficits and below there are surpluses.

2. A Monetary Disturbance   (Transitory Impact on P, H)

Suppose now that the money stock rose, from an initial full equilibrium at A to H'. Home goods market equilibrium at the initial price is disturbed. The higher level of money and spending imply an excess demand for home goods and as a result home goods prices will rise until we reach point A', at which internal balance is restored. But at point A' there is a deficit in the trade balance and therefore the money stock will be falling. Consequently, over time we move down along the NN schedule, as the decumulation of nominal money means that expenditure is falling, as are home goods prices. The process continues until the initial equilibrium at A is reattained.

The analysis above demonstrates that in deficit countries prices are high and falling. In these countries money stocks are above the equilibrium level as is spending. Prices are high as a reflection of the high spending levels, but because of the deficit, money and spending are falling over time.

Monetary Policy has no ultimate impact on money holding or relative prices (P_N/P_T).

3. A Devaluation

Consider next a devaluation in this extended model. This question is addressed in Figure 7-5, where the *NN* and *TT* schedules are drawn for a given price of traded goods or a given exchange rate. A depreciation will therefore affect these schedules. Using the homogeneity property of (18) and (19), we note that if money and both prices rose in the same proportion, *all* real variables would be unaffected. In particular, demand would still equal supply in each market. This implies that both schedules shift outward in proportion to the depreciation. If money and domestic prices rose to A'' there would be no real effect.

A devaluation does, however, have a real effect if the nominal money stock is fixed. At the initial money stock H_0 the devaluation raises traded goods prices and therefore shifts resources from the home goods sector

FIGURE 7-5

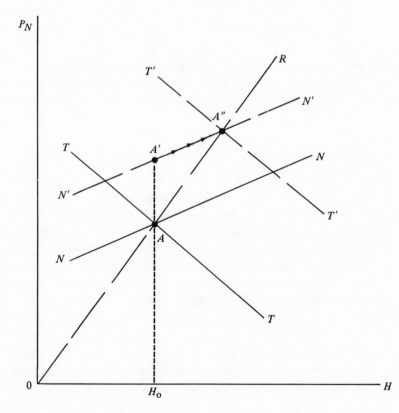

to the production of tradeables. The excess demand for home goods causes their price to rise, though less than proportionately to the depreciation. Short-run equilibrium thus obtains at point A'. At A' there is a trade surplus. Nominal income has risen but spending has not. Money flows in and, in response, prices rise until we reach A''.

As before, when there were no non-traded goods, a devaluation has only transitory effects. In addition to the trade balance effect of the last section we note now the additional effect on the relative price of home goods. The impact of a devaluation is to reduce the *relative* price of home goods, although their absolute price will rise.

See Dornbusch (AER, 1973).

4. Productivity Growth

As another application of this augmented model we consider the case of productivity growth in the traded goods sector. We noted in the previous chapter that at constant relative prices productivity growth in the traded goods sector raises the supply of traded goods and reduces the supply of home goods. In terms of Figure 7-6 this implies that the TT schedule shifts

FIGURE 7-6

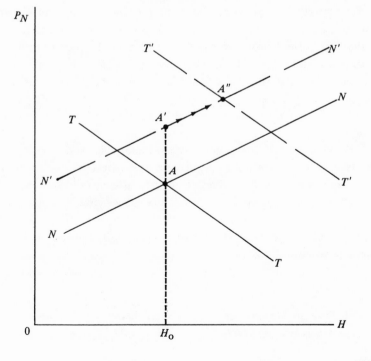

out and to the right, since given relative prices, higher money and spending is required to maintain external balance. In the home goods market the reduced supply creates imbalance and calls for reduced spending thus shifting the *NN* schedule up and to the left.

The short-run equilibrium is at point A'. With a given money stock and nominal spending level there is an excess demand for home goods that raises their price. The trade balance at A' is in surplus and thus money accumulates. In the long-run money and prices will rise. Thus productivity growth in the traded goods sector, with fixed exchange rates, is inflationary and countries with rapid growth in productivity would show a consumer price index (incorporating both traded goods and nontraded goods) which rises faster than that in the rest of the world.

III. THE MONETARY MECHANISM AND THE TERMS OF TRADE

In this section we extend the one commodity model to include terms of trade effects. The main message is quite straightforward. We saw above that redistribution of money raises spending in one country and reduces it in the other. The immediate question, in light of the transfer problem, is to ask what happens to individual commodity demands. In the previous section we studied the case of nontraded goods, an extreme case since the foreign propensity to spend on these is by definition zero. Accordingly, home goods prices moved unambiguously with the domestic level of money and spending.

Now we make the distinction between importables and exportables and ask whether the payments adjustment process affects the terms of trade. There are two sources of distribution effects—differences in spending velocities and differences in marginal propensities. As we already explored in the section above, the role of differences in velocities—they affect the level of prices—we will now concentrate on marginal propensities and assume therefore common velocities $V = V^*$.

1. The Model

With these preliminary remarks we write market equilibrium conditions for exportables and importables:

Money, Prices, and Payments Adjustment

$$V[\delta H + \delta^* e H^*] = PY \qquad (20)$$

$$V[(1-\delta)H + (1-\delta^*)eH^*] = P^*Y^* \qquad (21)$$

where we have assumed complete specialization and fixed supplies and where P and P^* are the domestic currency prices of domestic and foreign goods. The expenditure shares δ and δ^* are assumed decreasing functions of the relative price:

$$\delta = \delta(P/P^*) \qquad \delta^* = \delta^*(P/P^*) \qquad (22)$$

To complete the model we add (20) and (21) to obtain the balance of world income and spending:

$$PY + P^*Y^* = V(H + eH^*) = V\overline{H} \qquad (23)$$

where $\overline{H}$ is again the world money stock measured in home currency. We can use any two of the three equilibrium conditions. It will be convenient to take (20) and (23) shown in Figure 7-7 for a given distribution of money stocks and exchange rate. The WW schedule shows the balance of world income and

FIGURE 7-7

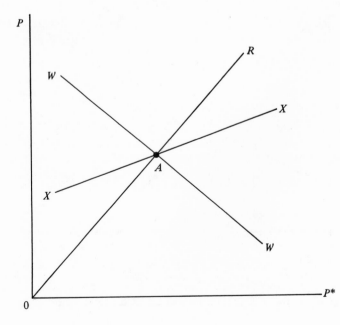

spending. The world money stock fixes world nominal spending, so that if income is higher in one country it must be lower in the other.

Along *XX* there is equilibrium in the market for domestic output. The schedule is flatter than a ray through the origin because an equiproportionate rise in prices, leaving expenditure shares unaffected, raises the price level, reduces real balances, and therefore creates an excess supply of both goods. To restore equilibrium in the domestic goods market the relative price of our goods must fall thereby inducing expenditure switching to restore market equilibrium. Associated with the equilibrium price levels at point *A* is the trade balance, which in this case equals the balance of payments and rate of increase in money:

$$T = PY - VH = \dot{H} \tag{24}$$

2. A Demand Shift

Consider a shift in demand from domestic goods to imports. Such a shift is shown for a given distribution of world money and spending in Figure 7-8. From an initial equilibrium at point *A* we move to point *A'*. The home

FIGURE 7-8

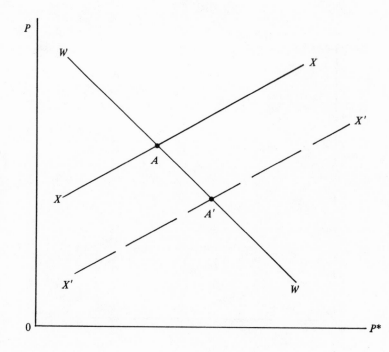

country's terms of trade must worsen, because only at a lower absolute and relative price can domestic output be sold. The short-run effect is thus unambiguously a deficit and a loss of money balances.

The deficit and money flows will next affect the level of spending on our goods. From (20) spending will rise with the redistribution of money toward the foreign country if the foreign propensity to spend on our goods δ^* exceeds our own propensity δ. If that were the case the XX schedule would start shifting backward, offsetting in part the impact effect on the terms of trade. Conversely, if the foreign propensity to spend on our goods falls short of our own, the money flows will lead to a further worsening of the terms of trade.

3. Stability and Adjustment

The redistribution of money supplies implied by the trade deficit at A' changes prices, income, and spending and thus feeds back to the trade balance itself. Is that adjustment process in fact stable? To answer that question, we use (24) to calculate the impact on the balance of payments of a redistribution of monies:

$$d\dot{H} = YP \; \hat{P} - VH \; \hat{H} \tag{25}$$

For stability, in a neighborhood of equilibrium, we require that a redistribution of money toward the home country not raise our price level too much. For stability, our price level must rise proportionately less than the quantity of money.

The change in the equilibrium price level induced by a redistribution of monies can be calculated from (20) and (23) and is

$$\hat{P} = (\delta - \delta^*) \left\{ \theta(1 - \theta)/[\theta(1 - \theta) + \Psi] \right\} \hat{H} \tag{26}$$

where Ψ is a measure of the relative price elasticity of demand for domestic goods defined as

$$\Psi \equiv -[\eta\delta\theta + \eta^*\delta^*(1 - \theta)] \gtrless 0 \tag{27}$$

The relative price elasticity is the weighted sum of the elasticities of expenditure shares, with the weights given by each country's share in world income:

$$\eta \equiv [d\delta/d(P/P^*)] (P/P^*)/\delta \qquad \eta^* \equiv [d\delta^*/d(P/P^*)] (P/P^*)/\delta^* \tag{27a}$$

$$\theta \equiv PY/V\overline{H}$$

What can be said about the sign of Ψ? If the price elasticities are unity and cross price elasticities are zero then we have the case where $\eta = \eta^* = \Psi = 0$.* In this case, as verified from (26), the sign and size of the relative price change is given just by the difference in expenditure shares, $\delta - \delta^*$.

If the expenditure shares do depend on the relative price we distinguish two possibilities. First, the case in which a rise in the relative price reduces the expenditure share of domestic goods so that η and η^* are negative. This corresponds, of course, to the case of demand elasticities larger than one in absolute value. The alternative case, with increasing expenditure shares, represents less than unit elastic demand and will appear as a potential source of instability.

Using now the expression for the equilibrium change in domestic prices derived in (26) in the balance of payments equation yields

$$d\dot{H} = -VH\left\{ [\Psi + \theta(1 - \theta)(1 - \delta + \delta^*)]/[\Psi + \theta(1 - \theta)] \right\}\hat{H} \quad (25a)$$

We observe that for the case where Ψ is positive or zero, we must have stability.

The stability properties of our model depend on a variant of the Marshall-Lerner condition. We observe immediately that if Ψ is positive or zero an increase in our money holdings *must* lead to a deficit in the external balance and thus to an outflow of money and a return to the initial equilibrium. Conversely, if demand is insufficiently elastic, so that Ψ is negative, there is the possibility of instability. For example, if the domestic propensity exceeds that abroad and $\theta(1 - \theta) + \Psi$ is positive then the domestic price level may rise more than proportionately to the increase in money. If so, nominal income rises more than expenditure and the trade balance actually improves, thereby leading to a further rise in money.

The stability problem then arises in the following manner: Distribution effects $\delta - \delta^*$ give rise to relative price changes. With insufficient price elasticity, these relative price changes can be large and thereby more than offset the direct expenditure changes. Relative prices and price elasticities thus *do* play a critical role even in an otherwise quite monetarist model. Even if we set aside the issue of stability, price responses as influenced by elasticities affect the speed of adjustment. This point is illustrated in Figure 7-9.

Equation (26) showed that the domestic equilibrium price level is a func-

---

*The demand for domestic goods from (20) is $V[\delta H + \delta^* eH^*]/P$, and hence is a function of P and P^*.

FIGURE 7-9

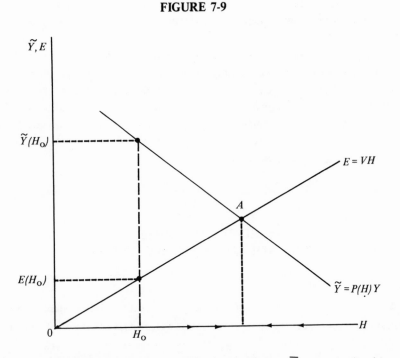

tion of the distribution of monies. Given world money $\overline{H}$, our price level is a function of our money stock:

$$P = P(H) \tag{26a}$$

For the stable case, a rise in money changes prices less than proportionately. The direction of change in prices depends only on the difference in spending propensities. In Figure 7-9 we thus show domestic nominal income, the equilibrium price $P(H)$ times given real output Y, taking the case where our propensity to consume domestic goods falls short of that abroad. Accordingly, nominal income is a decreasing function of our nominal money stock.* We also show domestic nominal spending, $E = VH$, as an increasing function of our nominal money.

For any given money stock, such as H_0, we have an equilibrium price level and nominal income, $\tilde{Y}(H_0)$, a spending level VH_0, and therefore a balance of payments $\tilde{Y}(H_0) - VH_0$, given by the vertical distance between income and spending. The balance of payments of course affects the money stock over

---

*The other stable case is represented by a schedule for nominal income that is flatter than a ray through the origin, and positively sloped.

time and thus leads us to converge to the steady state at point A. Over time, the redistribution of money lowers nominal income and raises expenditure until we achieve external balance. Where do price elasticities enter in this adjustment process? The larger the price elasticities of demand, the smaller the changes in relative (and absolute) prices. Accordingly, the flatter is the nominal income schedule in Figure 7-9. But with a flatter schedule for nominal income it is apparent that at any level of money there is a smaller balance of payments imbalance and thus a slower adjustment process. Price elasticities thus affect not only the stability, but the speed of adjustment of the price-specie flow mechanism as well.

IV. MONEY, CREDIT, AND THE WORLD QUANTITY THEORY

We conclude this chapter with a model of world inflation based on the monetary approach. We look at two countries, a single (composite) commodity, full employment and fixed exchange rates. In such a world inflation is determined by growth in the world money stock and growth in world real income. The balance of payments of individual countries is related to their growth in domestic credit relative to the growth in money demand.

1. The World Rate of Inflation

In the world economy equilibrium requires the balance of world income and spending:

$$(H + H^*)V = P(Y + Y^*) \tag{28}$$

where we have assumed a fixed exchange rate ($e = 1$) and a common velocity in the two countries. We can solve the equation for the equilibrium world price level:

$$P = V(H + H^*)/(Y + Y^*) \tag{29}$$

In an open economy under fixed exchange rates and in the absence of sterilization the money supply is endogenous. What the central bank does control is not the supply of money but rather domestic credit. Thus we can use the identity

Money, Prices, and Payments Adjustment

$$H \equiv C + R \tag{30}$$

where C is domestic credit (of the consolidated banking system) and R is the stock of net foreign assets or reserves. Suppose now we have no *net* reserves in the world so that one country's net foreign assets are liabilities of the other country (say the dollar standard). In that case, adding the money supplies and using (30) leaves us with

$$H + H^* = C + C^* \tag{31}$$

since in the aggregation reserves will cancel out. The world money stock thus equals world "domestic" credit.

Substituting (31) in (29) and differentiating the equation with respect to time yields an expression for the world rate of inflation $\pi = d\ln P/dt$:

$$\pi = (\beta c + \beta^* c^*) - (\rho\lambda + \rho^*\lambda^*) \tag{32}$$

where

$$\beta \equiv C/(C + C^*) \qquad \rho \equiv Y/(Y + Y^*) \qquad \lambda \equiv d\ln Y/dt$$

$$c \equiv d\ln C/dt$$

The world rate of inflation in (32) is determined by the weighted average growth in domestic credit less the weighted average of real income growth. The higher the growth rate of credit and money in the world the higher the rate of inflation. The higher real growth, and hence the growth rate of real money demand, the lower the rate of inflation.

2. The Balance of Payments, Domestic Credit, and Money Demand

In the home country we are in monetary equilibrium when money demand equals money supply, or

$$V(C + R) = PY \tag{33}$$

Differentiating that relation with respect to time yields

$$\beta(c + \xi r) = (\pi + \lambda)\rho \tag{34}$$

where $r \equiv (1/R)\, dR/dt$ is the balance of payments as a ratio of the stock of reserves and $\xi \equiv R/C$ is the ratio of reserves to domestic credit.

Equation (34) states a relation between the sources of money growth—the balance of payments and domestic credit growth—and the growth in nominal money demand due to inflation and real growth. The higher inflation and real growth the higher must be domestic credit creation or the balance of payments surplus, or both.

3. Inflation, Domestic Credit, and the Balance of Payments

We turn to an individual country and ask what contribution is made by domestic credit policy to world inflation and what such credit policies imply for the balance of payments. We take as given real growth (λ and λ^*) as well as the rate of foreign credit creation c^*. In Figure 7-10 we plot the equilibrium world rate of inflation shown in (32) as a function of our rate of domestic credit expansion c. This is the $\pi\pi$ schedule. The relation is positive with a slope determined by our relative size β. A small country will have only

FIGURE 7-10

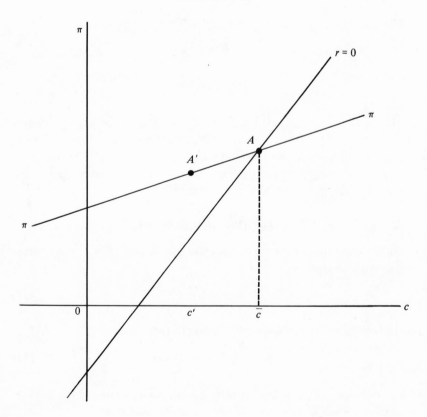

Money, Prices, and Payments Adjustment

a minor effect on world inflation, while a large country dominates world inflation by the choice of its rate of credit expansion.

We also show in Figure 7-10 the schedule $r = 0$ along which the home country is in balance of payments equilibrium. Higher rates of world inflation, and hence growth in nominal money demand, require higher rates of credit expansion to provide sufficient monetary growth. This is shown in equation (34), where the schedule has a slope β/ρ and thus is steeper than the $\pi\pi$ schedule. Above the schedule we have combinations of inflation and credit expansion that imply a balance of payments surplus, below the schedule we have points of deficit.

Given growth and foreign credit expansion the home country's choice of credit policy will set world inflation and our balance of payments. There is a unique rate of credit expansion $\bar{c}$ at which we have balance of payments equilibrium. For a lower rate of credit expansion, say c', we would be at point A' with a balance of payments surplus and conversely for a higher rate of credit expansion. The balance of payments can be solved for from (32) and (34).

Two basic propositions emerge from the model. First, increased domestic credit expansion raises world inflation and worsens the balance of payments. This corresponds to a movement along the $\pi\pi$ schedule in Figure 7-10. Second, increased foreign credit creation—an upward shift of the $\pi\pi$ schedule—raises world inflation and improves (for given credit policy) our balance of payments. This is the case of imported inflation.

The sharp implications of the model, in particular the tight link between credit policy and the balance of payments, are emphasized in policy decisions that use credit control as *the* balance of payments policy.

REFERENCES AND SUGGESTED READING

Collery, A. 1971. International adjustment, open economies and the quantity theory of money. *Princeton studies in international finance*, No. 28.

Dornbusch, R. 1973a. Currency depreciation, hoarding and relative prices. *Journal of political economy* 81:893-915.

Dornbusch, R. 1973b. Money, devaluation and nontraded goods. *American economic review* 63:871-80.

Dornbusch, R. 1975a. Alternative price stabilization rules and the effects of exchange rate changes. *Manchester School of economics and social studies* 43:275-92.

Dornbusch, R., and Mussa, M. 1975b. Consumption, real balances and the hoarding function. *International economic review* 16:415-21.

Frenkel, J., and Johnson, H. G., eds., 1976. *The monetary approach to the balance of payments.* London: Allen and Unwin.

International monetary fund 1977. *The monetary approach to the balance of payments.* Washington, D.C.

Krueger, A. O. 1974. The role of home goods and money in exchange rate adjustment, *International trade and finance.* ed. W. Sellekaerts. New York: International Arts and Sciences Press.

Michaely, M. 1960. Relative prices and income-absorption approaches to devaluation: a partial reconciliation. *American economic review* 50:144-47

Mundell, R. A. 1968. *International economics* [Chapter 8]. New York: Macmillan Publishing Co.

Mundell, R. A. 1971. *Monetary theory* [Chapters 9, 10]. Santa Monica: Good Year Publishing Co.

Swoboda, A. 1976. Monetary approaches to worldwide inflation. *Worldwide inflation.* eds. L. Krause and W. Salant. Washington: Brookings Institution.

CHAPTER

8

Money, Exchange Rates, and Employment

Here we extend the analysis of the monetary adjustment mechanism introduced in chapter 7. This chapter serves as an integration of the material presented in the preceding chapters in that it picks up the key elements: the
link between income and spending, the influence of relative prices on
the composition of spending, traded and nontraded goods, and (under
conditions of sticky prices) the determination of output through aggregate
demand. We choose as a vehicle for this integration a Ricardian model with
many goods, or more specifically, with a continuum of goods.* The model,
as we will see presently, is a very simple general equilibrium model with
enough structure to consider the most interesting disturbances and questions
in the area of trade and payments.

In section I we develop the basic model of this chapter and analyze the

*This chapter draws on Dornbusch, Fischer and Samuelson (1977).

monetary adjustment process. Section II deals with the question of purchasing power parity (*PPP*). In sections III and IV we study the effects of real disturbances when wages are inflexible and we assess the role of exchange rate flexibility in this context. In particular we demonstrate that flexible rates, in these circumstances, do not isolate a country from foreign real or monetary disturbances.

I. A RICARDIAN MODEL OF TRADE AND PAYMENTS

The setting for this chapter is a world with many goods. We choose the framework to show how two-commodity models are convenient analytical devices but that a more general analysis is possible and that it is rewarding in terms of the insights it yields. The first section develops the supply side of the economy and shows the relationship between wages and trade patterns. Section I(2) brings in the demand side and section I(3) studies the price-specie flow mechanism in this setting.

1. The Production Side

Labor is the only factor of production in this model and with constant returns there is a constant unit labor requirement for each industry. Across countries technology and hence unit labor requirements differ. To deal with the many-commodity case we choose a technique that seems a bit ambitious, but that in fact turns out to simplify matters greatly. In particular we assume that there is an infinity or a *continuum* of goods. In Figure 8-1 we choose as our horizontal axis the unit interval (0, 1) and we assume that to each point on the interval there corresponds a particular commodity. Let z be an index that ranges from zero to one. Then we can index commodities by z.

We now define the unit labor requirement of commodity z by $a(z)$ in the home country and $a^*(z)$ abroad. The relative unit labor requirement is defined as

$$A(z) \equiv a^*(z)/a(z) \tag{1}$$

and is a measure of the relative *technical* efficiency at home and abroad.

There is a degree of freedom in choosing how to place the various commodities along the (0, 1) interval. We use that degree of freedom by aligning

FIGURE 8-1

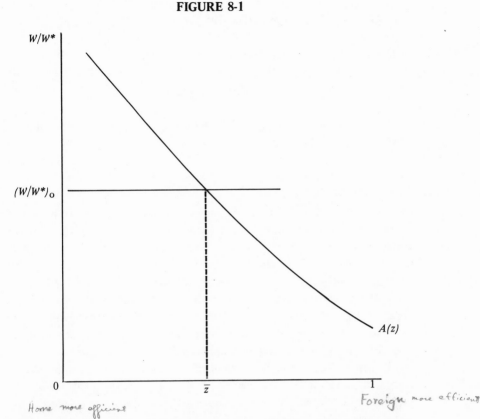

commodities in the order of decreasing relative efficiency. This is shown by the downward-sloping schedule $A(z)$ in Figure 8-1. Thus we place toward the origin the commodities for which the home country has relatively low unit labor requirements. Conversely, toward unity we place commodities for which the foreign country is relatively more efficient. The question we are building up to is who produces which commodities. We will see now that the home country produces commodities in the range $(0,\bar{z})$ and the foreign country those goods in the range $(\bar{z},1)$. The competitive margin or the dividing line $\bar{z}$, is determined jointly by demand and supply conditions as shown in section I(3).

Efficient geographic specialization implies that commodities be produced in the least cost location. If wages were equal between countries we would simply compare unit labor requirements. With wages not necessarily equal we have to compare costs and prices. With competition and constant returns, as we assume, prices are equal to unit labor costs. Thus for any commodity z produced at home, the price is equal to the wage W times the unit labor

145

requirement $a(z)$, or $Wa(z)$. If the commodity were produced abroad, the cost and price would be $W^*a^*(z)$. Here W and W^* are wages measured in a common currency. The home country will produce all those goods for which cost is less or equal than that abroad. Thus

$$Wa(z) \leqslant W^*a^*(z) \tag{2}$$

The borderline commodity $\bar{z}$ is defined by (2) holding with equality. Thus using (1) and (2) with equality we have:

$$W/W^* = A(\bar{z}) \quad \text{or} \quad \bar{z} = \phi(W/W^*) \qquad \phi' < 0 \tag{3}$$

Equation (3) is a central result of our model. It states that the efficient geographic specialization pattern is determined by technology, $A(z)$, and relative wages W/W^*. The higher our relative wage the smaller the range of goods we can efficiently produce and the larger the range of goods produced abroad. This is shown in Figure 8-1, where for a given relative wage, $(W/W^*)_o$ we have the competitive margin $\bar{z}$. It is apparent from the figure that a higher relative wage will reduce the range of goods produced at home. With a higher relative wage we lose cost competitiveness at the margin and goods that previously were exported now will be imported.

Before proceeding to the demand side of the economy we note that the range of goods defined in Figure 8-1 is that of *traded* goods. There is a separate and independent range of goods that at *all* relative wages are assumed nontraded.

2. The Demand Side and Market Equilibrium

We continue with the assumption of the previous chapter in respect to nominal spending. Nominal expenditure is proportional to nominal money holdings and velocities are the same across countries. As to the composition of expenditure across commodities, we assume constant expenditure shares $b(z)$ for each commodity. Furthermore, these expenditure shares are equal across countries. (By comparison with the previous chapter we assume that $\delta = \delta^*$ and are constant.)

A fraction k of expenditure falls on traded goods and a fraction $1 - k$ on nontraded goods. What part of the traded goods expenditure falls on goods that are produced by the home country? As the home country produces commodities in the range $(0, \bar{z})$ the fraction of spending falling on traded goods produced at home is equal to θ defined as

$$\theta \equiv \int_{0}^{\bar{z}} b(z)dz = \theta(W/W^*) \qquad \theta' < 0 \tag{4}$$

where we have used the fact that from (3) the competitive margin $\bar{z}$ is a function of the relative wage. Equation (4) thus states that the share of expenditure falling on our traded goods is lower the higher our relative wage. With a higher relative wage the home country is less cost competitive, thus producing a smaller range of goods.

We proceed now to the conditions of market equilibrium. In the home country equilibrium requires that the value of output produced equal spending on domestically produced goods. The value of output produced is equal to the value of labor services WN. Expenditure on our goods equals world spending on our traded goods $\theta V\bar{H}$ plus home spending on nontraded goods $(1-k)VH$:

$$WN = \theta(W/W^*)V\bar{H} + (1 - k)VH \tag{5}$$

where $\bar{H}$ is again the world money stock and H the domestic money balance.

Note that the assumption of equal velocities and equal tastes allows us to write on the right-hand side of (5) world spending on domestic traded goods rather than the separate domestic and foreign components. Note also that the spending on our traded goods, $\theta V\bar{H}$, is independent of the distribution of world money. That is not the case, however, for nontraded goods expenditure. The latter does depend on *our* money holdings.

Figure 8-2 shows the schedule YY along which the home country is in goods and labor market equilibrium. The schedule is flatter than a ray through the origin since an equiproportionate increase in wages leaves relative prices and demand unchanged—θ does not change—but reduces real balances and hence real demand. To eliminate the excess supply, our relative wage must fall, thus extending the range of goods produced at home. Extending the range of goods produced by the home country restores equilibrium, because it raises the demand for labor in the new marginal industries.*

We also show in Figure 8-2 the schedule WW along which world income, $WN + W^*N^*$, is equal to world spending $V\bar{H}$:

$$WN + W^*N^* = V\bar{H} \tag{6}$$

---

*The slope of the YY schedule is equal to $\hat{W} = [\theta\Psi/(\alpha + \theta\Psi)]\,\hat{W}^*$. It depends on the elasticity of θ with respect to the relative wage: $\Psi \equiv -\theta'(W/W^*)/\theta$ and on the share of our income in world spending $\alpha \equiv WN/V\bar{H}$.

FIGURE 8-2

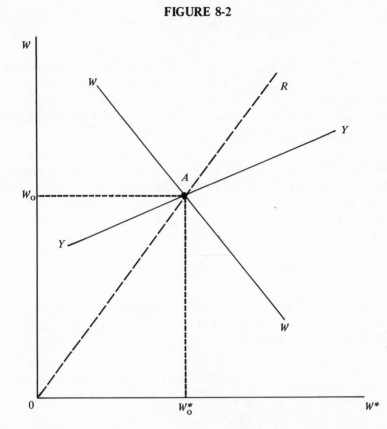

The schedule is downward sloping since a higher nominal income in one country, given spending, requires a lower level in the other country. Point *A* shows the equilibrium absolute and relative wages at which goods markets clear. The relative wage, given by the slope of a ray *OR*, determines the equilibrium specialization pattern and thus the allocation of world spending. The equilibrium at point *A* is dependent on technology and taste patterns and on the distribution of world money between countries. Next we investigate the price specie-flow mechanism in this model.

3. The Price Specie-Flow Mechanism

Suppose an initial equilibrium at point *A* such that all markets clear and income equals expenditure. There will be a unique distribution of the world money stock between countries that will ensure such a long-run equilibrium. Imposing the constraint that income equals expenditure, $VH = WN$, in (5) yields the long-run equilibrium relation

$$WN = \theta(W/W^*)(WN + W^*N^*) + (1-k)WN \qquad (5a)$$

Equation (5a) together with (6) defines the long-run equilibrium levels of wages and the long-run distribution of world income. The question we address now is whether the economy will, in fact, converge to the long-run equilibrium. We investigate that question by considering a redistribution of money toward the home country, starting from an initial full equilibrium. If the redistribution induces a deficit and thus a money outflow, the adjustment process is stable.

From equations (5) and (6) we calculate the effect of a redistribution of money on home wages as*

$$\hat{W} = (1-k)\left\{\alpha(1-\alpha)/[\alpha(1-\alpha) + \theta\Psi]\right\}\hat{H} \qquad (7)$$

Equation (7) is of interest in several respects. It states that a redistribution of money toward the home country will raise wages at home, but proportionately less than the increase in money. The extent of the wage increase depends on the share of nontraded goods in expenditure $1-k$. If there are no nontraded goods $k=1$ then a money redistribution has no effects on wages and prices. As money is redistributed our spending on all goods rises and foreign spending on all goods falls. Assuming there are identical spending patterns for traded goods, there would be no distribution effects. Our demand increase precisely offsets the foreign reduction in demand. This is, however, not the case for home goods. Our increased spending raises home goods demand and thus home demand for labor while the opposite occurs abroad. Therefore our wage rises while it declines abroad. The larger the share of nontraded goods the stronger the distribution effect, and hence the more pronounced the absolute and relative wage changes.

Consider next the balance of payments. When the goods markets clear the trade balance is equal to the excess of income over spending:

$$\dot{H} = WN - VH \qquad (8)$$

It is immediately apparent from (8) and (7) that an increase in our money

---

*Differentiation of the system yields

$$\begin{bmatrix} \alpha + \theta & -\theta\Psi \\ \alpha & 1-\alpha \end{bmatrix}\begin{bmatrix} \hat{W} \\ \hat{W}^* \end{bmatrix} = \begin{bmatrix} (1-k)\alpha \\ 0 \end{bmatrix}\hat{H}$$

where α and Ψ were defined in the preceding footnote.

stock, starting from initial equilibrium, will lead to a balance of payments deficit and thus an outflow of money:

$$d\dot{H} = VH(\hat{W} - \hat{H}) = -VH\left\{[k\alpha(1-\alpha) + \theta\Psi]/[\alpha(1-\alpha) + \theta\Psi]\right\}\hat{H} \quad (9)$$

How can we think of this adjustment process in terms of exports and imports? There are two distinct effects. The first is the direct expenditure effect of the redistribution of money. This leads the home country to spend more on imports and to have a reduced export revenue. The second effect arises from the change in relative wages:

$$\hat{W} - \hat{W}^* = \left\{\alpha(1 - k)/[\alpha(1-\alpha) + \theta\Psi]\right\}\hat{H} \quad (10)$$

Because our relative wage rises, the range of goods produced at home declines and this further reduces our export revenue and raises our import spending. The shift in the competitive margin is clearly an important part of the adjustment process. What about the role of price changes in this context?

The model, in assuming constant expenditure shares, implicitly assumes unit price elasticities. The change in relative wages and prices thus leaves import and export spending independent of prices except for the changing of competitive margins already referred to.

II. PURCHASING POWER PARITY

Let us now investigate the relationship between various prices in the adjustment process to a monetary disturbance and in response to real changes. The purpose is to establish that even though consumers in both countries face the same prices of traded goods—there are no tariffs or transport costs and no failure of spatial arbitrage—price levels can still diverge.

1. Relative Price Levels and Payments Adjustment

We start with the definition of consumer price levels. Assume the price level is an expenditure weighted index of the three sets of prices—importables, exportables, and nontraded goods:

$$P = P_m^{(k-\theta)}P_x^\theta P_n^{(1-k)} \qquad P^* = P_m^{(k-\theta)}P_x^\theta P_n^{*(1-k)} \quad (11)$$

where P_i is a price index of all the commodities in a particular group. In comparing the two countries' indexes we note immediately that they face the same traded goods prices and have the same expenditure pattern. Accordingly, the relative price level is simply a function of the home goods price levels:

$$P/P^* = (P_n/P_n^*)^{1-k} \tag{12}$$

The next step is to recognize that the level of home goods prices is determined by the pattern of unit labor requirements in that sector and by the level of wages. For simplicity we can imagine a single home good with a unit labor requirement c per unit of output and c^* abroad. With prices equal to unit costs we then have:

$$P/P^* = (cW/c^*W^*)^{1-k} \equiv \beta(W/W^*)^{1-k} \tag{12a}$$

where $\beta \equiv (c/c^*)^{1-k}$ represents the relative level of labor productivity in the home goods sector. Equation (12a) shows that relative price levels are determined by labor productivity in the home goods sector and by relative wages. We now take technology as given and ask what the monetary adjustment process implies for relative wages and hence relative price levels.

In the preceding section we showed that an increase in the domestic money supply raises our relative wage. From (12a) it thus follows that the consumer price level at home rises relative to that abroad. The reason for the divergent behavior of price levels is that our home goods prices rise absolutely, whereas abroad they decline. Again from (12a) it is clear that the existence of a home goods sector is essential for this result. The divergent behavior of price levels is entirely due to the presence of nontraded goods, not to a failure of spatial arbitrage—the law of one price—for traded goods.

2. Productivity Growth

We next turn to the role of productivity changes and investigate their impact on relative price levels. Here there is an important distinction between productivity growth in traded versus nontraded goods. Consider first an increase in domestic productivity in the home goods sector only. The productivity growth will lower, at the initial wage, the cost and price of home goods. With unit elastic demand, quantity demanded will increase in proportion to the price decline which in turn equals the growth in productivity or labor saving. Total employment in home goods therefore remains unchanged and accordingly there is no need for adjustments in absolute or relative wages. In terms of (12a) the price level at home falls relative to that abroad as β declines.

The case of productivity growth in the traded goods sector is considerably more complicated. Interestingly, it yields the opposite effect on relative price levels. Inspection of Figure 8-1 shows that growth in domestic productivity in the traded goods sector shifts the $A(z)$ schedule upward as domestic labor requirements are reduced. For a given relative wage that implies an increase in the range of goods produced at home and, from (3) and (4), a higher expenditure share θ for domestic goods.

We just have shown that at the initial relative wage, growth in productivity in our traded goods sector raises the demand for goods and labor at home. The demand increase is centered on the range of goods where the productivity growth has made us cost competitive. With an excess demand for domestic goods at the initial equilibrium we now have an adjustment in relative wages. Our relative wage rises, thereby partially offsetting the gain in cost competitiveness. (In terms of Figure 8-2 our argument corresponds to an upward shift of the YY schedule.)

The rise in the home country's equilibrium relative wage implies by (12a) that our price level rises relative to that abroad. We thus have the puzzling case where a gain in productivity in the traded goods sector, and a gain in competitiveness through the cost reduction, leads at the same time to a rise in the relative price level. The reason is that the increased labor productivity in the traded goods sector leads to a rise in money wages and therefore to a rise in costs and prices of nontraded goods where productivity has not changed. As relative price levels are determined by home goods prices, the relative price level of the country experiencing productivity growth must increase.

Balassa (1964) has shown that the theoretical argument has empirical support. Taking the GNP deflator as a comprehensive price index, including both nontraded and traded goods, he showed that countries with high productivity growth experience a rise in the GNP deflator relative to wholesale prices in manufacturing, where the latter serve as an index for traded goods prices.*

Returning to (12a) we can ask what are the implications of productivity growth for comparative inflation rates. Note that the relative price levels in (12a) are measured in a common currency. To translate foreign wages and prices into foreign currency we substitute $\overline{W}^*e = W^*$ and $\overline{P}^*e = P^*$ in (12a) to obtain after some manipulation:

*See also Kravis *et al.* (1978), who use the argument for the international comparison of real income levels.

Money, Exchange Rates, and Employment

$$P/\bar{P}^* = e^k \beta (W/\bar{W}^*)^{1-k} \tag{13}$$

where $\bar{W}^*$ and $\bar{P}^*$ are foreign wages and prices in terms of foreign currency. Equation (13) shows that home inflation will exceed that abroad if our wages rise faster or if our exchange rate is depreciating.

III. STICKY WAGES AND FIXED EXCHANGE RATES

Earlier in this chapter we discussed the adjustment to nominal and real disturbances on the assumption of wage and price flexibility, thus ensuring full employment. Here, we look instead at employment determination when wages are sticky. Section III(1) shows the determination of equilibrium nominal income and employment. Section III(2) considers the adjustment to an exogenous increase in wages abroad.

1. Employment Determination

With fixed nominal wages and fixed exchange rates the relative wage W/W^* is given and so is accordingly our expenditure share $\theta(W/W^*)$. Let $\bar{\theta}$ be our share for the given relative wage. Defining nominal income as the given wage times the endogenous level of employment:

$$\tilde{Y} = WN \tag{14}$$

Equilibrium in the home goods market requires that nominal income equal spending on domestic goods:

$$\tilde{Y} = \bar{\theta} V\bar{H} + (1-k)VH \tag{15}$$

With given relative wages and the implied distribution of spending across traded goods our employment and income level just depend on our money holdings. Once again home goods play a critical role. A rise in our money holdings raises expenditure on nontraded goods, thereby raising the level of employment. The absence of distribution effects rules out any employment effects in the traded goods sector.

Figure 8-3 shows the demand for domestic output as a function of nominal money, given $\bar{\theta}$ and world money. The intercept term is world spending on domestic traded goods, $\bar{\theta}V\bar{H}$. The slope of the demand schedule depends on the expenditure share of nontraded goods, $1 - k$. Without nontraded goods the schedule is flat.

Suppose now that the home country has a level of money holdings H_0 and a level of spending VH_0. Equilibrium output is determined at point A' and, at that level of spending, income exceeds expenditure. Accordingly there is a trade surplus and nominal money holdings rise, raising income and spending while reducing the trade surplus. The economy converges over time to the steady state equilibrium at point A_1. Throughout the adjustment process the expansion in output and employment takes place entirely in the home goods sector. The home country does spend more on all goods, but our increased spending on traded goods is offset by reduced foreign demand. Therefore, the only employment creation is in the home goods sector.

FIGURE 8-3

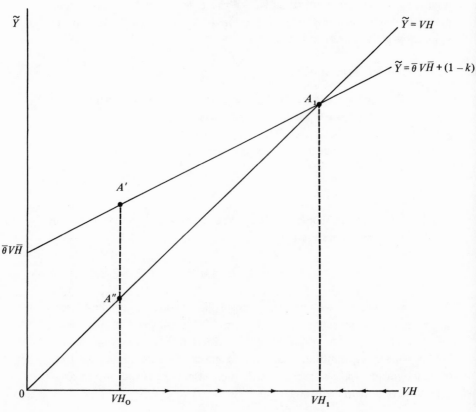

FIGURE 8-4

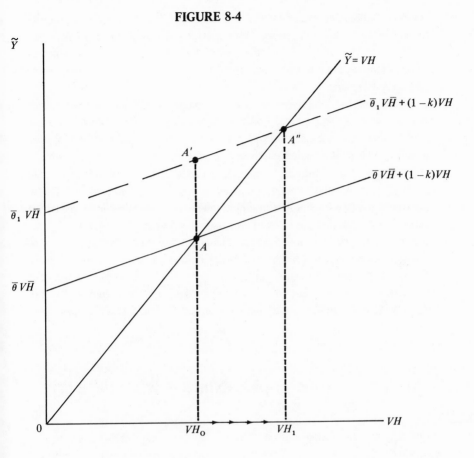

2. A Rise in Foreign Wages

In this section we study the impact of a change in foreign wages. The discussion is conducted in terms of Figure 8-4, where we begin with an initial equilibrium at point A, where trade is balanced.

The increase in foreign wages lowers our relative wage and therefore raises domestic cost competitiveness. Given technology, the home country will be able to efficiently produce a wider range of goods. Accordingly the expenditure share of domestically produced traded goods increases to $\bar{\theta}_1$. In Figure 8-4 this increase in demand for domestic goods is shown by an upward shift of the demand schedule.

The impact effect of increased foreign wages is to raise domestic cost competitiveness, output and employment. Nominal income immediately rises to point A'. But with spending VH_0 as yet unchanged income now exceeds spending, money balances accumulate and there is a further induced expansion as the economy moves from A' to A''.

What are the effects of higher wages abroad? It is readily shown that abroad nominal income and employment must fall and that the foreign trade balance deteriorates.

Where are the employment changes concentrated? Abroad the higher wages raise costs and prices. For a given nominal level of expenditure the level of real spending falls, making for a decline in the real demand for non-traded goods. In the traded goods sector we have to distinguish price effects and shifts in the competitive margin. The higher prices of foreign traded goods—for those that remain produced—are offset by reduced demand so that here, too, we have a loss in employment. A further loss in employment occurs from the shifting competitive margin where the home country displaces foreign production and employment. Initially this is the only source of domestic employment creation. Accordingly the impact effect of the wage change is to reduce foreign employment by more than the gain in employment at home. Subsequent adjustments through changes in money and spending reinforce the home employment gains and further reduce employment abroad.

IV.

~~III.~~ FIXED WAGES AND FLEXIBLE EXCHANGE RATES

Under flexible exchange rates and in the absence of capital flows or intervention, the current account of the balance of payments must be in equilibrium. In our model that implies the equality of the value of imports M and exports M^*. Our imports and foreign demand for domestically produced traded goods are, respectively*

$$M \equiv (k - \theta)VH \qquad M^* \equiv \theta VH^* e \qquad \theta = \theta(W/\overline{W}^* e) \qquad (16)$$

where H^* is the foreign money supply measured in foreign currency and where e is the exchange rate or domestic currency price of foreign exchange. With money wages given it is apparent that the relative wage, measured in a common currency $W/\overline{W}^* e$ is just a function of the exchange rate. A depreciation by the home country lowers our relative wage and thereby expands

---

*Total spending on traded goods amounts to a fraction k of expenditure. With a fraction θ spent on domestically produced goods, the expenditure share of foreign traded goods is $k - \theta$.

the range of goods we can competitively produce. Thus a depreciation raises exports and reduces imports. There is a second effect of a depreciation and that is to raise the value of foreign expenditure in terms of domestic currency VH^*e, and thus to raise our nominal export revenue.

In Figure 8-5 we show the foreign exchange market for given nominal wages and nominal money in each country. An exchange depreciation reduces import spending by the home country owing to the shifting competitive margin. Export revenue is an increasing function of the exchange rate because of the shifting competitive margin and because the domestic currency value of foreign spending rises. The equilibrium obtains at point A, where trade is balanced:

$$\theta(W/\overline{W}^*e)VH^*e \ = \ [k - \theta(W/W^*e)] \ VH \qquad (17)$$

The exchange rate now plays the key role of determining relative wages, relative prices, and therefore the allocation of resources. Employment levels, however, are determined by money and wages independently of the exchange rate. That point is apparent from the fact that when trade is balanced income equals expenditure $WN = VH$, or $N = VH/W$. Thus employment in each coun-

FIGURE 8-5

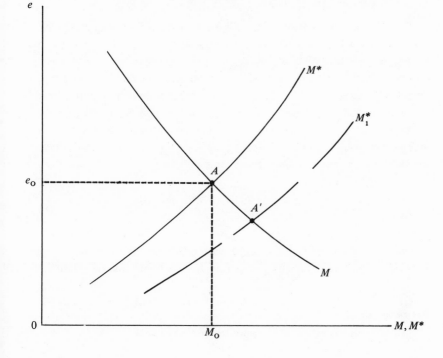

try is determined by the real money supply in terms of wage units. The exchange rate assures that the employment levels thus determined are consistent with market equilibrium in each country.

1. An Increase in Nominal Money Abroad

To see the operation of the flexible rate model we start with an increase in foreign money. From (16) we note that foreign nominal spending and therefore our export revenue rises. The export revenue schedule in Figure 8-5 shifts downward and to the right.* The trade surplus at the initial exchange rate leads to appreciation until the new equilibrium at A' is reached.

At point A' the foreign monetary expansion has led to a rise in our relative wage and therefore to a contraction in the range of goods produced at home. With the exchange rate appreciating less than the rise in foreign money, there is increased foreign real spending on our goods. The loss in employment in marginal industries is offset by increased employment in the industries that we maintain. Abroad employment rises from the expansion of the range of foreign exports, but in their traditional exports and their home goods sector employment rises as well.

2. A Change in Foreign Wages

The next disturbance we consider is an increase in the foreign wage. Here we want to compare our results to the case of fixed exchange rates studied above. The rise in foreign wages, at the initial exchange rate, lowers foreign cost competitiveness and therefore raises our exports and reduces our imports. It is apparent from (16) that the home country's import demand schedule in Figure 8-6 will shift down in proportion to the foreign wage increase. The foreign import schedule though will shift down by less.†

The new equilibrium is shown at point A'. From (17) we can calculate the change in the equilibrium exchange rate as

$$\hat{e} = -[\Psi\theta/(1 + \Psi\theta)]\,\hat{\overline{w}}* \tag{18}$$

With the equilibrium exchange rate appreciating proportionately less than the increase in foreign wages, our relative wage falls. The gain in competitiveness implies an increased range of production for the home country. Home em-

---

*It is readily shown that the downward shift is proportionately less than the rise in foreign money.

†From (16) the downward shift is equal to $\hat{e} = -[\Psi/(1 + \Psi)]\,\hat{\overline{w}}*$.

FIGURE 8-6

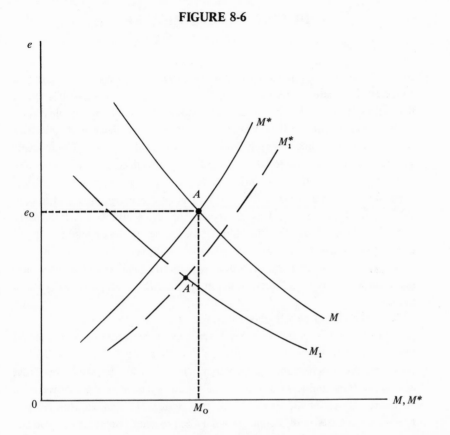

ployment is constant and the expanded output in the new industries is off-set by a reduction in traditional export industries. Here employment falls because the real value of foreign spending declines due to the appreciation. Abroad, of course, employment falls in all industries due to the reduction in the real money supply in terms of wage units.

How do fixed and flexible rates compare? With flexible rates the foreign wage increase is partially offset by our appreciation. There is no gain in employment at home, but there is still a shifting in the competitive margin. Flexible rates dampen the relative price and trade effects of foreign wage-price disturbances. But they do not fully offset these effects. The reason? A foreign wage increase, given foreign nominal money, is a real disturbance. Only if *both* money and wages increased abroad in the same proportion would a flexible rate provide full insulation. As long as we are dealing with real disturbances, flexible rates can dampen their transmission but they cannot eliminate the spillover of all real effects.

III. CONCLUDING REMARKS

In concluding we emphasize two important aspects of this chapter. The first concerns the strategic use of assumptions. Although we dealt with a model that allowed for a variety of effects—income and spending, employment, trade patterns, productivity growth, and money—we dealt with all these issues at the same time and even did so in a two-country setting. The strategic simplifications were three. The Ricardian production structure naturally reduces the continuum of goods to a few composite commodities, exportables, importables and nontraded goods. The next assumption is that of constant expenditure shares. This cuts out cross price effects and immensely simplifies the analysis. The final simplification lies in the expenditure function that excludes income and thus prevents multiplier effects. Some of these assumptions can be relaxed, of course. The merit of making them in the first place, however, is to address issues in a reasonably complex and realistic model.

The second and closely related aspect of this chapter concerns the integration of real and monetary issues of trade and macroeconomics. The model laid out here achieves that integration and thus shows that trade balance problems are macroeconomic problems. It shows at the same time that correcting trade imbalances will invariably imply changing the relative price structure, allocation of demand and production. This integration of perspectives contrasts with simple monetary approaches that represent balance of payments problems as "purely" monetary.

REFERENCES AND SUGGESTED READINGS

Balassa, B. 1964. The purchasing power parity doctrine, a reappraisal. *Journal of political economy* 72.

Dornbusch, R., Fischer, S., and Samuelson, P. A. 1977. Comparative advantage, trade and payments in a Ricardian model with a continuum of goods. *American economic review* 67:823-39.

Kravis, I., Heston, A., and Summers, R., 1978. Real GDP per capita for more than one hundred countries. *Economic journal* 88:215-41.

Samuelson, P. A. 1964. Theoretical notes on trade problems. *Review of economics and statistics* 46:145-54.

CHAPTER

9

Monetary and Exchange Rate Policy for Macroeconomic Stability

This chapter concludes our macroeconomic models emphasizing the interaction of relative prices and aggregate spending in determining output and the trade balance. We approach that question once more to ask what monetary and exchange rate policies can be used to attain internal or external balance. In section I we look at monetary and exchange rate policy from a perspective of dynamics. Here we ask how the time path of adjustment is influenced by an employment oriented monetary policy in contrast to the classic adjustment process. In section II stabilization policy is addressed from the vantage point of modern Phelps-Friedman macroeconomics. The question posed there is whether monetary and exchange rate policies that accommodate price disturbances have undesirable side effects. We show, extending the work done by Taylor (1979), that this is indeed the case. Exchange rate rules that closely follow purchasing power parity do offset the employment effects of price disturbances, but they do so at the cost of increased instability of prices.

I. WAGES, MONEY, AND THE EXCHANGE RATE

The early chapters of this book showed the determination of employment by demand and emphasized the role of wages and relative prices in this context. Later chapters added money as another determinant of spending and employment. We now combine these two aspects and show how monetary and exchange rate policy are used in the adjustment to external and internal imbalance. Section I(1) shows the basic model, while section I(2) discusses the adjustment process.

1. Employment and the Trade Balance

We assume an economy where employment is determined by demand and where the unit labor requirement, once again, is a constant a. Denoting employment by N we have

$$N = a(D + M^*) \qquad (1)$$

where D and M^* are domestic and foreign demand for home output. Domestic price is determined by unit labor costs:*

$$P = aW \qquad (2)$$

The trade balance is equal to the excess of export receipts over import spending:

$$T = PM^* - P^* e M \qquad (3)$$

*The pricing formula is readily adjusted to include a profit markup π to obtain $P = a(1 + \pi)W$, or to include indirect taxes and the like.

where $P*$ is the given foreign currency price of our imports, assumed constant and equal to unity, and e is the exchange rate.

[handwritten: Assume: $P^* = 1$.]

Our behavioral assumptions are that foreign demand depends on the relative price of our exports P/e. Domestic demand for our own goods and for imports depend on income WN, money balances H, and prices of our goods and imports. Moreover, the demand functions are homogeneous of degree zero in money, income and prices. Accordingly we can write the behavioral equations in terms of relative prices, and the real value of money and labor income in terms of import prices. The choice of import prices as a numeraire is a convenience without *any* economic significance or implication:*

$$D = D(\overset{\ominus}{P/e}, \overset{(+)}{WN/e}, \overset{(+)}{H/e}); \quad M = M(\overset{(+)}{P/e}, \overset{(+)}{WN/e}, \overset{(+)}{H/e}); \quad M* = M*(\overset{\ominus}{P/e}) \quad (4)$$

[handwritten: relative prices — Real income — Real balances]

The behavioral equations in (4), together with the price equation in (2) allows us to solve for the level of employment in (1) and for the associated trade balance in (3). The solutions are readily derived by substitution, and we state here merely the result and the properties that we assume: equilibrium employment N is a function of the wage and the money stock, relative to the exchange rate:

$$N = N(W/e, H/e) \qquad N_1 < 0, N_2 > 0 \qquad (5)$$

A rise in the nominal money stock, given the exchange rate and wage rates raises real balances, spending, and employment. A rise in wages, given money and the exchange rate raises the relative and absolute price of domestic goods. With substitution and real balance effects dominating the real income effect, as we assume, employment declines. Exchange depreciation raises employment. *[handwritten: (Again, because substitution outweighs other effects.)]*

Likewise, the trade balance depends on wages and money relative to the exchange rate. A rise in wages is assumed to worsen the trade balance as is a rise in money. An exchange depreciation, given money and wages, will improve the external balance, because it creates demand for domestic goods while reducing expenditure via the adverse real balance effect:

$$T = T(W/e, H/e) \qquad T_1 < 0, T_2 < 0 \qquad (6)$$

In Figure 9-1 we show a schedule TT along which trade is balanced. The slope reflects the assumption that a rise in the relative price of domestic

---

*The reader will want to demonstrate that we could use equally any price index as a deflator.

FIGURE 9-1

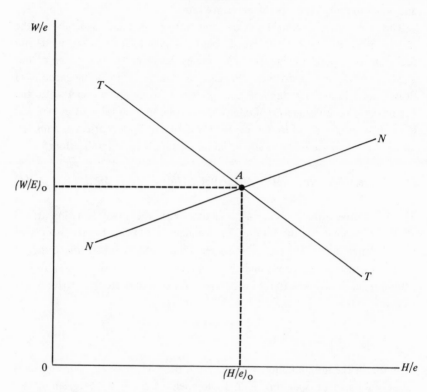

goods worsens the trade balance and therefore must be offset by a reduction in real balances, which lowers spending and thus maintains external balance. Points above the schedule correspond to a deficit and points below the schedule to a surplus.

Figure 9-1 shows also the schedule *NN* along which labor market equilibrium obtains. Along that schedule the demand determined level of employment N equals the existing labor force $\bar{N}$. The schedule is positively sloped since a rise in the relative price of our goods reduces employment so that higher real balances and thus higher spending are required to maintain labor market equilibrium. Above the schedule there is unemployment while below and to the right there is overemployment (overtime).* At point A real balances and relative prices are such as to ensure internal and external balance.

---

*Exchange appreciation is represented by a movement up and along a ray through the origin. The *NN* schedule is flatter than a ray through the origin on the assumption that an appreciation lowers employment, substitution effects dominating real income and real balance effects.

2. *The Adjustment Process*

We now study alternative adjustment processes. In particular we compare the "classical" adjustment process with one of a "managed" system. The classical adjustment process relies on money wage changes induced by unemployment and money supply changes induced by the balance of payments. The managed system, by contrast, has the money supply and the exchange rate managed with a view to attaining internal and external balance along preferred paths.

Under fixed exchange rates and in the absence of sterilization, money balances rise at a rate equal to the balance of payments surplus:

$$\dot{H}/\bar{e} = T(\bar{W}/e, \bar{H}/e) \qquad (7)$$

" $-$ " Denotes fixed.

Thus anywhere above the TT schedule the money supply is falling absolutely and in terms of importables and conversely below the TT schedule. The corresponding arrows are indicated in Figure 9-2.

Wage behavior is governed by unemployment. The rate of wage change is proportional to the difference between employment and the labor force:

FIGURE 9-2

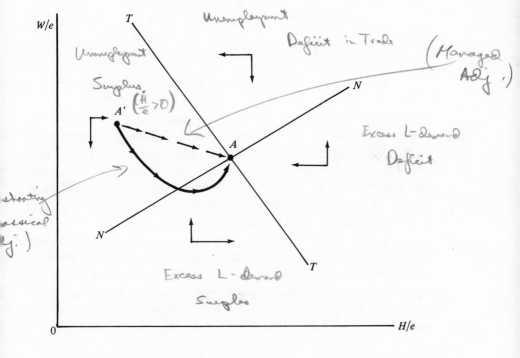

$$\dot{W}/e = \phi[N(W/e,H/e) - \bar{N}]\qquad(8)$$

Above the *NN* schedule wages are thus falling absolutely and in terms of the exchange rate, while below the *NN* schedule real wages are rising. Again the arrows in Figure 9-2 indicate the dynamics.

Suppose now that we start at a point like A' in Figure 9-2, with unemployment and a surplus. Unemployment implies falling real wages while the surplus implies a rising money supply, absolutely and in real terms. At point A' both the real depreciation and the gain in real balances create employment. The external balance may initially worsen or improve. The solid path $A'A$ shows the adjustment, possibly cyclical, for the classic case. It is essential to recognize that this process does assume flexible *real* wages and the absence of sterilization. Under these assumptions, and given time to adjust, the system will converge to internal and external balance.

A managed system will involve rules for the behavior of the money stock and the exchange rate that supplement the wage dynamics so as to achieve a preferred path. In Figure 9-2 we show as an example the dashed path $A'A$ that avoids the overdepreciation of the real exchange rate and is potentially faster than the classical adjustment process. *(Nom. exch. rate is fixed.)*

The managed system would be represented by the following dynamics:

$$(\dot{W}/e) = \phi[N(W/e,H/e) - \bar{N}]\qquad(6)$$

and

$$(\dot{H}/e) = T(W/e,H/e) + k[\bar{N} - N(W/e,H/e)]\qquad(7)$$

It is apparent that the system is more employment oriented than is the classic adjustment process. Now depreciation supplements nominal wage changes in moving the real wage. The real money stock is managed both with a view to the trade balance but also with respect to employment. At a point like A' real balances are allowed to grow more rapidly than under the classical adjustment process and thus employment recovers more rapidly.

Important features of the classic and managed systems, are on one hand that there is flexibility in real wages and that accordingly the long-run equilibrium at A can be attained. The other point concerns dynamics. The managed system can be implemented without offsetting or dampening responses from the private sector. The next part shows an alternative model that centers on the interaction of private wage setting and monetary and exchange rate policy.

166

Elements of "Overshooting"

II. ACCOMMODATION AND MACROECONOMIC STABILITY

This part develops an alternative approach to exchange rate policy. We take here a longer-run perspective and ask how policy rules for exchange rates and money contribute to the stability of output and the persistence of price disturbances. The approach follows important work on the closed economy by Taylor (1979). Extending Taylor's model to the open economy, we find that monetary and exchange rate policies that accommodate price disturbances will tend to stabilize output, but they do so at the cost of increased persistence in wage and price disturbances. The reason is that the wage-setting process is influenced by expectations about the extent to which policies are accommodating. The more policies are accommodating, the less labor has to be concerned about the unemployment consequences of wage policy and hence the slower is the adjustment of wages and prices.

In section II(1) we develop a simple log-linear macroeconomic model of the open economy along the lines already encountered in the preceding section. Section II(2) introduces the wage behavior and discusses the stability of output and prices. Taylor's model that serves as a background is sketched in the appendix.

1. Demand, Policy Rules, and Equilibrium Output

The model studies deviations of output, relative prices and real balances from their long-run equilibrium levels. The model is formulated in a log-linear version for computational convenience. Here y, h, p, and e denote respectively the logs of real output, nominal money, domestic prices and the exchange rate.

Equilibrium output is determined by the real exchange rate $e - p$, real balances $h - p$, and a random term v:

$$y = a(e - p) + b(h - p) + v \qquad a, b > 0 \qquad (8)$$

Following the assumptions of previous chapters a real depreciation, a rise in $e - p$, raises demand and output as does a rise in real balances. The shift term v represents shifts in the demand for domestic output resulting either from shifts between domestic and foreign goods or from changes in the aggregate level of spending. Note that all variables represent deviations from their long-run equilibrium. In long-run equilibrium $y = p = e = h = 0$.

In chapter 8 monetary and exchange rate policies were formulated in terms of differential equations describing the behavior of real balances and the real wage as functions of employment and the trade balance. Here we formulate policy rules in terms of the extent to which the authorities accommodate disturbances in the price level through an increase in money and a depreciation of the exchange rate.

These policy rules are shown in (9):

$$h = \beta p \qquad e = \alpha p \tag{9}$$

where β and α represent the elasticities of the nominal money stock and the nominal exchange rate with respect to the price level. Thus if the price level doubled the authorities would accommodate the price disturbance by a β percent increase in nominal money and an α percent increase in the exchange rate.

Substitution of the policy rules in (8) yields the equilibrium level of output as a function of the price level and the random demand term:

$$y = -\theta p + v \qquad \theta \equiv a(1 - \alpha) + b(1 - \beta) \tag{8a}$$

The reduced form equation for output shows that an increase in the level of prices will reduce demand and output unless money and the exchange rates are *fully* accommodating, $\alpha = \beta = 1$. With partial accommodation ($\alpha, \beta < 1$), a rise in prices reduces real balances and appreciates the *real* exchange rate, thereby lowering demand for domestic output. The coefficient θ summarizes the responsiveness of output to price disturbances.

2. Wage-Price Behavior

In this section we discuss two related issues. The first is why, in response to unemployment, wages and prices do not adjust immediately. The second concerns the manner in which expectations about accommodating macroeconomic policies affect the process of wage-price adjustment. The argument we develop follows directly the model of Taylor and uses long-term, overlapping wage contracts combined with rational expectations as the framework for wage-price setting.

There are two-period contracts and two groups, each having a contract coming up every other year for renegotiation. In this manner there are always two contracts overlapping, one in its first year, the other in its terminal, second year. The group that negotiates or sets a new wage has three points of reference. One is the ongoing second year contract that is still in force.

The second is the new contract, which is expected to come into force when the currently negotiated contract is in its second year. The third point to consider is the unemployment consequence of current wage setting.

The current wage contract x will thus be set with reference to ongoing contracts entered into last period, x_{-1}, expected future contracts, $\tilde{x}_{+1}$, and expected employment $\tilde{y}$ and $\tilde{y}_{+1}$ during the length of the current contract. Here a tilde (~) denotes the expectations operator and u is an error term:*

$$x = f(x_{-1}, \tilde{x}_{+1}, \tilde{y}, \tilde{y}_{+1}) + u \tag{10}$$

The higher are current and expected employment, the higher is our *relative* wage. Conversely, with higher unemployment we are prepared to take a *relative* wage cut.

The price level is proportional to the average wage. The average wage in turn is formed by the currently effective contracts, x and x_{-1}. Thus the price level is equal to

$$p = 0.5(x + x_{-1}) \tag{11}$$

Now suppose that last period, starting from trend equilibrium, there was a wage disturbance u. Wage settlements turned out high relative to trend. As a consequence prices last period were above trend by $p_{-1} = 0.5x_{-1}$. What are the implications for current wage settlements? We recognize that there will be unemployment if the price level is above trend, $p > 0$, because there is less than full accommodation. One wage strategy, clearly, is to take a wage cut sufficiently large to maintain the price level on trend: $x = -x_{-1}$. That policy ensures full employment but it implies a relative wage cut both in terms of the contract x_{-1} and in terms of the contract coming up. The latter is true because our low settlement would allow that contract to be high.

An alternative policy is to strike a balance between some cut in the *relative* wage and some unemployment. Thus our wage contract will imply some increase in money wages, though not fully matching last period's contract. Similarly the next period's contract will imply some wage settlement above trend, though again less than the present one. Thus over time the wage returns to trend as does the average wage and the price level. The question is what determines the speed with which prices return to trend or to put it in other words, what determines the persistence of price disturbances.

---

*The model is stated in terms of deviations from trend. This applies equally to wage contracts so that x denotes the deviation from the long-term wage trend along which $x = x_{-1} = x_{+1} = 0$.

Taylor shows that two structural characteristics determine persistence. The first is the extent of accommodation. The more fully policies accommodate disturbances—the smaller the θ—the smaller are the unemployment consequences of wage-price disturbances and hence the smaller the incentive to return rapidly to the trend price level. Indeed with full accommodation the price level becomes a random walk, since there is no restraint on wage setting. The second characteristic that matters is the extent to which contracts are forward or backward looking. The more contracts are backward looking the stronger is persistence.

The model is important because it provides an explanation for short-run wage-price stickiness even in a framework of rational expectations. It is especially important in pointing to accommodative stabilization policies as one of the reasons for wage-price stickiness.

We now return to exchange rate policy and ask what role it plays in this context. The answer is quite immediate. A policy of maintaining near purchasing power parity (*PPP*) implies that we follow price disturbances by accommodating exchange rate adjustments. Such a policy keeps the real exchange rate relatively constant and thus reduces this source of employment variation. But because it prevents these employment effects, or because it *validates* the price increase, it abolishes much of the incentive for prices to return rapidly to their trend. *PPP* oriented exchange rate rules thus promote price level instability.

In concluding this section we note that the stability of output and the persistence of price disturbances depend on the total accommodation provided by monetary and exchange rate policy as summarized in the coefficient θ in (8a). This leaves room, therefore, to use subsidiary considerations to allocate the stabilization role between money and the exchange rate. If real exchange rate variability is seen as much more costly than variability in real balances then exchange rate policy should be very close to *PPP* and money balances would respond hardly at all to the price level.* There is nothing, however, in the present model to make such a choice.

---

*For an alternative exchange rate rule that takes into account the trade balance, see Dornbusch (1979).

APPENDIX: PRICING A LA TAYLOR

This appendix reproduces Taylor's model of the wage process. Aggregate demand, for the closed economy, is represented by the deviation of output from normal:

$$y = -\theta p \qquad (A\text{-}1)$$

where θ varies between zero and one depending on the extent of monetary accommodation.

Wages are set according to a relative wage equation:

$$x = (1-d)x_{-1} + d\tilde{x}_{+1} + \gamma[(1-d)\tilde{y} + d\tilde{y}_{+1}] + u \qquad (A\text{-}2)$$

where γ represents the responsiveness of the wage contract to employment prospects. Note from (A-2) that wages are purely forward looking if $d=1$ and purely backward looking for $d=0$. The term u represents random movements in wages.

The model is completed by the price equation:

$$p = 0.5(x + x_{-1}) \qquad (A\text{-}3)$$

which states that the price level equals the average wage.

Rational expectations are now used to derive a wage equation. The employment predictions will be made, using the economic model that determines output. That means we use equation (A-3) in (A-1) and take expectations:

$$\tilde{y} = -0.5\theta(x + x_{-1}) \qquad \tilde{y}_{+1} = -0.5\theta(x + \tilde{x}_{+1}) \qquad (A\text{-}4)$$

Substituting the result in (A-3) yields an equation in wages with coefficients that reflect the economic model in which wages and employment are determined:*

$$\tilde{x} = (1-d)\tilde{x}_{-1} + d\tilde{x}_{+1} - \gamma[0.5(1-d)\theta(\tilde{x} + \tilde{x}_{-1}) + 0.5d\,\theta(\tilde{x} + \tilde{x}_{+1})] \qquad (A\text{-}5)$$

Collecting terms gives us an equation for wages:

$$(1-d)\tilde{x}_{-1} - c\tilde{x} + d\tilde{x}_{+1} = 0, \qquad c \equiv (1+0.5\theta\gamma)/(1-0.5\theta\gamma) \qquad (A\text{-}6)$$

*Note that $x = \tilde{x}$ and $x_{-1} = \tilde{x}_{-1}$.

with a solution:

$$x = \rho x_{-1} + u \qquad \rho \equiv (\tfrac{1}{2}d) \ \left\{ c - [c^2 - 4d(1-d)]^{\tfrac{1}{2}} \right\} \qquad \text{(A-7)}$$

Substitution of (A-7) into the price equation gives the stochastic process for prices:

$$p = \rho p_{-1} + 0.5(u + u_{-1}) \qquad\qquad \text{(A-8)}$$

It follows from (A-8) that the process generating price is a function of the extent to which policy is accommodating. The more accommodating the monetary and exchange rate policy, the more persistent or drawn out the price disturbances.

REFERENCES AND SUGGESTED READING

Barro, R. 1978. A stochastic equilibrium model of an open economy under flexible exchange rates. *Quarterly journal of economics* 92:149-64.

Dornbusch, R. 1979. Exchange rate policy and macroeconomic stability. *The crawling peg: future prospects and past performance,* ed. J. Williamson. New York: Macmillan Publishing Co.

Fischer, S. 1973. Stability and exchange rate system in a monetarist model of the balance of payments. *The political economy of monetary reform,* ed. R.A. Aliber. London: Allen and Unwin.

Flood, R., 1979. Capital mobility and the choice of exchange rate system. *International economic review* 20:405-416.

Lapan, H., and Enders, W. 1979. Random disturbances and the choice of exchange rate regimes in an intergenerational model. Unpublished manuscript, Iowa State University.

Taylor, J. 1979. Staggered wage setting in a macro model. *American economic review,* papers and proceedings. 108-18.

Weber, W. 1979. Output variability under monetary policy and exchange rate rules in a rational expectations international trade model. Unpublished manuscript, University of Virginia.

Part 4

Assets Markets, Capital Mobility, and Stabilization Policy

CHAPTER

10

Stabilization Policy Under Fixed Exchange Rates and Capital Mobility

This chapter introduces interest-bearing assets in addition to money and investigates the implications of trade in securities for monetary and fiscal policy in a world of fixed exchange rates. The time perspective is strictly short-run. There is no consideration here of price adjustment or of the implications of balance of payments disequilibrium regarding the ability of the central bank to finance these flows. Nor do we take into account the implications of the private sector's current account imbalance for changes in wealth.

The literature we draw on developed during the sixties. The seminal work was done by Mundell (1968), McKinnon and Oates (1966), and Fleming (1962). This literature showed that a small country, faced with perfect capital mobility, will find fiscal policy particularly effective and monetary policy entirely ineffective. These results are due to the endogeneity of the money stock via fixed rates and integration of assets markets. In a two-country setting, where repercussion effects can be taken into account, monetary expansion in one country will expand aggregate demand and output in the world. Fiscal expansion, by contrast, may lead to lower income abroad.

In section I we review the concept of capital mobility and consider the implications of assets market integration for the "small" country case. The effects of monetary and fiscal policy are studied for a country too small to affect the world interest rate. In section II the analysis moves to the world capital market and the effects of monetary and fiscal policy in a two-country setting. The chapter concludes, in section III, with the case where domestic and foreign securities are imperfect substitutes.

I. CAPITAL MOBILITY

Consider a world where there are two assets: money and bonds. Bonds are an aggregate of all interest earning assets and are distinguished from money by the fact that they *do* bear interest. We assume for the present that domestic and foreign bonds are *perfect substitutes*. Perfect substitution means that holders of securities are indifferent between domestic and foreign bonds and that their yields must be equalized accordingly. For the present, there is no exchange rate uncertainty; accordingly interest rates must be the same.

We also assume that portfolio adjustments are *instantaneous*. Given a change in the determinants of portfolio composition, say a change in the interest rate, there will be an immediate portfolio shift that leads to the preferred asset holdings. We will call the combination of perfect substitution and instantaneous adjustment *perfect capital mobility*. It implies that yields are continuously equalized and that asset holders are continuously in portfolio equilibrium. We will later contrast this view of assets markets with two alternatives. One arises when portfolio adjustments are slow although assets are perfect substitutes. The other obtains if adjustments are instantaneous with assets being imperfect substitutes. These alternatives have important implications for the central bank's ability to conduct monetary policy.

Stabilization Policy/Fixed Exchange Rates

1. Monetary Equilibrium under Fixed Exchange Rates

We take the standard representation of money demand:

$$L = L(r, Y) \tag{1}$$

where L denotes the demand for real balances, r is the rate of interest, and Y denotes real income. An increase in the rate of interest on alternative assets lowers real money demand, while a rise in real income, via the transactions motive, increases the demand for real balances. The inclusion of only one interest rate reflects the assumption of perfect substitutes.

Equilibrium in the money market requires that money demand equals the supply of money. The latter is equal to net foreign assets R plus domestic credit D:

$$R + D = L(r, Y) \tag{2}$$

For the moment we forget the existence of a banking system and accordingly the left hand side corresponds to high-powered money.*

Take now domestic credit D and also the level of income as given. The equilibrium stock of reserves R is drawn in Figure 10-1 as a function of the rate of interest. The schedule L-D corresponds to equation (2a):

$$R = L(r, Y_o) - D_o \tag{2a}$$

For every level of the interest rate there is an equilibrium money supply. Given domestic credit D_o, there is a unique level of reserves that will establish that supply of money.

The next step is to recognize that perfect capital mobility implies that our interest rate will equal the world rate of interest, or

$$r = r^* \tag{3}$$

A given rate of interest in the world r_o^* thus establishes the equilibrium reserve level at which we have asset market equilibrium. In Figure 10-1 the reserve level is R_o.

We can immediately use Figure 10-1 to derive three important results: First, a rise in our income, by raising money demand, leads to an increase in the equilibrium supply of money and, for given domestic credit, to a reserve

*We also neglect the distinction between nominal and real balance, since prices will be assumed given and constant.

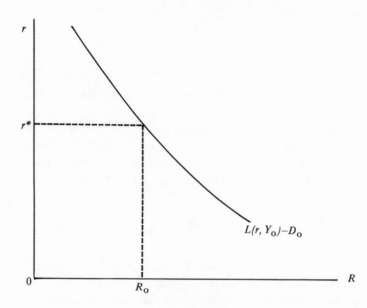

Fiscal , Expansion

Fixed Exchange Rate Policy

Monetary Expansion

inflow. The mechanism though which this monetary expansion occurs is as follows: as income rises, the transactions demand for money increases. To finance the expansion of their money holdings, domestic residents sell off bonds in the world market. The repatriation of the proceeds leads to an incipient exchange appreciation that forces the central bank to buy foreign exchange and create domestic money. The monetary expansion meets the increased money demand.

The second implication of the model is that domestic credit creation will lead to an offsetting reserve outflow and leave unchanged interest rates and the equilibrium money stock. This result is entirely due to the fact that the home country is deemed too small to change the world rate of interest. Thus money demand is given as well as the equilibrium money stock. If the central bank conducted an open market operation leading to an incipient decline in interest rates below the world level, there would be an instantaneous capital outflow and reserve loss until the initial interest rate had been restored. With an unchanged money stock, reserve losses offset the credit expansion. Under fixed rates and perfect capital mobility a small country cannot conduct monetary policy. In terms of Figure 10-1 the analysis amounts to a leftward shift of the L-D schedule. Accordingly, at an unchanged interest rate there will be an equal and offsetting reserve loss.

Stabilization Policy/Fixed Exchange Rates

The third implication of the model concerns interest rates. A decline in the world rate of interest—a movement along the *L-D* schedule of Figure 10-1— will lead to an increase in money demand and hence to an increase in equilibrium reserves.

2. Monetary and Fiscal Policy: the Small Country Case

We continue to look at the effects of monetary and fiscal policy for a country that is sufficiently small so as not to affect the world rate of interest. We also assume that repercussion effects deriving from changes in domestic income can be ignored.

We retain the assumption of perfect capital mobility and the specification of monetary equilibrium in (2) and add an equation for the determination of equilibrium output. This is the conventional open economy *IS* equation:

$$Y = E(r,Y) + T(Y....) \tag{10}$$

where E denotes aggregate spending by domestic residents, now a function of income *and* the rate of interest. The trade balance is denoted by T. Figure 10-2 shows the equilibrium condition in the goods market as the downward sloping *IS* schedule. Moving down and along the schedule a lower interest rate increases aggregate demand and requires an expansion in equilibrium output. The trade balance worsens as we move down along the schedule since import spending rises relative to the given level of exports.

With a world and domestic interest rate $r=r^*$ the initial equilibrium output is Y_0. The interest rate determines the level of demand and hence the equilibrium level of production. Suppose there is a fiscal expansion, raising aggregate demand and thus shifting the *IS* curve to the right to *IS'*. At the unchanged world and domestic interest rate, output expands to Y'. The expansion of output is given by the standard open economy multiplier $1/(s+m)$.

Perfect capital mobility will ensure that point A' is compatible with equilibrium in the money market. To recognize this, imagine that the real expansion puts upward pressure on interest rates as the transactions demand for money rises relative to the prevailing money stock. There will immediately be a capital inflow and a need for the central bank to prevent currency { Sterilization appreciation by a monetary expansion. The central bank buys foreign exchange and creates domestic money until the money supply equals money demand at the higher income level and unchanged interest rates. Once again, under fixed rates and capital mobility the money stock is fully and instantaneously endogenous. In terms of Figure 10-2 this implies that the *LM* curve

FIGURE 10-2

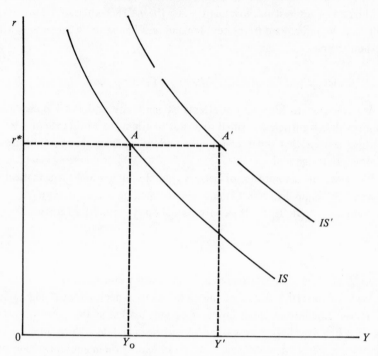

is perfectly elastic at the world interest rate. The elasticity derives from the perfectly elastic supply of money.

Consider next monetary policy. We have already seen that an expansion of domestic credit will be fully offset by a loss of exchange reserves. There is no need to consider this result further.

Under fixed exchange rates, perfect capital mobility, and small country conditions, fiscal policy is very effective and monetary policy is not effective at all. We next consider how these results are modified once we look at a model of the world economy.

II. THE WORLD ECONOMY UNDER CAPITAL MOBILITY

We now abandon the small country assumption and look at an integrated world capital market. Equilibrium requires the world demand for money to equal the world supply of money:

$$D + D^* + \bar{R} = L(r,Y) + L^*(r,Y^*) \qquad (4)$$

$\bar{R}$ is the world stock of reserves. Interest rates in the two countries are equated thus reflecting the assumption of perfect asset substitutability between domestic and foreign bonds. In (4) we treat world reserves $\bar{R}$ as outside assets–*SDR*s or gold.

1. Monetary Equilibrium

Incomes are given, as are domestic credit in each country and the world stock of reserves. We have to determine the equilibrium interest rates and the distribution of reserves that will clear the assets market. This is done in Figure 10-3.

FIGURE 10-3

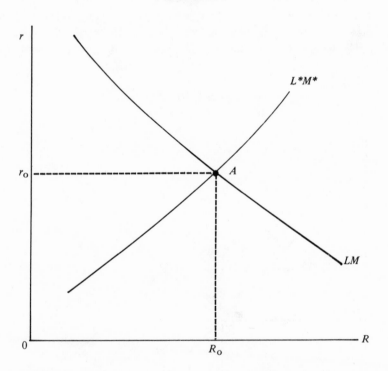

The schedule *LM* shows, for given domestic credit D_0, the equilibrium stock of reserves at which we have domestic monetary equilibrium. At a lower interest rate there is a higher level of money demand; accordingly we require a higher level of reserves to yield a higher money supply.

Figure 10-3 also shows the foreign money market equilibrium schedule L^*M^*. Given the world supply of money $\bar{R} + D + D^*$, the foreign money stock is larger the lower are domestic reserves, and hence the higher are foreign reserves. Accordingly the foreign money market equilibrium schedule is positively sloped, being derived from:

$$D^* + \bar{R} - R = L^*(r, Y^*) \tag{5}$$

Equilibrium obtains at point A, where both money markets clear. The equilibrium stock of reserves for the home country is R_o.

Consider now an expansion in domestic credit in the home country. To maintain monetary equilibrium at unchanged interest rates the money stock would have to remain unchanged. In terms of Figure 10-4, we require a leftward shift of the LM schedule equal to the credit expansion. In section II(1) we concluded that for the small country, because of the inability to affect the world interest rate, there is an equal offsetting reserve loss. In the present case there is, however, an effect on the equilibrium rate of interest in the world. At the initial equilibrium there is a world excess supply

FIGURE 10-4

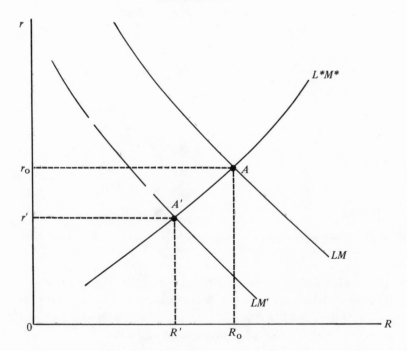

of money and a world excess demand for debt; the equilibrium interest rate declines to point A'. At A', of course, there is a reserve loss. It is important to note, though, that the reserve loss falls short of the credit expansion. The reason is that the decline in the world interest rate raises our money demand and therefore requires some expansion in the domestic money stock. Accordingly there is only a partial offset through reserve losses. The partial offset is necessary because money demand rises abroad as well, requiring an expansion in the foreign money stock.

What determines the extent to which a credit expansion is offset by reserve losses? The "offset coefficient" dR/dD will depend on two factors: relative interest response of money demand and relative size. Suppose first that interest elasticities of money demand are the same. Then the decline in interest rates raises money demand in the same proportion in both countries. It raises money demand absolutely by more in the larger country and accordingly the monetary expansion must be larger in that country. It follows that if the home country is relatively large, then a relatively small portion of the credit expansion will be offset by reserve losses. The other extreme is the case where the home country is very small and where accordingly almost the entire credit expansion is lost through reserve drain.

The other determinant of the offset coefficient is the elasticity of money demand. The country with the larger interest elasticity will experience the larger proportional increase in money demand and the larger absolute increase. That country accordingly will have the larger monetary expansion.*

2. Monetary and Fiscal Policy in the World Model

How are the small country results of monetary and fiscal policy modified once interaction between countries is recognized? The complete model consists of the two goods market equilibrium conditions and the world money or capital market equilibrium condition discussed above:

$$Goods \qquad Y = E(r,Y) + T(Y,Y^*) \qquad (5)$$

$$Goods \qquad Y^* = E^*(r,Y^*) - T(Y,Y^*) \qquad (6)$$

$$Money \ (or \ capital) \qquad D + D^* + \bar{R} = L(r,Y) + L^*(r,Y^*) \qquad (7)$$

*Using the equilibrium condition in (4) to obtain the change in the interest rate induced by a credit expansion, $dr/dD = 1/(L_r + L_r^*)$ and substituting into the change in home money demand we have: $dL/dD = L_r/(L_r + L_r^*)$ and $dR/dD = -L_r^*/(L_r + L_r^*)$. Using the definition of the interest elasticity $\beta = -L_r r/L$ and denoting by $\alpha = L/L + L^*)$ our share in the world money stock, we obtain the following expression for the change in money demand induced by a credit expansion: $dL/dD = \alpha\beta/(\alpha\beta + \alpha^*\beta^*)$.

The interdependence of income determination is explicitly recognized by the fact that the trade balance depends on income levels in both countries. The model differs from that of chapter 3 only by the fact that now income and interest rates are determined simultaneously.

For expository purposes it will be convenient to solve equation (6) for the equilibrium level of foreign income as a function of interest rates and the level of income at home. We write that equilibrium level as

$$Y^* = \phi^*(Y,r) \tag{8}$$

An increase in our income level raises foreign equilibrium output while higher interest rates reduce aggregate demand and equilibrium output abroad. Next we substitute the equilibrium foreign income level from (8) in (5) to obtain the *reduced form* equation of our *IS* schedule:

$$\text{Goods} \qquad Y = E(r,Y) + T(Y, \phi^*(Y,r)) \tag{5a}$$

Equation (5a) reflects equilibrium in the domestic *and* foreign goods market. It is shown in Figure 10-5 as the downward sloping schedule *IS*. How does

FIGURE 10-5

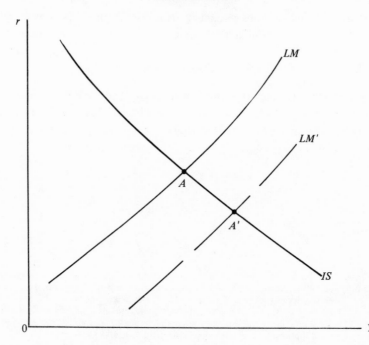

the *IS* schedule compare with that of the small country case in Figure 10-2? Here foreign income is *not* held constant. As the interest rate declines, foreign income and hence our exports expand. Similarly, a rise in our income induces a foreign expansion and consequently increases exports at home. The schedule thus fully reflects the repercussion effects in the rest of the world. The slope of the *IS* schedule is

$$\left. \frac{dr}{dY} \right|_{IS} = [(s + m) - mm^*/(m^* + s^*)] / [E_r + E_r^* m^*/(m^* + s^*)] \quad (9)$$

The *IS* schedule is flatter than the one of the small country case. A decline in interest rates is more expansionary once the induced effects in the rest of the world are taken into account.

We proceed in a similar manner to derive our *LM* schedule along which monetary equilibrium obtains. Our money stock is the world stock $D + D^* + \bar{R}$ less equilibrium foreign money holdings determined by money demand. For monetary equilibrium the supply has to equal money demand, or

$$D + D^* + \bar{R} - L^*(r, \phi^*(r, Y)) = L(r, Y) \quad (10)$$

where we have substituted the equilibrium level of foreign income in the foreign money demand. The *LM* schedule will be upward sloping, because higher interest rates reduce money demand but raise the supply of money since foreign money demand also falls. Accordingly, to return to monetary equilibrium, income has to rise. This raises our money demand and lowers the available supply due to the foreign money demand expansion. The slope of our *LM* schedule is

$$\left. \frac{dr}{dY} \right|_{LM} = [L_Y + L^*_{Y*} m/(m^* + s^*)] / \quad (11)$$
$$[L_r + L_r^* + L^*_{Y*} E_r^*/(m^* + s^*)]$$

Equilibrium is determined at point *A* in Figure 10-5, where the goods and money markets clear for the world economy—this is the implication of using the reduced form equations.

A credit expansion in the home country is depicted in Figure 10-5. The world money stock rises and accordingly the *LM* schedule shifts down and to the right. The new equilibrium is at point *A'* and output at home increases along with a decline in interest rates. Output abroad similarly expands since both lower interest rates and higher domestic income provide a stimulus to foreign income and spending. We thus have our first result: Credit expansion leads to an increase in output in both countries. Moreover, it is immaterial whose domestic credit expands. It is true, though, that the expanding country will suffer reserve loss as we noted in section I.

Consider next the effects of a domestic fiscal expansion. This is shown in Figure 10-5 by the rightward shift of the *IS* schedule. With unchanged world money our income rises as does the world interest rate. What can be said about the foreign country? The higher interest rate will dampen foreign demand and prove deflationary abroad. Our income expansion, however, will tend to spill over and expand foreign income. The net effect is uncertain.

We conclude then that once repercussion effects are taken into account both monetary and fiscal policy are effective. Monetary policy spreads in an expansionary way to the rest of the world while fiscal policy may lower income abroad.

III. IMPERFECT SUBSTITUTABILITY

We return now to the small country case to explore the implications of imperfect substitutability between domestic and foreign securities. We take the world rate of interest r^* as given. The rate on domestic securities is determined by the equilibrium in the home security market. Domestic securities can be held either by domestic residents only (nontraded securities) or by both domestic and foreign residents. Because they are not perfect substitutes for foreign securities their equilibrium yield is determined endogenously.

1. Capital Market Equilibrium

Equilibrium in the domestic financial markets is determined by money market equilibrium and equilibrium in the home security market. The equilibrium determines the money stock or, for given domestic credit, the stock of reserves and the yield on home securities. The equilibrium condition in the security market is stated in (12):

$$K = \sigma(r, r^*, Y, W) + \sigma^*(r, r^*, Y^*, W^*) \tag{12}$$

where K is the existing stock of domestic securities to be held by the private sector, and W is our wealth. The demand for our securities σ is a function of

FIGURE 10-6

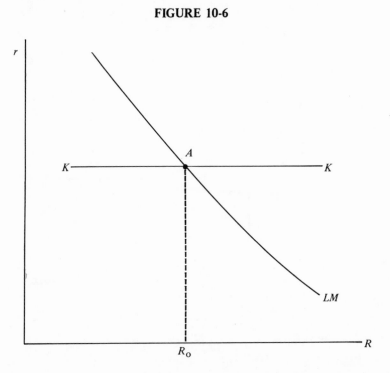

wealth, rises with the rate on domestic assets, and is a declining function of the yield on foreign assets. The same is true of the foreign demand for our securities σ^*. Wealth and income are given.

Figure 10-6 shows the asset market equilibrium schedule KK, drawn for given wealth, incomes, foreign interest rates, and the existing supply of domestic securities. There is a unique interest rate at which the market achieves equilibrium. We also show the LM schedule corresponding to (2a). The equilibrium interest rate on domestic securities determines the money stock and, given domestic credit, the level of reserves R_o.

Consider now the effects of a domestic credit expansion. The central bank buys domestic debt and creates money. The reduction in the existing stock of debt to be privately held, as shown in Figure 10-7, creates an excess demand for debt and thereby lowers the equilibrium interest rate to r'. The extent of the downward shift of the KK schedule will depend on the degree of asset substitutability. If domestic and foreign securities are near perfect substitutes then the domestic rate will remain nearly constant at the world level. Conversely, if they are very imperfect substitutes then it will take a relatively large change in the interest rate to accept the shift in portfolio composition.

187

FIGURE 10-7

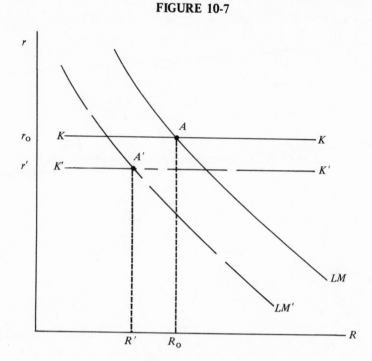

The *LM* schedule shifts to the left, as in Figure 10-1, by the amount of credit expansion. The new equilibrium at point A' is therefore one where we have a loss of reserves. The interesting question now concerns the offset coefficient dR/dD. The extent of offset will depend on the substitutability between assets. The change in reserves from (2a) is given by:

$$dR/dD = -1 + L_r dr/dD \tag{13}$$

The change in the equilibrium interest rate in turn can be calculated from the domestic security market equilibrium in (12) as:

$$dr/dD = -1/(\sigma_r + \sigma_r{}^*) \quad (dK = -dD) \tag{14}$$

Combining the two equations yields:

$$dR/dD = -1 - L_r/(\sigma_r + \sigma_r{}^*) \tag{15}$$

The *offset coefficient* dR/dD will fall short of minus unity provided assets are less than perfect substitutes. In terms of Figure 10-7 this implies that the

KK schedule does shift down and that the domestic interest rate declines in response to a fall in the supply of domestic securities to be held.

The ratio $\pi \equiv -L_r/(\sigma_r + \sigma_r^*)$ must be less than unity in absolute value since, with gross substitutes assumptions, σ_r exceeds L_r in absolute value. The assets budget constraint is

$$W = L(r, r^*, Y) + \sigma(r, r^*, Y, W) + \theta(r, r^*, Y, W) \tag{16}$$

where θ is the domestic demand for foreign securities. The budget constraint implies that:

$$0 = L_r + \sigma_r + \theta_r \qquad L_r, \theta_r < 0, \ \sigma_r > 0 \tag{17}$$

It follows that π must be less than unity both because of the gross substitute assumption and because of the foreign asset substitution term σ_r^*.

2. Empirical Estimates of Offset Coefficients

There has been a considerable amount of empirical work on offset coefficients. The work attempts to measure the extent to which asset substitution or capital flows offset variations in domestic credit. The empirical equations start from the balance sheet:

$$\Delta R = \Delta L - \Delta D \tag{18}$$

where Δ denotes the first difference. Next we note that the change in reserves is equal to the current account CA plus the capital account CAP of the balance of payments:

$$\Delta R = CA + CAP \tag{19}$$

Combining the two equations and rearranging terms we have:

$$CAP = -CA - \Delta D + L_r \Delta r + L_Y \Delta Y + L_{r*} \Delta r^* \tag{20}$$

where we have substituted for the change in money demand in terms of income and interest rate changes. Next we eliminate the change in domestic interest rates by solving (12):

$$\Delta r = -[(\sigma_{r*} + \sigma^*_{r*})/(\sigma_r + \sigma^*_r)] \Delta r^* - [\sigma_Y/(\sigma_r + \sigma^*_r)] \Delta Y - $$
$$[1/(\sigma_r + \sigma^*_r)] \Delta D \tag{21}$$

and obtain our final equation:

$$CAP = -CA - (1 - \pi)\,\Delta D + a\Delta Y + b\Delta r^* \qquad (20a)$$

where a and b can be calculated as positive and negative from (20) and (21).

The equation is typically estimated taking the current account, income, domestic credit creation, and foreign interest rates as exogenous. Early work on offset coefficients was done by Kouri and Porter (1974). They estimated offset coefficients in the range of 0.4 to 0.8 for a number of industrialized countries. These results support the view that asset substitution is less than perfect and that accordingly there *is* scope for monetary policy.

Subsequent work on offset coefficients has emphasized two points. The first is that empirical work on structural asset demands, particularly on money demand, reveals slow adjustment. Recognition of this fact would lead to a specification of the capital flow equation that permits lagged adjustment. The second point, and one that is of central importance, concerns the endogeneity of domestic credit. To the extent that changes in domestic credit are designed to offset capital flows, induced for example by exchange rate expectations, we cannot treat the variable as exogenous. Work that remedies these deficiencies, in particular Herring and Marston (1977) and Obstfeld (1978), typically estimates a system of equations including a policy reaction function for domestic credit. Estimated offset coefficients turn out smaller than the unity coefficient of the perfect capital mobility and assets substitution case.

3. Monetary and Fiscal Policy Once More

The model of imperfect asset substitution is now applied to the question of monetary and fiscal policy. We saw earlier that the small country, because it cannot affect the world and hence domestic interest rate, cannot use monetary policy but finds fiscal policy particularly effective. We return now to the same question regarding the case of imperfect asset substitutability, but maintain the assumption that the world interest rate is given and that income repercussion effects can be neglected.

Figure 10-8 shows the standard open economy *IS* curve. It also shows the *KK* schedule along which the market for domestic securities is in equilibrium. We *cannot* draw the *LM* schedule because, as explained earlier, the money stock is fully endogenous.

Equilibrium obtains at point A, where the goods and security markets clear. Corresponding to the equilibrium level of income and interest rates

FIGURE 10-8

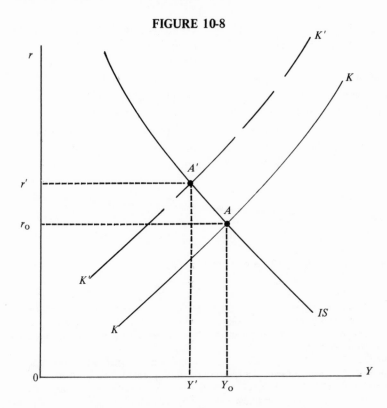

there is an associated level of money demand and hence a level of reserves, given domestic credit.

Suppose there is a domestic credit contraction so that the central bank sells domestic debt and reduces the money stock. The equilibrium interest rate rises to r' and output declines to Y'. Monetary policy now works; the extent to which changes in domestic credit affect the rate of interest and hence equilibrium output depend on asset substitutability or the offset coefficient. In the limit the KK schedule is flat, as it would be for perfect asset substitutability.

While monetary policy now works, the effects of fiscal expansion will be dampened. A fiscal expansion, because it raises income and therefore reduces the demand for domestic debt (see the budget constraint in [16]), leads to higher interest rates and hence to a dampening of the expansion. Again, the extent of asset substitutability determines how much interest rates increase and to what extent the fiscal expansion is dampened.

All the models explored in this chapter emphasize international interdependence not only through the current account but through the integration of capital markets and the resulting link of interest rates as well. The degree of asset substitutability determines the extent to which monetary policy is lost as an effective policy instrument.

The short-run perspective serves to emphasize that the balance of payments effects of domestic financial policies operate quite rapidly by comparison with the longer-run process of price adjustment or the effects of the current account on wealth and thereby on macroeconomic equilibrium. This latter aspect will be taken up in part 5 of this book.

REFERENCES AND SUGGESTED READING

Dornbusch, R. 1977. Capital mobility and portfolio balance. *The Political Economy of Monetary Reform*. ed. R. Z. Aliber. London: MacMillan Press Ltd. Co.

Fleming, M. 1962. Domestic financial policies under fixed and under floating exchange rates. *IMF staff papers* 9.

Henderson, D. 1977. Modeling the interdependence of national money and capital markets. *American economic review* papers and proceedings 67:190-99.

Herring, R., and Marston, R. 1977. *National monetary policies and international financial markets.* New York: Elsevier-North-Holland.

Kenen, P. 1976. Capital mobility and financial integration: a survey. *Princeton studies in international finance,* no. 39, Princeton: Princeton University Press.

Kouri, P., and Porter, M. 1974. International capital flows and portfolio equilibrium. *Journal of political economy* 86.

McKinnon, R., and Oates, W. 1966. The implications of international economic integration for monetary, fiscal and exchange rate policy. *Princeton studies in international finance,* no. 16. Princeton: Princeton University Press.

Mundell, R. A. 1968. *International economics.* New York: Macmillan Publishing Co.

Niehans, J. 1976. How to fill an empty shell. *American economic review* 66:177-83.

Obstfeld, M. 1978. Sterilization and offsetting capital movements: evidence from West Germany, 1960-1971. Unpublished manuscript, Massachusetts Institute of Technology.

Swoboda, A. 1973. Monetary policy under fixed exchange rates: the effectiveness, speed of adjustment and proper use. *Economica* 40:136-54.

Whitman, M. 1970. Policies for internal and external balance. *Special papers in international economics* no. 9. Princeton: Princeton University Press.

CHAPTER

11

Flexible Exchange Rates and Capital Mobility

This chapter continues the analysis of monetary and fiscal policy under conditions of perfect capital mobility and asset substitutability. Unlike in chapter 10, we now assume that the exchange rate is flexible, that payments are balanced and that the money stock is therefore fully under the control of the monetary authorities.

In section I we examine the *Mundell-Fleming model*—the flexible rate version of the standard *IS-LM* model with output demand determined and prices taken as given. We show for the small country that monetary policy is effective in that a monetary expansion raises output. Fiscal expansion, however, leads to full crowding out through a deterioration in the trade balance. These conclusions oppose those reached for the fixed exchange rate model in chapter 10. Extending the model to the world economy, we show that fiscal expansion in one country will spread abroad through a worsening of the trade balance. A monetary expansion, by contrast, will bring about a decline in income abroad.

The Mundell-Fleming model is stated in terms of fixed domestic prices and static expectations about the exchange rate. In section II we depart from these assumptions and allow price adjustment when the economy deviates from full employment. Exchange rate expectations enter prominently because asset holders look at the international interest differential adjusted for exchange depreciation. In a framework of rational expectations we draw on the differential speeds of adjustment in goods and assets markets to show how a monetary expansion leads to an initial <u>overshooting</u> of exchange rates. The increase in output brought about by expansionary monetary policy is shown to be only transitory.

I. THE MUNDELL-FLEMING MODEL

In this part we develop the <u>basic macroeconomic model of flexible exchange rates under conditions of perfect capital mobility</u>. The model is a direct extension of the *IS-LM* model. The openness of the economy is introduced through two already familiar channels. The relative price of domestic goods in terms of importables is a determinant of the composition of spending and net exports are a component of demand for domestic output. The other channel is the linkage of interest rates in an integrated world capital market. With static expectations in regard to the exchange rate, nominal interest rates are equated internationally. The exchange rate is flexible and affects macroeconomic equilibrium because, with given prices at home and abroad, changes in the exchange rate change the terms of trade and therefore the allocation of demand, output, and employment.

1. The Small Country Model

The small country faces a given price of its importables in terms of foreign currency but demand for domestic goods depends on the relative price and the rate of interest. It will be convenient for subsequent use to have a log-linear model and for that reason we use that formulation already here. Equilibrium in the goods market is described in (1) where output is determined by the rate of interest r and by the real exchange rate, or terms of trade e-p:

$$y = \delta(e\text{-}p) - \sigma r + u + f y^* \tag{1}$$

Flexible Exchange Rates and Capital Mobility

with y, e, and p the logs of output, the exchange rate, and the price of domestic goods, respectively.* A real depreciation, or a rise in e-p, raises demand for, and output of, domestic goods, while a rise in the interest rate leads to a fall in demand and output. The term u denotes an exogenous demand shift parameter such as an increase in exports or in government spending.

Monetary equilibrium is described in equation (2) by the equality of the real money stock h-p and the demand for real money balances. Real money demand depends on real income and the rate of interest:

$$h\text{-}p = -\lambda r + \phi y \qquad (2)$$

where h is the log of nominal money.

The model is closed by the requirement that domestic interest rates equal the given rate of interest in the world:

$$r = r^* \qquad (3)$$

In Figure 11-1 we show the model in an initial full equilibrium at point A. The LM schedule shows monetary equilibrium according to (2), the schedule being drawn for a given real money stock. The IS schedule is drawn for a given real exchange rate, a given foreign income, and exogenous spending u. In the initial equilibrium, our interest rate equals that in the rest of the world. We will now show how changes in money or aggregate demand change equilibrium income and the exchange rate.

2. Monetary and Fiscal Policy

Here we demonstrate that in the Mundell-Fleming model a monetary expansion leads to an increase in output while a fiscal or export expansion has no effect at all on the level of output. These results are the opposite of the small country model under perfect capital mobility and fixed exchange rates. The striking difference is attributable to the fact that under fixed exchange rates the money stock is fully endogenous, while under flexible rates it is exogenous.

Figure 11-1 shows the case of a monetary expansion. Starting from an initial equilibrium at point A, nominal balances increase. Because prices are given, a rise in nominal balances is a rise in real balances. The ensuing mone-

---

*The relative price more properly is $e + p^* - p$. Here we assume that the given foreign price level is unity and hence its log is zero. y^* is the log of foreign output which, for the time being, is exogenous.

FIGURE 11-1

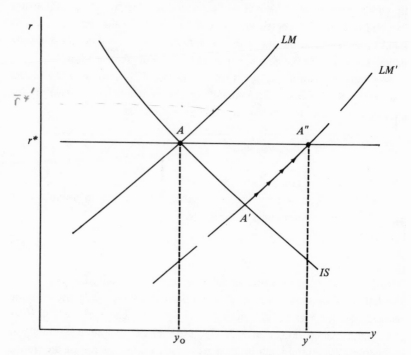

tary disequilibrium leads to a fall in interest rates and an expansion in income as the *LM* schedule shifts out to the right. Disregarding capital mobility and the linkage of interest rates, the economy moves to a point like A' where goods and money markets clear and where the trade balance has deteriorated.

Point A' is, of course, not an equilibrium because our interest rate has fallen below that in the rest of the world. There is a tendency for capital to flow out, creating a deficit in the balance of payments and thus leading to exchange depreciation. The depreciation in turn lowers the relative price of domestic goods, raises the demand for domestic output and thus shifts the *IS* curve up and to the right. Depreciation, induced by incipient capital outflows, leads to a rise in income. As indicated by the arrows in Figure 11-1 the depreciation continues until income has expanded sufficiently to restore monetary equilibrium at the world rate of interest. This is the case at point A''.

The income expansion induced by an increase in nominal money is due entirely to exchange depreciation and the trade balance improvement associated with a fall in the relative price of our goods. Monetary expansion raises output and employment through an improvement in the balance of trade.

FIGURE 11-2

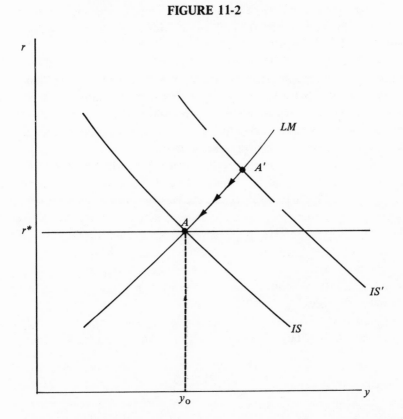

Consider next the case of a fiscal expansion or a rise in exports shown in Figure 11-2. At the initial level of interest rates, exchange rates, and income, there is an excess demand for goods and accordingly the *IS* curve shifts outward, raising income and the rate of interest. Again, this cannot be the final equilibrium since the interest rate has risen above the world level. Incipient capital inflows now lead to exchange appreciation and thus to a loss in competitiveness. Demand shifts away from domestic goods leading the *IS* curve to shift back toward its initial position.

The process of exchange appreciation will continue as long as the interest rate exceeds the world level. Given the money stock, exchange appreciation will continue as long as output is above its initial level. It follows then that exchange appreciation will proceed until the *initial* equilibrium is reestablished. The exchange appreciation leads to a trade balance deterioration that *fully offsets* the initial demand expansion. With full crowding out, demand expansion leaves output unaffected as long as there is no accommodating increase in real balances.

What do these comparative static results imply concerning the proper policy mix for internal and external balance? Internal balance is readily defined as full employment. External balance, of course, is no problem if we think of it as overall balance of payments equilibrium that is insured by the flexible rate. External balance remains an objective, though, if we think of current account targets. A country may wish a particular current account or trade balance because it may not wish to borrow or lend abroad excessively. Consider, then, a particular target for the trade balance T_0, and hence a corresponding rate of capital outflow or lending abroad.

In Figure 11-3 we show the vertical schedule $\bar{y}$, which corresponds to the full employment level of output. Along T_0T_0 we satisfy the current account target. Higher income worsens the current account, calling for a real exchange depreciation to restore the current account to the target level. Above the schedule we have an excessive current account surplus, below the schedule the current account is below target. Region I is thus an area with unemployment and too strong a trade balance or excessive net foreign lending. In region II, by contrast, there is insufficient net foreign lending along with unemployment.

Regions II and IV correspond to circumstances where monetary policy is appropriate. A monetary expansion in region II leads to exchange deprecia-

FIGURE 11-3

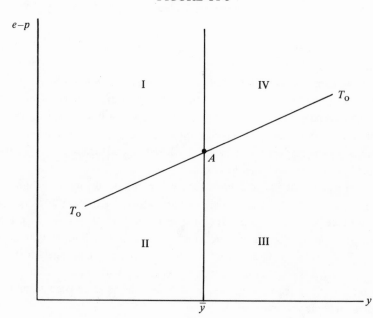

tion and a rise in income and thus moves us toward the target at point A. In region IV, with too strong an external balance and overemployment, a monetary contraction is called for. A reduction in the money stock leads to exchange appreciation and thus to a deterioration in the current account and a fall in output and employment.

Regions I and III call for a policy mix. In region I, for example, we need a monetary and fiscal expansion. The monetary expansion leads to a rise in income but also to a further inprovement in the external balance. The fiscal expansion that is part of the package displaces the trade improvement without affecting income. Thus it can be used to achieve the correct compósition of demand for domestic output.

3. The Two-Country Model

In the discussion of the small country case we showed that monetary and fiscal policy affect the exchange rate and thereby the balance of trade. Monetary and fiscal policy affect net exports and this is the channel through which policy disturbances spread to the rest of the world. In the preceding sections we ignored repercussion effects, which now are taken up briefly.

The foreign country's goods and money market equilibrium conditions parallel those of the home country:

$$y^* = -\delta^*(e-p) - \sigma^*r + f^*y \qquad (1a)$$

and

$$h^* - p^* = -\lambda^*r + \phi^*y^* \qquad (2a)$$

where we have made use of the equilibrium condition requiring equalization of interest rates. The four equations determine equilibrium output levels, the equilibrium terms of trade, and the world rate of interest.

For comparative static purposes we build up a simple diagram in Figure 11-4.* The two schedules represent reduced forms along which the respective countries' goods and money markets clear simultaneously. The first step to derive these schedules is to solve (1) and (1a) for income levels in terms of interest rates and relative prices:

$$y = \alpha(e-p) - \beta r + ku \qquad y^* = -\alpha^*(e-p) - \beta^*r + k^*u \qquad (4)$$

where we *assume* all coefficients to be positive so that a real depreciation

*For an alternative diagram see Dornbusch and Krugman (1976).

FIGURE 11-4 *(Monetary Equil.)*

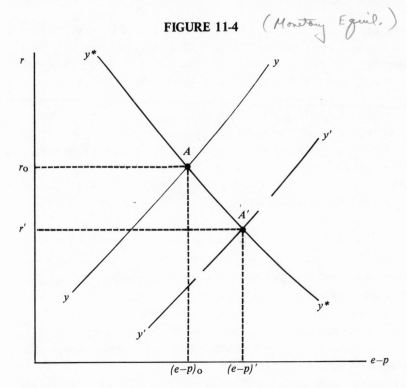

raises our income while lowering income abroad. Higher interest rates lower income in both countries. Next, we solve the conditions of monetary equilibrium for income levels in terms of real balances and interest rates. Equating these income levels to those in (4) yields the market equilibrium schedules shown in Figure 11-4. The equations are, respectively:

$$\alpha(e-p) - \beta r + ku = (1/\phi)(h - p + \lambda r) \tag{5}$$

and

$$-\alpha^*(e-p) - \beta^* r + k^* u = (1/\phi^*)(h^* - p^* + \lambda^* r) \tag{6}$$

From our assumptions it is apparent that the equilibrium schedule for the home goods and money market in (5) is positively sloped. Exchange depreciation, taking into account repercussion effects, raises income and thus requires a higher rate of interest for monetary equilibrium. Conversely, for the foreign country our exchange depreciation lowers their income and thus requires a fall in the rate of interest to maintain monetary equilibrium. At point A in Figure 11-4 all markets clear and interest rates are equalized across countries.

Flexible Exchange Rates and Capital Mobility

Consider now a monetary expansion at home. In Figure 11-4 this is shown by a downward shift of the home country's market equilibrium schedule. Interest rates must fall, or the exchange rate must depreciate, thereby raising income and money demand. The new equilibrium is at point A', where the world interest rate has fallen and our terms of trade have deteriorated. Both the fall in interest rates and the real depreciation, by (4), raises income at home. Abroad, strikingly, the opposite is true. As Mundell has shown, foreign income *must* decline. This is easily verified from the condition of foreign monetary equilibrium. With unchanged money abroad and lower interest rates, the equilibrium level of income must have declined. This implies that the expansionary effects of lower interest rates and higher income at home are more than offset by the appreciation of the foreign currency.

The effects of a fiscal expansion at home are shown in Figure 11-5. At the initial relative price, the fiscal expansion, as seen in the context of the foreign trade multiplier with repercussions, will raise income in both countries. To maintain monetary equilibrium interest rates must rise. Both market equilibrium schedules in Figure 11-5 shift upward. The equilibrium interest rate

FIGURE 11-5

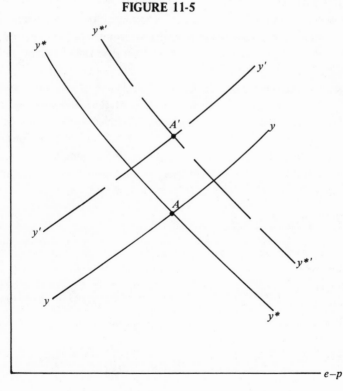

rises, but the effect on the terms of trade is uncertain as it depends on the relative shifts of the market equilibrium schedules. What can be said about the effects of the fiscal expansion on incomes? With money given in each country and equilibrium interest rates increased, monetary equilibrium requires higher levels of income. Thus we have established that a fiscal expansion *must* raise income in each country.

The two-country model qualifies our earlier results. A country sufficiently large to affect the world rate of interest now recaptures some of the effects of its own fiscal policy, as there is less than full crowding out. Monetary expansion still raises home income but it now exerts adverse employment effects abroad. Monetary expansion becomes a beggar-thy-neighbor policy.

II. EXPECTATIONS AND EXCHANGE RATE DYNAMICS

In this part we return to the small country case to explore the adjustment process of exchange rates and prices. The model we develop here emphasizes three points.* The first is the role of price adjustment. We assume that domestic prices, rather than being given, adjust over time to goods market disequilibrium. The second point concerns the differential speeds of adjustment of prices and exchange rates. The third is the role of exchange rate expectations. Section II-(1) introduces exchange rate expectations and develops the conditions of asset market equilibrium in this extended model. Sections II-(2)(3) discuss *rational expectations* and the effects of a monetary expansion under conditions of full employment. In section IV we complete the analysis by allowing transitory employment effects. An appendix deals with an alternative solution method to rational expectations paths.

1. Asset Market Equilibrium

In preceding sections we assumed that nominal interest rates, under conditions of perfect capital mobility, are equalized across countries. This condition clearly ignores the possibility that there is a differential that precisely offsets the anticipation of appreciation or depreciation. Portfolio holders will be indifferent between securities denominated in domestic and foreign

---

*This section draws on Dornbusch (1976b). Rational expectations in the context of flexible exchange rates were first proposed by Black (1973).

Flexible Exchange Rates and Capital Mobility

currency if an interest differential in favor of the home country r-r^* is exactly offset by the expected rate of depreciation of our currency μ. The equilibrium condition, taking into account expectations, then is

$$r = r^* + \mu \tag{7}$$

where μ denotes the expected rate of depreciation of our currency. The expected rate of depreciation has the dimension of an interest rate and is thus dimensionally commensurate with r and r^*.

Equation (7) implies that nominal rates for the home country are no longer fixed. Our interest rate can be low when appreciation is anticipated or high if there is an expectation of depreciation. The next step is to make an assumption about the formation of exchange rate expectations. The exchange rate is expected to depreciate in proportion to the discrepancy between the long-run equilibrium exchange rate $\bar{e}$ and the current actual rate e:

$$\mu = \theta(\bar{e} - e) \tag{8}$$

where θ is the adjustment coefficient. The long-run equilibrium exchange rate is assumed known and will be derived below.

The expectations equation (8), the arbitrage equation in (7), and the money demand equation:

$$h - p = -\lambda r + \phi \bar{y} \tag{2b}$$

are now combined to yield the condition of *asset market equilibrium*:

$$h - p = -\lambda r^* - \lambda \theta(\bar{e} - e) + \phi \bar{y} \tag{9}$$

where output $\bar{y}$ is taken as given. Equation (9) ensures three separate conditions: that money demand equal the money supply, that interest rates adjusted for depreciation be equated internationally, and that expectations be formed according to (8).

It will now be convenient to express (9) in terms of deviations from long-run equilibrium. With money, foreign interest rates, and output given, the long-run equilibrium relation is

$$h - \bar{p} = -\lambda r^* + \phi \bar{y} \tag{9a}$$

since, in the steady state, actual and expected depreciation are assumed to be zero. Subtracting (9a) from (9) yields one of the key equations:

$$p - \bar{p} = \lambda\theta(\bar{e} - e) \tag{10}$$

or

$$e = \bar{e} - (1/\lambda\theta)(p - \bar{p}) \tag{10a}$$

Equation (10a) is shown in Figure 11-6 as the downward sloping schedule *AA*. The equation shows that if the actual price level exceeds the long-run level then the actual exchange rate falls short of the long-run rate. These relations reflect the simultaneous conditions of money market equilibrium and yield equalization, given the expectations formation process. A higher price level implies a lower level of real balances, a higher interest rate and therefore, with equalized yields, the expectation of depreciation. An expectation of depreciation, however, must imply that the spot rate falls short of the long-run equilibrium rate.

Consider next the goods market. Here we assume that output is given and that prices rise in proportion to excess demand. This assumption is stated in (11):

$$\dot{p} = \pi\left[u + \delta(e - p) - \sigma r + \gamma y + f y^* - \bar{y}\right] \tag{11}$$

FIGURE 11-6

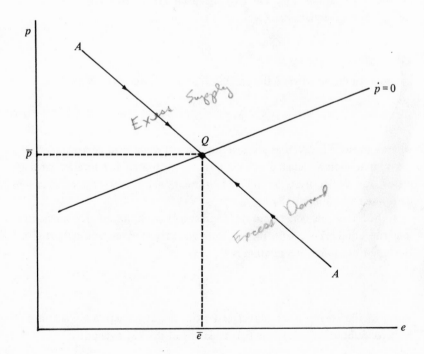

Flexible Exchange Rates and Capital Mobility

where u is a constant and $e - p$ measures the relative price of domestic goods so that the term $\delta(e-p)$ reflects the substitution between domestic and foreign goods. Solving (2b) for the rate of interest and substituting into (11) yields:

$$\dot{p} = \pi[u + \delta(e-p) + (\sigma/\lambda)(h-p) + fy^* - \rho\bar{y}] \qquad (12)$$
$$\rho \equiv \phi\sigma/\lambda + 1 - \gamma$$

or in terms of deviations from the noninflationary long-run equilibrium:

$$\dot{p} = \pi[\delta(e-\bar{e}) + (\delta + \sigma/\lambda)(\bar{p}-p)] \qquad (12a)$$

The schedule $\dot{p}=0$ is shown in Figure 11-6 as positively sloped. An increase in the price level creates an excess supply because it raises the relative price of domestic goods and raises interest rates through reduced real balances. To restore equilibrium the exchange rate must depreciate proportionally more, so as to offset the deflationary impact of higher interest rates. Accordingly the schedule is positively sloped and flatter than a ray through the origin.*

2. The Adjustment Process

The strategic assumption is that assets markets clear continuously and that prices adjust slowly over time. That implies, in terms of Figure 11-6, that we are always on the AA schedule. Above the $\dot{p}=0$ schedule there will be excess supply since the relative price of our goods and the interest rate are too high. Hence prices will be falling. The converse is true below the $\dot{p}=0$ schedule. It follows, as the arrows indicate, that we will converge to long-run equilibrium at point Q.

We can solve explicitly for the rate of adjustment of prices by substituting the equilibrium exchange rate derived in (10a) (this is the equilibrium rate along AA) into the equation for price adjustment to obtain:

$$\dot{p} = -v(p-\bar{p}) \qquad v \equiv \pi[(\delta + \sigma\theta)/\theta\lambda + \delta] \qquad (13)$$

---

*The model makes two special assumptions that are easily generalized. The first is that domestic prices are the deflator for real balances. An alternative is to write real balances as $h - qp - (1-q)e$, where q and $1-q$ are the shares of domestic goods and imports in expenditure. The other assumption is that demand for domestic output depends on the nominal interest rate rather than on the real rate, $r - \dot{p}$. The alternative formulation has the same form as (12a) with $\pi' = \pi/(1-\pi\sigma) > 0$.

Equation (13) describes the adjustment of prices. The speed of adjustment of prices depends on all the structural coefficients of the model and it also depends on the manner in which expectations are formed. This is evidenced by the fact that θ is one of the determinants of the adjustment speed of prices v. We turn now to the question of rationality of expectations. First, we show that the adjustment process for prices in (13) implies, by (10a), an adjustment process of the actual exchange rate. Next we verify whether, and under what conditions, the adjustment process for the exchange rate coincides with the expectations assumption formulated in (8).

Differentiating (10a) with respect to time (noting that $\bar{e}$ and $\bar{p}$ are constant) yields an equation for the actual rate of depreciation. Using (10) the actual rate of depreciation is equal to:

$$\dot{e} = -(1/\lambda\theta)\dot{p} = (v/\lambda\theta)(p-\bar{p}) = v(\bar{e}-e) \qquad (14)$$

Equation (14) shows that the *actual* rate of depreciation is proportional to the discrepancy between the long-run equilibrium value of the exchange rate and the current value, just as was assumed in (8) for the *expected* rate of depreciation. There will be no expectational errors provided $v=\theta$. If that condition is satisfied, actual and anticipated exchange depreciation coincide. Using the definition of v in (13) and equating v and θ yields:

$$v(\theta) \equiv \pi[(\delta + \sigma\theta)/\lambda\theta + \delta] = \theta \qquad (15)$$

The solution to the equation is illustrated in Figure 11-7. From (15) the equation $v(\theta)$ is a decreasing function of θ, going to infinity as θ tends toward zero and approaching a positive asymptote as θ tends to infinity. There is accordingly a fixed point $\tilde{\theta}$ for which $v(\tilde{\theta}) = \tilde{\theta}$. This point is shown by the intersection of the function $v(\theta)$ and the 45° line. The solution is given in (16) by the positive root of the quadratic equation in (15). The solution is:

$$\tilde{\theta} = \frac{1}{2}\pi(\sigma/\lambda + \delta) + \frac{1}{2}[\pi^2(\sigma/\lambda + \delta)^2 - 4\pi\delta/\lambda]^{1/2} \qquad (16)$$

The speed of adjustment of expectations, and the rate of convergence to the steady state, will be faster the lower is the interest response of money demand, the higher is the interest response of aggregate demand, and the higher is the price elasticity of demand for domestic output. The reason? With a low elasticity of money demand, a given change in the price level and real balances yields both a larger interest rate change and, via the interest

FIGURE 11-7

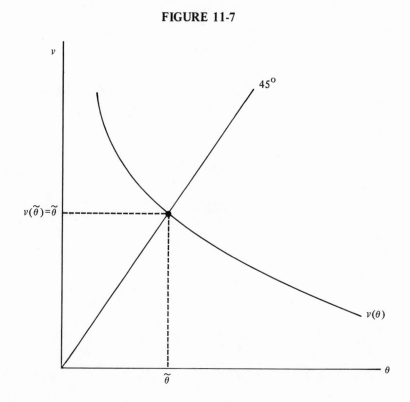

elasticity of aggregate demand, a higher excess demand. Thus there is a faster price adjustment. The price elasticity enters because a given change in the interest rate will require an offsetting expectation of appreciation and there- fore a given change in the actual rate relative to the long-run rate. The larger the price elasticity of aggregate demand, the more the change in the actual rate will affect aggregate demand and therefore the rate of inflation.

3. Monetary Disturbances and Overshooting

We use now our model to investigate the adjustment process to an increase in the nominal money stock. In particular we are interested in expectations and their implications for the adjustment process. Suppose now that money increases. The public immediately recognizes, that the *long-run* equilibrium price level and exchange rate will rise in the same proportion—in the long-run money is neutral. In terms of Figure 11-8 this implies that everybody recog- nizes that the economy will move from Q to Q'.

The economy cannot instantaneously jump to the new long-run equi-

FIGURE 11-8

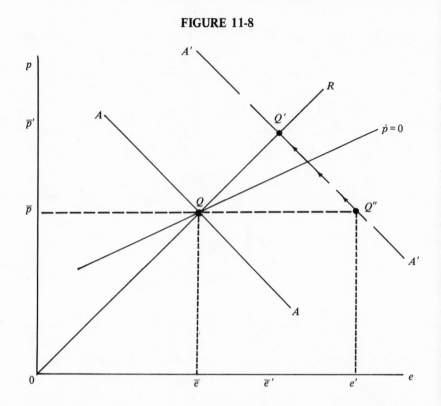

librium because, by assumption, prices can only move gradually. In the short run, the level of prices is given and an increase in nominal money therefore is an increase in real money. The equilibrium interest rate will fall. What happens to the exchange rate? The current exchange rate will depreciate because, using (10a), there is the recognition of an increase in both the long-run equilibrium exchange rate *and* the long-run price level. Accordingly, the exchange rate immediately depreciates by

$$de/dh = 1 + 1/\theta\lambda \qquad (17)$$

noting that $d\bar{e} = d\bar{p} = dh$ because of the long-run neutrality of money.

"*Overshooting*" The exchange rate in the short run *overshoots* or rises by more than the increase in the long-run equilibrium rate. That result is depicted in Figure 11-8. Here we show that the money increase shifts the assets market equilibrium schedule (and the goods market equilibrium schedule, not drawn) upward in proportion to the money increase. In the short run, the price level is given and therefore, to obtain assets market equilibrium, the exchange rate must depreciate to point Q'', or it must overshoot. *Overshooting results from the requirement that the interest differential equal the anticipated rate of appreciation. Thus the spot rate has to go beyond the long-run equilibrium rate to yield an expectation of appreciation.*

The extent of overshooting is determined by the structural parameters. Substituting in (17) from (16) yields

$$de/dh = 1 + 1/\{ \pi(\sigma + \delta\lambda)/2 + [\pi^2(\sigma + \delta\lambda)^2/4 + \pi\delta\lambda]^{\frac{1}{2}}/2 \} \quad (17a)$$

Accordingly, the extent of overshooting is larger, the smaller are price and interest elasticities of aggregate demand and the smaller is the interest elasticity of money demand.

The interesting point of (17a) is the fact that parameters not related to the money market—price elasticities or interest elasticities of aggregate spending—appear as determinants of the short-run adjustment of the exchange rate. This reflects rational expectations, since the initial overshooting and the subsequent path of appreciation are jointly determined by the whole system.

At point Q'' there is an excess demand for domestic output, both because of lower interest rates and a lower relative price of our goods. The excess demand leads to price inflation and the economy adjusts along $A'A'$ until the new long-run equilibrium at Q' is reached.

4. Output and Price Adjustment

We conclude this chapter with an extension of the model to allow for short-run adjustments in output. Output now is demand determined yielding the goods market equilibrium condition:

$$y = u + \delta(e-p) + \gamma y - \sigma r + fy^* \quad (18)$$

In terms of deviations from long-run equilibrium this becomes

$$y - \bar{y} = \delta(e - \bar{e}) - \delta(p - \bar{p}) + \gamma(y - \bar{y}) - \sigma(r - r^*) \quad (18a)$$

By maintaining our assumptions about exchange rate expectations formation we can use (7)-(10) to rewrite the equation as:

$$y - \bar{y} = -\Phi(p - \bar{p})$$
$$\Phi \equiv [\lambda(\sigma + \delta/\theta) + \delta]/[1 - \gamma + \phi(\delta/\theta + \sigma)] \quad (19)$$

The schedule YY in Figure 11-9 shows the goods *and* assets market equilibrium condition reflected in (19).

For price adjustment we assume that prices rise in proportion to the deviation of output from full employment. The vertical schedule in Figure 11-9 corresponds to the full employment level of output, at which prices are constant.

The adjustment path for the economy is along YY. Goods and assets markets continuously clear. When prices are high, interest rates are high because the real money stock is low. Also, exchange rates will be relatively low because there must be the expectation of depreciation. The combination of high prices and low exchange rates—and hence a low relative price of imports—imply a low level of demand and hence low equilibrium output. With output that is low, prices will be falling and thus move the economy toward long-run equilibrium at Q. Conversely, when prices are low interest rates are low, the exchange rate is high so as to yield the expectation of appreciation. Demand for domestic goods, and hence output, is high and prices are rising.

How will a monetary expansion work out in this extended framework? In Figure 11-10 we show the effect of a monetary expansion as an upward shift of the YY schedule. In the long run a monetary expansion is, once more, fully reflected in prices and exchange rates. Accordingly the YY schedule shifts up in proportion to the monetary expansion. In the short run, though, the price level is given. The reduction in the interest rate and the depreciation that will immediately occur raise demand for domestic output and lead us to point Q''. Here there is overemployment and therefore inflationary pressure. The process continues until the initial equilibrium is reached at point Q'. The monetary expansion thus exerts only a transitory effect on output. The expansion in output arises through two channels, one being the reduction in interest rates due to the increased real money stock. The other, closely related, is the depreciation in the exchange rate due to the long-run expected depreciation and the need to balance yields internationally.

APPENDIX

In section II we assumed an explicit process for the expectations formation:

$$\mu = \theta(\bar{e} - e)$$

FIGURE 11-9

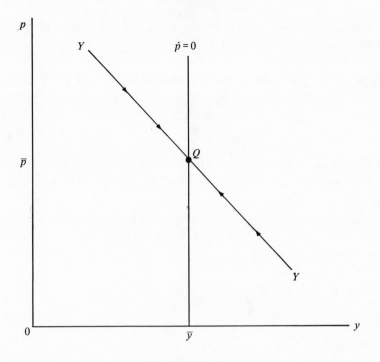

FIGURE 11-10

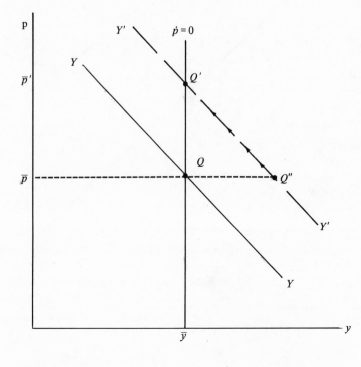

and then showed how to solve for the value of θ consistent with perfect foresight. The general (graphic) analysis of a perfect foresight model is sketched in this appendix.

We reproduce here the equation describing the rate of price increase, given monetary equilibrium:

$$\dot{p} = -a(p - \bar{p}) + b(e - \bar{e}) \tag{A-1}$$

where a and b are defined in (12a). For assets market equilibrium, under perfect foresight, we require that the actual rate of depreciation e equal the interest differential, or:

$$\dot{e} = -\mu(p - \bar{p}) \tag{A-2}$$

FIGURE A-1

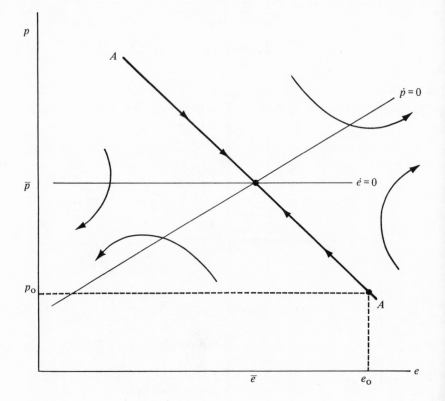

where we have expressed both (A-1) and (A-2) in terms of deviations from the long-run equilibrium.

In Figure A-1 we show the schedules AA along which we have assets market equilibrium: There is only one price level $\bar{p}$, at which our interest rate is equal to the world rate and hence expected depreciation is zero. We also show the schedule $\dot{p}=0$ along which we have goods and money market equilibrium. The schedule is exactly the same as that in Figure 11-8. The arrows indicate the adjustment process on the assumptions of our model; continuous asset market equilibrium, perfect foresight, and slow adjustment of goods prices.

It is apparent from the phase diagram that there is only one trajectory, the solidly drawn line, along which the economy will converge to the steady state. All other paths *are* perfect foresight paths, but they do not converge. The convergent path corresponds to selection of the positive root in solving equation (15). The stable branch is the AA line of Figure 11-8. For any initial condition on the price level, say p_0, there is a unique level of the exchange rate e_0, that will ensure that the economy will converge to long-run equilibrium with perfect foresight.

REFERENCES AND SUGGESTED READING

Argy, V., and Porter, M. 1972. The forward exchange market and the effects of domestic and external disturbances under alternative exchange rate systems. *IMF staff papers*, November.

Black, S. 1973. *International money markets and flexible exchange rates.* Princeton studies in international finance, No. 32.

Caves, R. 1963. Flexible exchange rates. *American economic review*, papers and proceedings. 53:120-29.

Dornbusch, R. 1976a. Exchange rate expectations and monetary policy. *Journal of international economics* 6:231-44.

Dornbusch, R. 1976b. Expectations and exchange rate dynamics. *Journal of political economy* 84:1161-76.

Dornbusch, R., and Krugman, P. 1976. Flexible exchange rates in the short run. *Brookings papers on economic activity*, No. 3.

Ethier, W. 1979. Expectations and the asset-market approach to the exchange rate. *Journal of monetary economics*, 5:259-82.

Fleming, M. 1962. Domestic financial policies under fixed and under floating exchange rates. *IMF staff papers*, November.

Giersch, H. 1973. On the desirable degree of exchange rate flexibility. *Weltwirtschaftliches archiv*, 109 (2):191-213.

Isard, P. 1978. *Exchange rate determination*, Princeton studies no. 42, Princeton: Princeton University Press.

Mundell, R. A. 1967. *International economics*. New York: Macmillan Publishing Co.

Niehans, J. 1975. Some doubts about the efficacy of monetary policy under flexible exchange rates. *Journal of international economics* 5:275-81.

Willet, T., and Tower, E. 1970. Currency areas and exchange rate flexibility. *Weltwirtschaftliches archiv*, 105(1):48-65.

Wilson, C. 1979. Exchange rate dynamics and anticipated disturbances. *Journal of political economy*, June, vol. 79:639-47.

CHAPTER

12

Monetary Stabilization, Intervention, and Real Appreciation

This chapter investigates the adjustment process to a reduction in the rate of credit creation in an open, flexible exchange rate economy. The framework of analysis is one of rational expectations with respect to interest rates, inflation, and depreciation. The special feature of the model is the role of exchange market intervention and the resulting endogeneity of the growth rate of the money stock.

The model is of empirical interest because of the growing experience, for example, in Israel, Spain, and Latin America, with the fact that monetary disinflation rapidly leads to real appreciation, unemployment, and money creation induced by exchange intervention. With capital flows and induced money creation threatening attempts at stabilization policy, there is a need to understand the interaction of stabilization and intervention.

Table 12-1 shows the facts to be explained. Although these facts are becoming well known, there appears to have been little formal modeling to

TABLE 12-1

Some Facts

	ė	ṗ	Ṙ/H	Ḣ/H
Spain				
1977	18.5	24.5	17.5	21.6
1978	−13.4	19.7	26.7	24.9
79/I-78/I	−14.8	16.3	27.6	37.8
Israel				
1977	31.1	34.6	119.0	42.5
1978	67.0	50.6	179.9	27.8
79/I-78/I	21.8	58.1	259.3	17.5
Argentina				
1977	117.7	176.1	52.0	140.3
1978	67.9	175.5	60.5	109.7
79/I-78/I	60.4	169.0	81.8	131.1

NOTES: ė = % change in the local currency price of the $ US;
ṗ = % CPI inflation;
Ṙ/H = change in central bank foreign assets as % of "reserve money";
Ḣ/H = % change in "reserve money".
SOURCE: IMF *International Financial Statistics*, August 1979 Lines ae, 11, 14, and 64.

date. Work by Liviatan (1979), however, has addressed these issues and the present model is directly stimulated by that contribution.

Here we also add to rational expectations models of flexible exchange rate systems. At present there are three main avenues of modeling. Following Black (1973) there are models of the "asset market approach" that emphasize the fast adjustment of financial relative markets relative to goods markets as a basis of exchange rate dynamics. The previous chapter explores that approach. A second line of theory emphasizes the current account as a basis of exchange rate dynamics and is dealt with in the last two chapters of this book. The third approach is concerned primarily with imperfect substitutability between domestic and foreign securities and takes portfolio composition effects as an important source of exchange rate movements and variability. Work along these lines has been done by Kouri (1975) and Dooley-Isard (1979), Branson (1976), Calvo and Rodriguez (1977), and Henderson (1979).

This chapter is most nearly in the spirit of this third approach, especially in its emphasis on exchange market intervention. It does, however, differ in a critical respect. Rather than modeling imperfect capital mobility as the instantaneous, but imperfect, substitutability of domestic and foreign securities, we take the older approach that focuses on capital flows in response to interest differentials. The theory is less clear cut than portfolio balance approaches, but it commands an empirical plausibility.

Section I sets out the model, adapting the assets market approach developed in the previous chapter to a world of inflation, exchange market intervention that is "leaning against the wind" and finite capital mobility. The model is used to show the adjustment to a sustained reduction in the rate of domestic credit creation. We show that the adjustment process involves an initial overshooting in the rate of exchange depreciation relative to the trend rate of inflation, real appreciation, and unemployment. The rate of monetary growth, fed by intervention, may actually expand for some time. The monetization of reserve gains constitutes part of the rise in real balances that takes place during the adjustment.

In section II we study for comparison the adjustment process when there is no intervention. The exchange rate immediately appreciates and the unemployment level rises instantaneously. The difference between the two regimes is therefore seen to be one of timing. The concluding part and the appendixes deal with a more general model.

I. THE MODEL

Output is demand determined and depends on relative prices and the real rate of interest. Deviations of output from full employment and money creation are the sources of inflation. Nominal interest rates are determined in the standard *LM* curve manner, by real income and the real money stock.

1. The Structural Equations

The nominal interest rate i is determined by real income y and real balances $h - p$:

$$i = ky - f(h - p) \tag{1}$$

where y, h, and p are all in logs. Aggregate demand is a function of relative prices and the real rate of interest $i - \dot{p}$:

$$y = a'(e - p) - b'(i - \dot{p}) \tag{2}$$

or, substituting from (1) for the nominal interest rate:

$$y = a(e - p) + b(h - p) + c\dot{p} \qquad a, b, c > 0 \tag{2a}$$

Here, e is the nominal exchange rate and $e - p$ is the real exchange rate or the relative price of our goods. For the time being, we concentrate on a special case where aggregate demand is independent of the rate of interest, $b = c = 0$. Only in section III do we return to the general case. For our special case then, the equilibrium level of output is solely determined by the real exchange rate:

$$y = a(e - p) \tag{2b}$$

The full employment level of output, by choice of units, is set at the level $\bar{y} = 0$. Then y can be interpreted as the deviation of output from normal and similarly, $e - p$ is the deviation of the real exchange rate from the level consistent with full employment.

Inflation is determined by the output gap y and the rate of monetary growth $\dot{h}$. Inclusion of money growth in the inflation equation is required for steady state full employment inflation, although the steady state growth rate of credit could serve the same purpose:

$$\dot{p} = \phi y + \dot{h} \tag{3}$$

Equation (4) shows the intervention policy of "leaning against the wind." The rate of accumulation of reserves as a fraction of the money stock $\dot{R}/H$ is negatively proportional to the excess of the rate of depreciation $\dot{e}$ over the rate of domestic credit creation, v:*

---

*An alternative intervention rule is $\dot{R}/H = -\theta(\dot{e} - \dot{p})$. See Appendix B.

Monetary Stabilization, Intervention, and Real Appreciation

$$\dot{R}/H = -\theta(\dot{e} - v) \tag{4}$$

The intervention rule can be looked at in a slightly different way by defining total adjustment as the sum of reserve accumulation plus appreciation relative to trend: $\dot{R}/H - (\dot{e} - v)$.* With that definition of total adjustment, and using (4), we have the fraction of adjustment that is effected through reserve changes as:

$$(\dot{R}/H)/[\dot{R}/H - (\dot{e} - v)] = \theta/(1 + \theta) \equiv \lambda \tag{4a}$$

Active intervention or a value of λ close to unity thus implies that the exchange rate is maintained close to the long-run inflation trend $\dot{e} \doteq v$. A low value of λ by contrast allows the exchange rate to deviate substantially from trend inflation. We refer to λ as the "intervention coefficient."

Estimable ?

The balance of payments is a function of the real exchange rate, real income, and the nominal interest differential adjusted for exchange depreciation:

$$\dot{R}/H = g(e - p) - my + n(i - \dot{e} - i^*) \tag{5}$$

(See Dornbusch [1980] and Girton and Roper [below].)

Replacing the intervention, $\dot{R}/H$, by the rule given in (4) allows us to write:

$$\theta(\dot{e} - v) = -[g(e - p) - my + n(i - \dot{e})] \tag{5a}$$

where, for convenience, we have set the foreign interest rate equal to zero. In (5) and (5a) it is the excess of the nominal interest rate over the rate of depreciation that governs capital flows. Capital mobility is measured by the coefficient n.[†] A rise in the nominal interest rate leads to a capital inflow while increased depreciation leads to a capital outflow. Capital mobility is less than perfect in that, in the short run, interest differentials can persist.

Rational expectations are used here in two places. The actual real rate of interest $i - p$ determines aggregate spending and the actual interest differential $i - \dot{e} - i^*$ governs capital flows. It is readily apparent that the assumption of rational expectations simplifies the analysis since it dispenses with the need for additional equations describing the formation of expectations about inflation and depreciation.

Assump. of Rat. Expectations

---

*Total adjustment corresponds to what Girton and Roper (1977) call "exchange market pressure."

†The coefficient n is to be interpreted as the rate of capital inflow, as a fraction of the money stock, generated by a change in the interest differential. Even with high capital mobility, it is thus likely to be a fraction. The same normalization on the nominal money stock applies to the coefficients g and m.

Finally, monetary growth is equal to the growth of domestic credit plus the monetary growth derived from exchange market intervention. Thus:

$$\dot{h} \equiv v + \dot{R}/H = v - \theta(\dot{e} - v) \tag{6}$$

The monetary growth equation shows that when exchange depreciation is high, the resulting intervention leads to a slowdown in monetary growth. Conversely, high appreciation leads to growth over and above the scheduled rate of credit creation.

Our model is simplified in three respects. First, we do not allow for a role of import prices, and hence the exchange rate, in the real balance deflator. Second, we exclude depreciation from the definition of the real interest rate in aggregate demand. Third, we do not allow for a *direct* effect of depreciation on domestic inflation. An alternative model is explored in Appendix B and shows some of these extensions.

2. Dynamics

We now have completed the description of our structural model and can turn to the equilibrium conditions and the dynamics. At any point in time the levels of the exchange rate, prices, and nominal money are exogenously given. So are the growth rates of domestic credit and the intervention coefficient which are policy parameters.

For given levels of the stated variables we can solve the system for the current rates of inflation, depreciation, and money growth and thus for the rate of change of the real exchange rate and the rate of change of real balances. Using (1), (2b), (3), and (5) we obtain:

$$\dot{h} - \dot{p} = -\phi a(e - p) \tag{7}$$

$$\dot{e} - v = \mu(e - p) + \nu(x - \bar{x}) \tag{8}$$

$$\mu \equiv - [g - a(m - nk)]/(\theta - n) < 0$$

$$\nu \equiv nf/(\theta - n) > 0$$

where $x \equiv h - p$ and $\bar{x}$ denotes steady-state real balances.* The rate of change of the real exchange rate is given by:

---

*Equation (8) is derived in terms of deviations from long-run equilibrium, recognizing that in the steady state $\dot{e} = \dot{p} = v$.

Monetary Stabilization, Intervention, and Real Appreciation

$$\dot{e} - \dot{p} = \delta(e - p) + (1 + \theta)\,v(x - \bar{x}) \qquad \delta \equiv (1 + \theta)\mu - \phi a < 0 \qquad (9)$$

For the stability of this system, we assume that $\delta < 0$ and that $\theta - n > 0$.

In Figure 12-1 we show the schedule $\dot{e} = \dot{p}$ along which the real exchange rate is constant. An increase in real balances lowers the nominal interest rate. The resulting interest differential leads to a capital outflow, a balance of payments deficit—an increased deficit or a reduced surplus—and therefore increased exchange depreciation. Since by assumption there is no effect on income and inflation, there is unambiguously a depreciating *real* rate. To offset the effect of higher real balances, a higher level of the real exchange

FIGURE 12-1

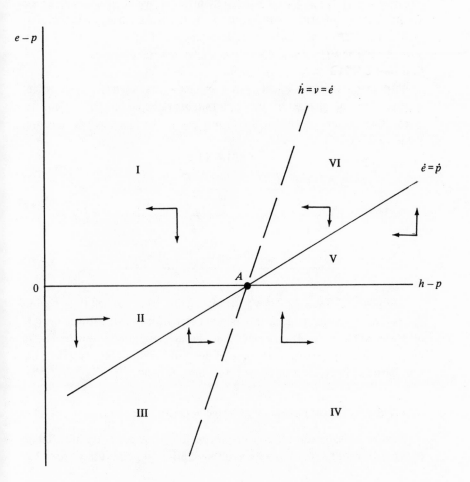

rate and hence a higher level of income and an improvement in the external balance, are required. Thus the schedule is positively sloped.

Real balances are constant along the horizontal axis where relative prices are such that output is at the full employment level. The steady state equilibrium is shown at point A. At A the rate of depreciation equals the rate of credit creation; there is no intervention and real exchange rates and real balances are constant.

We also show in Figure 12-1 the schedule $\dot{h}=v=\dot{e}$ along which growth of money derives only from domestic credit. Intervention and the balance of payments are zero and depreciation equals the rate of credit creation. The schedule is steeper than the $\dot{e}=\dot{p}$ locus as can be noted from equations (8) and (9). Above the horizontal axis there is overemployment, which by itself causes real appreciation. Along the $\dot{e}=\dot{p}$ schedule, the inflationary effect of the overemployment is precisely offset by the depreciation in excess of the rate of domestic credit creation. As the real exchange rate increases further the rate of depreciation declines and the first term in (9) becomes progressively smaller. Along the $\dot{h}=v$ schedule, the real exchange rate is therefore appreciating.

With these reference schedules we can now characterize the levels and relative rates of change of the endogenous variables in the various regions. With symmetry we can limit ourselves to the first three as shown in Table 12-2.

TABLE 12-2

The Road Map

I	II	III
$\dot{p}>\dot{h}>v>\dot{e}$	$\dot{h}>\dot{p}>v>\dot{e}$	$\dot{h}>v>\dot{e}>\dot{p}$
$y>0$	$y<0$	$y<0$
Surplus	Surplus	Surplus

One point of Table 12-2 is worth emphasizing. That is, in all three regions the rate of credit creation, or the long-run rate of inflation, exceeds the rate of depreciation, $v>\dot{e}$. Accordingly, there is exchange intervention leading to money creation in excess of the rate of domestic credit expansion. There are thus balance of payments surpluses in all three regions.

3. The Adjustment Process to a Change in Credit Creation

We now consider the adjustment process to a reduction in the growth rate of domestic credit v. We start with a full equilibrium at point A in Figure 12-2.

FIGURE 12-2

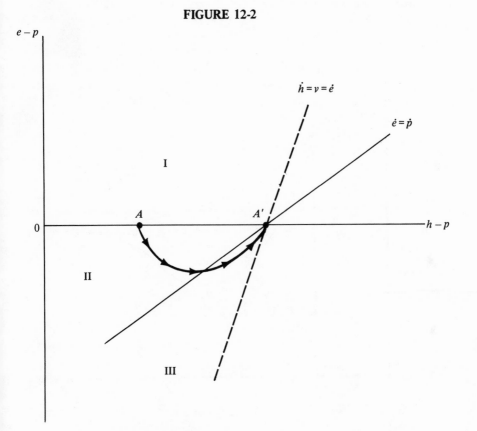

The reduced rate of credit creation will, in long-run equilibrium, lead to no change in relative prices or output, but will raise the equilibrium stock of real balances $\bar{x}$ because from (2), $d\bar{x} = -dv/f$. In addition, the new equilibrium inflation rate will be lower, as will be the nominal interest rate $di = dv$. Point A' thus indicates the new long-run equilibrium.

Starting from the initial equilibrium we have, as yet, unchanged real balances and an unchanged real exchange rate; output and nominal interest rates are at their initial level. This is the essential point for an understanding of the exchange rate implications of the stabilization. The authorities, in line with the intervention rule, reduce the rate at which the exchange rate is allowed to depreciate. In so doing they create an interest differential in favor of the home country—an interest differential adjusted for depreciation $i - \dot{e}$. Accordingly, there is a capital inflow or reduced outflow, creating pressure for a further reduction in the rate of depreciation and thus leading to intervention and money creation.

FIGURE 12-3

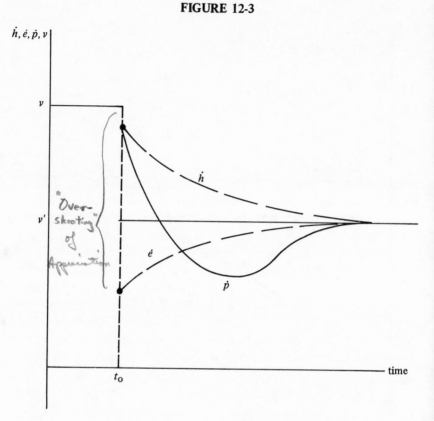

From (8) above the impact effect of reduced credit creation on the exchange rate, at the initial equilibrium, is

$$\left. d\dot{e}/dv \right|_{t=0} = 1 - v d\bar{x}/dv = \theta/(\theta - n) > 1 \qquad (10)$$

There is, accordingly, an *overshooting* not in the level of the exchange rate, but in its rate of change. As shown in Figure 12-3 a reduced rate of credit creation thus leads to a reduction in the rate of depreciation below its new trend level.

The impact effect of reduced credit creation on monetary growth must take into account the monetary expansion caused by intervention. From (6) and (10) we have:

$$\left. d\dot{h}/dv \right|_{t=0} = 1 - n\theta/(\theta - n) = [(1+\theta)/(\theta - n)] \, (\lambda - n) \lessgtr 0 \qquad (11)$$

224

A reduction in the rate of credit expansion need not reduce monetary growth unless $\lambda - n > 0$. With capital highly responsive to interest differentials, it is entirely possible that the intervention more than offsets the reduction in domestic credit creation.

Finally, the effect of reduced credit creation on inflation is, from (3), given by the change in monetary growth. Accordingly, with highly mobile capital and the intervention coefficient λ relatively small, it is possible that inflation in the first instance actually rises.

The impact effect of reduced credit creation thus involves real appreciation of the exchange rate, including the possibility of rising inflation with nominal appreciation. The real appreciation at point A will lead to a fall in demand and output. Once output falls and thus exerts a dampening effect on inflation, real balances will be rising. This is the adjustment process shown in region II.

Real appreciation and rising real balances will continue until we reach the $\dot{e} = \dot{p}$ schedule. Both inflation and depreciation are below the trend v, while monetary growth is above trend. Nominal interest rates have declined due to the fall in output and the rise in the real money stock. Depreciation and inflation now have converged. Depreciation has increased as the trade balance has worsened in response to the real appreciation, and the capital account has deteriorated because of lower interest rates. Inflation, by contrast, has declined due to the increased output gap.

From here on there is real depreciation. Money growth is still in excess of the reduced rate of credit creation and there is still intervention to keep the depreciation more nearly in line with the rate of credit creation. Continued real depreciation and real balance growth restore output. The real depreciation, in combination with rising real balances, brings the balance of payments more nearly into equilibrium.

By the time the economy reaches point A' relative prices are back to their initial level, but the stock of real balances has risen in adjustment to the lower rate of interest, inflation, and depreciation.

Thus in the long run, the reduction in credit creation is only reflected in a corresponding reduction in nominal interest rate, the trend rate of depreciation, and in a higher stock of real money balances. How is the gain in real balances achieved? Our model of inflation, allowing a full impact of money growth on prices, implies that the only way real balances can rise is through unemployment, or an output gap. It is true that intervention policy leads to nominal money growth, but that growth finds its way directly into inflation and thus does not help raise real balances. In Appendix B we explore an alternative model where depreciation directly affects inflation. In that model it is true that the deceleration of depreciation immediately contributes to real balance growth, although that effect is subsequently undone when the real exchange rate depreciates.*

In summary, we have shown that a reduction in the rate of credit creation will, in the long run, reduce inflation and depreciation. In the transition, however, unemployment is created as the real exchange rate initially appreciates in response to an interest differential that is created by the disinflation policy. Can the transitory unemployment and real appreciation be avoided? Liviatan has proposed an equalizing tax on capital flows that would eliminate the incentive for capital imports in the transition. An alternative, for the believer in rational expectations models as shown here, is a once and for all increase in the stock of nominal money along with a reduced rate of growth. The combination of the two would move the economy to point A' instantaneously, although at a higher price level than is implied by the adjustment path in Figure 12-2. Of course, it is hard to persuade the public that the true path to monetary stabilization is a big money bubble up front.

II. FULLY FLEXIBLE RATES

In this part we compare the adjustment process derived so far, with one where there is no intervention at all, where exchange rates are fully flexible and can jump in response to new information. We maintain all other assumptions of the model, including in particular the perfect foresight assumption concerning exchange rate expectations.

1. The Model Without Intervention

In the absence of intervention money growth is equal to the growth rate of credit because the balance of payments is identically equal to zero. The balance of payments in (5) can be set equal to zero and solved for the rate of depreciation. Setting $\theta = 0$ in (8) yields the rate of depreciation:

$$\dot{e} - v = \bar{\mu}(e - p) - f(x - \bar{x}) \qquad \bar{\mu} \equiv [g - a(m - nk)]/n > 0 \quad (12)$$

---

*In fact, this result holds independently of whether intervention is geared to the change in the real exchange rate $\dot{e} - \dot{p}$, or to trend inflation, $\dot{e} - v$. With the present intervention model and an inflation equation: $\dot{p} = \phi y + \alpha \dot{e} + (1 - \alpha)\dot{h}$ the impact effect on real balances is: $d(\dot{h} - \dot{p})/dv = -\alpha(1 + \theta)n/(\theta - n)$.

Monetary Stabilization, Intervention, and Real Appreciation

The important point to note is that (12) differs from (8) not only in that the intervention coefficient θ is zero, but also in the effect of the real exchange rate on the rate of depreciation. Since a real depreciation improves the balance of payments by assumption, and since the overall balance must be zero, a real appreciation must be accompanied by a deterioration in the capital account through increased anticipated depreciation. A rise in real balances lowers interest rates and worsens the capital account. It must be offset by a compensating reduction in anticipated depreciation that keeps the real interest $i - \dot{e}$, and hence the capital account, constant.

FIGURE 12-4

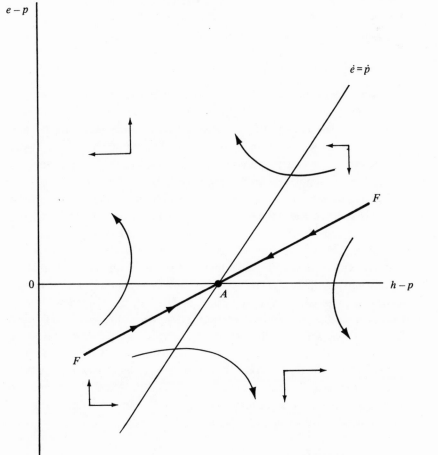

With real depreciation determined by (9) it is readily seen that the equation for the evolution of the real exchange rate $\dot{e} - \dot{p}$ now is given by:

$$\dot{e} - \dot{p} = \bar{\delta}(e - p) - f(x - \bar{x}) \qquad \bar{\delta} = \bar{\mu} - \phi\alpha > 0 \qquad (13)$$

Figure 12-4 shows the schedule $\dot{e} = \dot{p}$ along which the real exchange rate is content.* Above the schedule the real exchange rate is depreciating, and below the schedule it is appreciating. Above the horizontal axis real balances are falling, while below the axis the real money stock is rising. The arrows indicate the saddle-point instability characteristic of rational expectations models.

There is a unique trajectory FF along which the economy can converge to the steady state at point A. Any other trajectory does satisfy all equations, including the perfect foresight characteristic, but will not converge. We assume henceforth that the economy will in fact be on FF, although there is no process in our model that will guarantee this.

2. A Reduction in Credit Growth

Consider again the reduction in credit growth. Real balances across steady states will again be higher and, in long-run equilibrium, will be at $\bar{x}'$ in Figure 12-5. The adjustment process is as follows: Announcement of the reduced credit growth shifts the perfect foresight path down to $F'F'$. The exchange rate immediately appreciates and the level of the real exchange rate moves directly to point A'' on the new perfect foresight path.

The immediate real appreciation contrasts with the case of intervention. With intervention the real exchange rate starts appreciating while with fully flexible rates the level of the real rate directly rises. The freely flexible rate thus anticipates with a jump at the beginning the real appreciation process that builds up more steadily under intervention, as shown in Figure 12-2.

The impact effect of reduced credit growth at point A'' is to lower real income because of the real appreciation. The fall in real income, in turn, implies a decline in nominal interest rates. What then maintains overall balance of payments equilibrium? It is readily shown from (12) that at A'' the rate of depreciation of the nominal exchange rate is reduced. It is uncertain though whether the rate of depreciation declines below the new trend rate of inflation ν.

In the subsequent adjustment process, as the arrows indicate, the real exchange rate is depreciating. Accordingly nominal exchange depreciation

*We assume that $\bar{\delta} > 0$ and deal only with that case here.

FIGURE 12-5

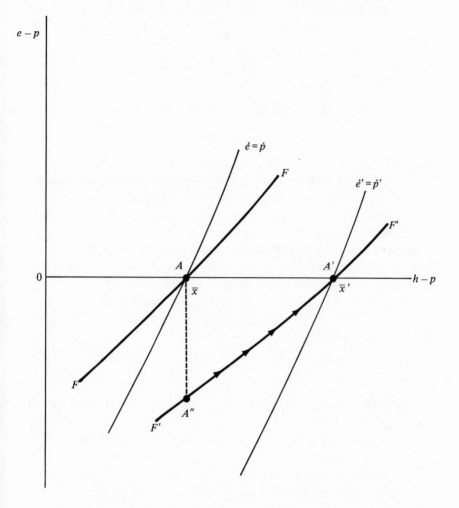

exceeds inflation. Since across steady states real balances have to rise it is also apparent that inflation falls short of money growth during the adjustment process.

The unemployment effects of the monetary stabilization arise under flexible rates just as much as they do under the intervention system. Here the unemployment shock is concentrated at the beginning with the subsequent real depreciation slowly eroding the economic slack. Cumulative deflation, to generate higher real balances, is just the same here as it is under the intervention system. Under both systems, deflation (or a once and for all rise in nominal money) is required to accommodate the reduction in velocity or the rise in real balances, associated with lower trend inflation. The real differences between the fully flexible rate and the intervention system thus lie in the time path of adjustment.

III. THE EXTENDED MODEL

In concluding this chapter we look at the extended model where the real interest rate, as well as the real exchange rate, are determinants of aggregate demand. The formal model is laid out in the appendix and we only comment here on some points regarding the structure and results.

The essential complication of this model arises from the link between the balance of payments, money growth, depreciation, and inflation. Appreciation, by raising money growth, raises inflationary expectations, reduces the real rate of interest, and therefore expands aggregate demand. These channels are captured in the reduced form equation for output derived from (2a), (3), and (6). The equation is, once again, expressed in terms of deviations from long-run equilibrium.*

$$y = \bar{a}(e-p) + \bar{b}(x-\bar{x}) - \theta\bar{c}(\dot{e}-v) \tag{14}$$

Equation (14) shows that real depreciation, or an expansion in the real money stock, raises output. A balance of payments deficit or a depreciating exchange rate (relative to trend), however, raises real interest rates through reduced money growth and inflationary expectations, and lowers output.

The second relationship we use is the balance of payments in (5a), having substituted for the nominal interest rate from (1):

$$\dot{e}-v = [-1/(\theta-n)][g(e-p) - (m-nk)y - nf(x-\bar{x})] \tag{15}$$

and where we assume here that the adverse expenditure effect of higher income on the current account outweighs the favorable capital account effect through higher nominal interest rates, $m-nk > 0$. Equations (14) and (15) are now used to show the impact effect of a change in credit growth on the depreciation rate and on output.

---

*The bar over a coefficient denotes that the coefficients in (2a) are multiplied by $(1-c\phi)^{-1} > 0$.

FIGURE 12-6

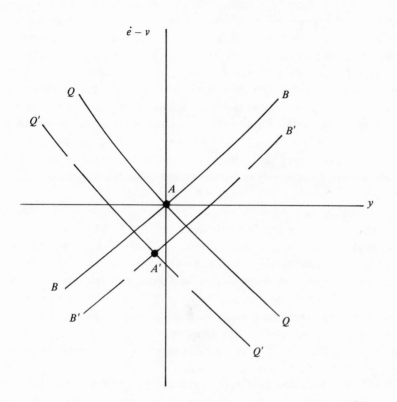

Figure 12-6 shows along the negatively sloped schedule QQ, the demand-determined output level of the economy shown in (14). The positively sloped schedule BB shows the balance of payments relation in (15). Both schedules, of course, represent reduced forms that take into account monetary equilibrium and the intervention rule. They are drawn for given real balances x and $\bar{x}$ and a given real exchange rate $e - p$.

A reduction in the growth rate of credit will raise steady state real balances and thus shifts both schedules in Figure 12-6. The output schedule shifts down and to the left because at each level of depreciation (relative to trend) there is now a reduction in inflationary expectations, higher real interest rates, and thus lower demand. The balance of payments schedule shifts down and to the right. Here, intervention around the new and lower trend of credit growth implies a real interest differential in favor of the home country and a capital inflow that must be offset by a deterioration in the external balance through higher income.

The reduction in credit growth in Figure 12-6, leads, in the short run, to a new equilibrium at point A'. The rate of depreciation once again has fallen below the new trend inflation rate so that we preserve here the overshooting property as well as the fact that there is, in the transition, a surplus and external money creation.

What determines the output effect of reduced credit creation? The higher expected real interest rate at home exerts an unambiguous deflationary effect shown by the downward shift of the output schedule. A high interest response of aggregate demand insures that this effect is large. The countervailing effect comes from the money supply side. The reduction in the rate of depreciation creates an international interest differential in favor of the home country, leading to capital inflows and external money creation which potentially offset the effect of reduced credit growth.

It is readily shown that the output schedule shifts down further than the balance of payments schedule provided $\lambda - n > 0$.* Thus output must fall initially if intervention is sufficiently vigorous relative to the degree of capital mobility. This condition ensures that a reduction in credit growth will reduce the rate of growth in nominal money. It is through this channel that the expected real interest rate rises and the contraction in demand occurs. In any event, it is apparent that for real balances to increase across steady states there must on average be unemployment in the transition. For the stable system, an initial output expansion, if it should occur, implies a subsequent recession that offsets the initial output gain.

The extended model once more draws attention to the importance of the intervention coefficient. The interaction of intervention, money growth and inflationary expectations makes the "intervention coefficient" a key parameter. Vigorous intervention implies small interest differentials, small capital flows, and therefore small external money creation. The other point that is to be emphasized, and this decidedly is a special feature of the model, is the direct link between money growth and inflation. The model is quite sensitive to the indicator of trend inflation expectations that we chose—$\dot{m}, v, \dot{e}$, or some combination of these. Any one formulation remains a special case, but it is certainly an area for more modeling.†

---

*The downward shift of the BB schedule, from (15) is $d(\dot{e} - v)/dv = -n/(\theta - n)$. We have used here the fact that $dx/dv = -1/f$, noting that increased trend inflation raises nominal interest rates. For the output schedule the downward shift is $d(\dot{e} - v)/dv = -\bar{b}/f\bar{c}\theta$ which, from the definitions of $\bar{b}$ and $\bar{c}$, is readily shown to equal $-1/\theta$. For the output schedule to shift down further than the BB schedule we thus require $1/\theta > n/(\theta - n)$ or $\lambda - n > 0$.

†To make the point, consider in place of (3) the inflation equation $\dot{p} = \phi y + \dot{e}$. What happens to relative price and output dynamics? Alternatively assume $\dot{p} = \phi y + \rho(\dot{e} - \dot{p})$ for a quite different inflation dynamics.

APPENDIX A

This appendix shows the reduced form equations of our complete model and develops the stability requirements. From equations (1) to (6) we derive the equations determining the level of output and the rate of depreciation at a point in time:

$$y = \pi_1(e-p) + \pi_2(h-p) + \pi_3 v \qquad (A-1)$$

$$\dot{e} = \sigma_1(e-p) + \sigma_2(h-p) + \sigma_3 v$$

where the following are the coefficients:

$$\pi_1 = [a(\theta - n) + c\theta g]/\Delta\gamma \qquad \pi_2 = b(1+\theta)(\lambda - n)/\Delta\gamma \quad (A-2)$$

$$\pi_3 = [c(1+\theta)(\lambda - n)]/\Delta\gamma \qquad \sigma_1 = -[g - a\beta]/\Delta$$

$$\sigma_2 = [nf + b\beta]/\Delta \qquad \sigma_3 = (1+\theta)[\lambda + c\beta]/\Delta$$

$$\Delta = (\theta - n) + \beta c\theta \qquad \beta = (m - nk)/(1 - c\phi);$$

$$\gamma = (1 - c\phi);$$

$$\lambda = \theta/(1+\theta)$$

The dynamics are defined by the evolution of relative prices and real balances, omitting the constant terms and using equation (3):

$$\dot{h} - \dot{p} = -\phi\pi_1(e-p) - \phi\pi_2(h-p) \qquad (A-3)$$

$$\dot{e} - \dot{p} = [\sigma_1(1+\theta) - \phi\pi_1](e-p) + [\sigma_2(1+\theta) - \phi\pi_2](h-p) \quad (A-4)$$

Stability of this system requires that all the coefficients of ξ in the characteristic equation be positive:

$$\xi^2 + \xi[\phi(\pi_1 + \pi_2) - (1+\theta)\sigma_1] + (1+\theta)(\pi_1\sigma_2 - \sigma_1\pi_2)\xi^\circ = 0 \qquad (A-5)$$

A sufficient condition for stability is

$$\sigma_1 < 0 \qquad \sigma_2\pi_1, \pi_2 > 0 \qquad (A-6)$$

APPENDIX B

Here we sketch an alternative model that allows (1) for a direct effect of depreciation on inflation and (2) uses an intervention rule geared to the rate of real depreciation. Equations (B-1) and (B-2) show the new specifications:

$$\dot{p} = \phi(y - \bar{y}) + \alpha\dot{e} + (1 - \alpha)\dot{h} \tag{B-1}$$

$$\dot{R}/H = -\theta(\dot{e} - \dot{p}) \tag{B-2}$$

As before, we assume here that output depends only on the real exchange rate and that money growth is determined by growth of domestic credit and by the balance of payments $\dot{R}/H$:

$$\dot{h} = v - \theta(\dot{e} - \dot{p}) \qquad y = a(e - p) \tag{B-3}$$

With these assumptions, it is readily shown that a reduction in the growth rate of domestic credit will lead to a reduction in the rate of depreciation, with the possibility of overshooting:

$$d\dot{e}/dv = (1 - \alpha)\theta/\Delta \qquad \Delta = \theta(1 - \alpha)(1 + n) - n > 0 \tag{B-4}$$

where we assume that $\Delta > 0$.

Next we note that the real exchange rate, on impact, will be appreciating as credit growth is reduced:

$$d(\dot{e} - \dot{p})/dv = n(1 - \alpha)/\Delta \tag{B-5}$$

Finally, real balances will, on impact, be growing due to the contribution of reduced depreciation in reducing domestic inflation:

$$d(\dot{h} - \dot{p})/dv = -n/\Delta \tag{B-6}$$

REFERENCES AND SUGGESTED READING

Black, S. 1973. *International money markets and flexible exchange rates.* Princeton Studies in International Finance.

Bilson, J. 1979. Virtuous and vicious circles. *IMF staff papers*, March.

Branson, W. 1976. Asset markets and relative prices in exchange rate determination. Unpublished manuscript, Institute for International Economic Studies, Stockholm.

Calvo, G., and Rodriguez, C. 1977. A model of exchange rate determination under currency substitution and rational expectations. *Journal of political economy* 85: 617-25.

Dooley, M., and Isard, P. 1979. The portfolio balance model of exchange rates. Unpublished manuscript, Board of Governors of the Federal Reserve.

Dornbusch, R. 1976. Expectations and exchange rate dynamics. *Journal of political economy* 84:1161-76.

Dornbusch, R., and Fischer, S. 1980. Exchange rates and the current account. *American economic review*, Massachusetts Institute of Technology.

Fair, R., 1979. A model of the balance of payments, *Journal of international economics* 9:25-46.

Flood, R. 1979. An example of exchange rate overshooting. *Southern economic journal* July, vol. 46:168-78.

Frenkel, J., 1979. On the mark; a theory of floating exchange rates based on real interest differentials, American economic review, Sept., vol. 69:610-22.

Girton, L., and Roper, D. 1977. A monetary model of exchange market pressure applied to the postwar Canadian experience. *American economic review* 67:537-48.

Henderson, D., 1979. The dynamic effects of exchange market intervention policy: two extreme views and a synthesis. Unpublished manuscript, Board of Governors of the Federal Reserve.

Kouri, P. K., 1976. The exchange rate and the balance of payments in the shortrun and in the longrun. *Scandinavian journal of economics*, 2, vol. 78:280-304.

Kouri, P. K., 1975. Three essays on flexible exchange rates, Unpublished Ph.D. dissertation, Massachusetts Institute of Technology.

Liviatan, N., 1979. Neutral monetary policy and the capital import tax. Unpublished manuscript, The Hebrew University.

Mussa, M., 1976. The exchange rate, the balance of payments and monetary and fiscal policy under a regine of controlled floating. *Scandinavian journal of economics* 2: 229-249.

Mussa, M. 1979. Macroeconomic interdependence and the exchange rate regime. *International economic policy*, R. Dornbusch and J. Frenkel, eds. Baltimore: Johns Hopkins University Press.

Rodriguez, C. 1977. The role of trade flows in exchange rate determination: a rational expectations approach. Unpublished manuscript, Columbia University.

Tobin, J. 1978. A proposal for international monetary reform. Unpublished manuscript, Yale University.

Part 5

Portfolio Balance and

the Current Account

CHAPTER

13

Exchange Rates, Assets Markets, and the Current Account

This chapter extends our discussion of exchange rate dynamics by bringing in a new element, the current account, as a factor determining the behavior of the exchange rate over time. The current account has always been recognized in popular discussion as an important determinant of exchange rates. Theoretical models such as those in chapters 11 and 12, however, seem to develop exchange rate theory without any role for the current account. The present chapter rounds out that earlier analysis by combining the assets market or stock market determination of exchange rates at a point in time with the implications of the current account for exchange rate behavior over time.

We draw here on more recent literature, starting with McKinnon (1969) and Tower (1972), and including Dornbusch (1975, 1976), Dornbusch and Fischer (1980), and the work by Kouri (1975, 1976), Flood (1977), and Rodriguez (1977) to name only a few.

This chapter assumes a very simple structure of the real sector. There is only one good in the world and attention thus focuses exclusively on the balance between income and spending—and thus on the current account—and not on the composition of spending and relative prices. In the assets markets there are only two assets, money and a real asset, claims to capital. We study the conditions of short-run equilibrium and the adjustment process that is brought into action by imbalance in the current account.

Two quite different models are studied. In section I we look at the inter-action of the current account and the exchange rate on the assumption of full employment. Here the emphasis is on exchange rate expectations and anticipations. In section II the current account is again a determinant of the exchange rate, but this time in a setting where real wages determine output and where wage adjustment is sluggish. Both parts serve to round out our understanding of factors important in exchange-rate dynamics.

I. THE SMALL-COUNTRY CASE

Here we introduce a relatively complete model of a small open economy that trades with the rest of the world in goods and assets.* There are no issues of goods market equilibrium or the terms of trade since the smallness assumption means that all output can be sold at the world market price. Full purchasing power parity obtains continuously and the interest rate, or the yield on capital, is continuously equal to that in the rest of the world. Output is fixed and prices are flexible, as is the exchange rate.

Section I (1 and 2) develops the basic model and discusses the adjustment process to long-run equilibrium when disturbances arise. Expectations are introduced in section I (3 and 4) where the perfect foresight assumption is formulated. Adjustment to anticipated future shocks is discussed in section I (5).

---

*For a two-country model see Dornbusch (1976).

Exchange Rates, Assets Markets, and the Current Account

1. The Model

Domestic residents allocate their portfolio between money and equity. Given wealth, the share of money in the portfolio θ is a function of the yield on capital. For the present we disregard inflation and depreciation as other determinants. This portfolio preference is shown in the money market equilibrium condition:

$$H/P \equiv x = \theta(r)\, w \tag{1}$$

where H and P are the nominal money stock and the price level, r is the world rate of interest, w denotes real wealth, and x denotes real balances. Real wealth is defined as the sum of real money balances x and the real value of equity holdings a/r:

$$w \equiv x + a/r \tag{2}$$

The number of income streams is a and each yields one *real* dollar indefinitely. Substituting (2) into (1) gives us the equilibrium value of real balances as a function of the stock of real assets:

$$x = [\theta/(1-\theta)]\ a/r = x(a,r) \qquad x_a > 0, x_r < 0 \tag{3}$$

A rise in the number of income streams raises wealth and therefore the demand for real balances. Monetary equilibrium therefore requires a rise in the real money supply. Conversely, a rise in the rate of interest reduces the equilibrium real money stock both because it lowers the preferred share of real balances in wealth and because it reduces the level of real wealth.

Next we look at income, savings, and the current account. Suppose a given labor income $\bar{Y}$. In addition there is the income from assets a. Total income Y is therefore:

$$Y \equiv \bar{Y} + a \tag{4}$$

Total income differs from the value of output to the extent that our income from assets exceeds or falls short of the income of capital domestically employed.

Saving depends only on wealth and the rate of interest. A rise in wealth lowers saving and raises spending, while a rise in the rate of interest raises saving:*

$$S = S(w,r) \qquad S_w < 0, S_r > 0 \tag{5}$$

*These are, of course, the assumptions of Metzler (1951).

The last point to note is that in an economy without investment, as we assume here, saving is equal to the excess of income over spending or the current account. The current account, in turn, is the rate at which we are acquiring claims on the rest of the world $\dot{a}/r$:

$$\dot{a}/r = S(w,r) \tag{6}$$

At any point in time, domestic residents hold a given number of income streams with a real value of a/r. By (3) there is implied an equilibrium stock of real balances and by (2) a level of real wealth. *Equilibrium* real wealth can therefore be written as a function of the number of income streams a:

$$w = x(a,r) + a/r = w(a,r) \qquad w_a > 0, \, w_r < 0 \tag{7}$$

A rise in the number of income streams raises real wealth, both directly and by means of the induced rise in real balances. A rise in the interest rate, by contrast, reduces real wealth.

The equilibrium level of real wealth in (7) implies a behavior of the current account or asset determination over time. Substituting equilibrium real wealth into (6) gives us the rate of accumulation of assets *given* that the assets market clears. Accordingly it gives us the equilibrium rate of asset accumulation:

$$\dot{a}/r = S(w(a,r),r) = \sigma(a, r) \qquad \sigma_a < 0 \tag{6a}$$

Since a rise in equities raises real wealth, and since a rise in real wealth lowers saving, we obtain the strong result that asset accumulation worsens the current account or $\sigma_a < 0$. The current account is shown in Figure 13-1 as a function of the number of equities. The relationship we show is obtained from (6a) by linearizing the equation around long-run equilibrium, $\bar{a}$, to obtain:

$$\dot{a} = S(w(\bar{a},r),r) + \sigma_a(a - \bar{a}) = \sigma_a(a - \bar{a}) \tag{6b}$$

where in long-run equilibrium, the level or real wealth is such that saving is zero. Accordingly, the approximation we show has the current account proportional to the discrepancy of equity holdings from their steady state level. If assets are above their steady state, the current account is in deficit and assets are being decumulated. Conversely, if assets are low initially then there is a current-account surplus and asset accumulation.

We have now shown that our economy will converge over time to a steady state with a balanced current account and a net holding of equities $\bar{a}$. What

FIGURE 13-1

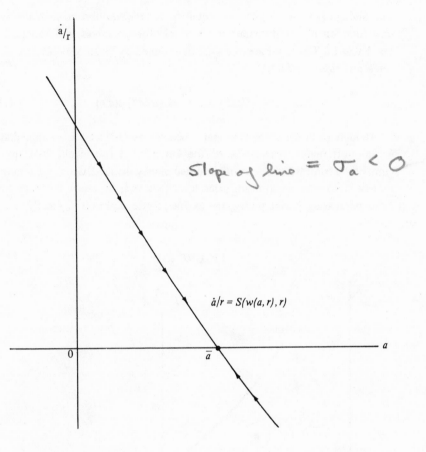

Slope of line = $\sigma_a < 0$

$\dot{a}/r = S(w(a,r), r)$

can be said about the behavior of real balances, prices, and exchange rates in the adjustment process? In (3) it was shown that equilibrium real balances are a function of equity holdings. Given nominal money H, the level of prices therefore depends on the value of equities.

We use the definition of real balances in (1) and the value of the equilibrium real money stock in (3) to write the equilibrium price level as follows:

$$P = H/x(a,r) \tag{8}$$

We also recognize that purchasing power parity, which we assume obtains continuously, implies a relation between our prices, the exchange rate, and foreign prices:

243

$$P = eP* \tag{9}$$

Combining (9) with (8) yields an equation for the equilibrium exchange rate as a function of the nominal money stock, foreign prices, and equilibrium real balances. The latter are of course determined by "real" variables, interest rates, and equity holdings:

$$e = (H/P*)/x(a,r) \equiv (H/P*)\,\phi(a,r) \tag{10}$$

An increase in the nominal money stock will by (10) lead to an immediate, equiproportionate depreciation of the currency. A rise in our holdings of equities, by contrast, raises wealth and real money demand. Given the nominal money stock, the equilibrium price level falls and, to offset the departure from purchasing power parity, the exchange rate appreciates. Finally, a rise

FIGURE 13-2

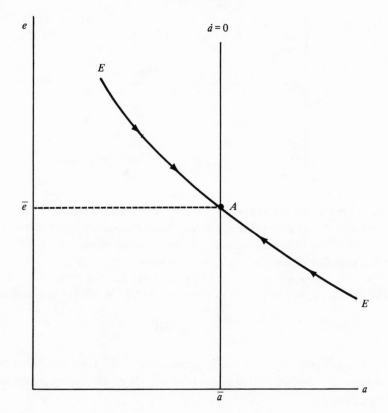

in the interest reduces real balances, raises prices, and thus leads to a depreciation of the exchange rate. We can rewrite the exchange rate in terms of its long-run value $\bar{e}$ and deviation of assets from their steady-state level:

$$e = \bar{e} + \phi_a(a - \bar{a}) \qquad \bar{e} = (H/P^*)/x(\bar{a}, r) \qquad \phi_a = -x_a/x^2 < 0 \quad (10a)$$

Schedule EE in Figure 13-2 shows the path of the equilibrium exchange rate in the adjustment process. If assets are above their steady-state level then the exchange rate will be depreciating, thus giving us the conventional association of depreciation and a current account deficit. Conversely with equities below their steady state level we have asset accumulation or a current-account surplus together with appreciation.

Three remarks are in order at this point. First, the exchange rate path is an "equilibrium path" because we have used in (10) both purchasing power parity and money market equilibrium—our only equilibrium conditions. Second, what determines the level of the exchange rate in the long run? The long-run determinants are domestic nominal money and the foreign level of prices as well as real variables. The real variables that enter come from the interaction of portfolio preferences and saving behavior. Portfolio preferences give us the equilibrium level of real balances associated with each level of equity holdings—equation (3). Saving behavior determines the long-run level of assets. The exchange rate thus reflects the entire general equilibrium interaction of the model.

The third point concerns the theory of exchange rate determination that is implicit in our model. At every point in time the *level* of the exchange rate is determined by the requirement of assets market or stock market equilibrium. Over time the exchange rate is moved by the current account. In a moment we extend this theory by introducing exchange rate expectations which establish an interdependence between the equilibrium level of the exchange rate and the path of the current account over time.

2. Comparative Statics

Before introducing exchange rate expectations we briefly consider some comparative static questions, in particular shifts in asset preferences and in saving behavior. From (3) a shift in preferences from equities to money— a rise in θ—will raise equilibrium real balances and therefore equilibrium real wealth associated with each level of equity holdings. This implies, in terms of (6a), that at each level of equity holdings, because of the higher real wealth, saving will be lower and therefore the current-account surplus will be less or the deficit larger. In terms of Figure 13-1, the current-account schedule shifts leftward and the steady value of equities declines. Steady state wealth will be unchanged since there is a unique level of wealth at which saving is zero. With real balances comprising a larger fraction of an unchanged steady state wealth, we must have a decline in the equilibrium price level and thus an appreciation of the exchange rate.

The adjustment process is shown in Figure 13-3, starting at point A. The shift in money demand immediately reduces the equilibrium price level and thus induces an offsetting appreciation as the economy moves to A'. Then, with the rise in real wealth arising from the higher real balances there is dissaving or a current-account deficit. The decumulation of assets implies falling wealth and real money demand and thus rising prices and a depreciating exchange rate. The economy comes to rest at point A''. In the short run the economy thus exhibits "overshooting".

FIGURE 13-3

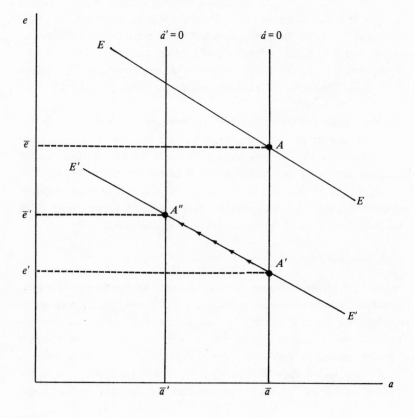

246

Exchange Rates, Assets Markets, and the Current Account

A shift in saving behavior is more easily handled. Inspection of (10) shows that the exchange rate schedule in Figure 13-2 will not shift. All that changes is the steady-state level of foreign assets. Accordingly, with a decline in saving there will be a decline in steady-state wealth and real balances and thus there will be a period of rising prices and exchange depreciation.

3. Expectations

In the adjustment process of asset accumulation or decumulation, prices are changing and so is the exchange rate. The alternative cost of holding money under these conditions is *not* the yield on equities r, which is the real rate of interest that is given in the world market, but rather the nominal rate:

$$i = r + \mu \tag{11}$$

where i is the nominal rate of interest and μ is the anticipated rate of inflation and depreciation. With purchasing power parity, inflation and depreciation are the same and we can talk interchangeably of exchange rate expectations or inflationary expectations.

We assume then that asset choice will depend on the holding cost of money and that accordingly the increased real rates or increased inflationary expectations will reduce the demand for real balances. Our equilibrium condition in the assets market then becomes:

$$x = \theta(r + \mu)w \tag{1a}$$

and therefore equilibrium real balances and equilibrium real wealth will be decreasing functions of the expected rate of inflation:

$$x = x(a, r + \mu) \qquad x_\mu < 0 \qquad w = w(a, r + \mu) \qquad w_\mu < 0 \tag{12}$$

An increase in inflationary expectations shifts the public out of money into equities and therefore reduces both equilibrium real balances and the equilibrium level of real wealth. Equation (12) in turn implies that both the equilibrium current account and the equilibrium exchange rate will depend on inflationary expectations:

$$\dot{a}/r = S(w(a, r+\mu), r) \qquad e = (H/P^*)/x(a, r+\mu) \tag{13}$$

Finally, to close the model we have to make an assumption about the formation process of expectations. We assume here perfect foresight so that expected and actual rates of depreciation are always equal $\mu = \dot{e}/e$.

Substitute now $\mu = \dot{e}/e$ in the exchange rate equation to obtain (10b):

$$e = (H/P^*)\phi(a, r + \dot{e}/e) \qquad \phi \equiv 1/x(a, r + \mu) \qquad (10b)$$

and invert the equation to solve for the rate of depreciation in terms of the level of the exchange rate:

$$\dot{e}/e = \phi^{-1}(eP^*/H, a, r) = \rho(eP^*/H, a, r) \qquad \rho_e > 0, \ \rho_a > 0 \qquad (14)$$

Equation (14) is one of our key equations. It describes the behavior of the exchange rate over time, given the assumption of perfect foresight. An increase in the level of the exchange rate leads to an increased rate of depreciation as does a rise in equity holdings. Figure 13-4 shows the $\dot{e} = 0$ schedule

FIGURE 13-4

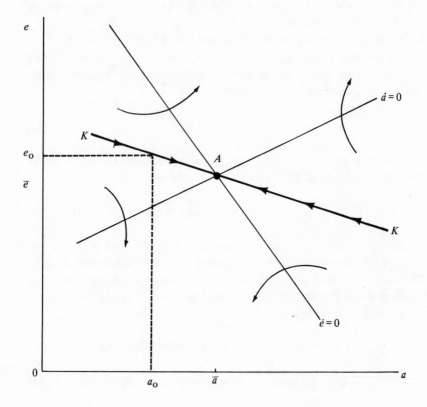

Exchange Rates, Assets Markets, and the Current Account

with a negative slope. (The schedule is the same as the *EE* schedule of Figure 13-2, along which, by assumption, expected depreciation was zero.)

Consider next the current account, given the assumption of perfect foresight. Using the equation for the equilibrium current account in (13) and substituting from (14) for $\mu = \dot{e}/e$ yields:

$$\dot{a}/r = S\left(w[a,r+\rho(eP^*/H,a,r)]\right) = \sigma(a,e,H,P^*,r)$$

$$\sigma_a = S_w w_a + S_\mu \rho_a < 0, \quad \sigma_e > 0 \tag{15}$$

A rise in assets raises wealth. Given the exchange rate and hence the real value of the money stock, the increased real assets and wealth lower saving and thus reduce the current-account surplus or the rate of increase in assets. A depreciation reduces real balances, lowers wealth, and thus leads to increased saving and accumulation. It follows that the $\dot{a} = 0$ schedule in Figure 13-4 must be positively sloped. Above the $\dot{a} = 0$ schedule real balances are low, saving is high, and there is asset accumulation. The converse is true below the current-account balance schedule.

4. The Adjustment Process Under Perfect Foresight

It is apparent from the phase diagram that the only stable trajectory is the perfect foresight path *KK*.* Given any initial level of equity holdings, such as a_0, there will be a unique level of the exchange rate e_0 (and the price level, and hence real balances), such that the economy will converge over time to the steady state. All other paths satisfy the equilibrium conditions and the assumption of perfect foresight, but they do not converge. We will assume that the economy will always be on the *KK* path.†

What difference is introduced by the presence of exchange rate and inflationary expectations? The difference can be assessed by comparing the perfect foresight path *KK* in Figure 13-4 with the level of the exchange rate along the path $\dot{e} = 0$ (corresponding to *EE* in Figure 13-2). Along the perfect foresight path the level of the exchange rate is lower when assets are below their steady state and conversely if they are above their long-run levels. This reflects the behavior of real money demand. With assets below their steady state level there is the expectation of rising assets and rising real money demand and hence the expectation of deflation and appreciation.

---

*The perfect foresight formulation of this model was introduced by Kouri (1975). See also Dornbusch (1976) and Dornbusch and Fischer (1980).
†For a further discussion of these issues see Fischer (1978).

This reduces the cost of holding real balances and therefore raises the level of desired real money holdings. Given nominal money, the equilibrium level of prices and the exchange rate must be lower.

The equilibrium current account is equal to the rate of saving. Saving depends on real wealth, and real wealth, as we have just argued, is affected by inflationary expectations. Along the perfect foresight path real wealth is higher when assets are below their long-run level (compared to an economy with static or long-run equilibrium expectations). Accordingly, with wealth high, saving and the current account will be lower. Thus along the perfect foresight path there is a smaller current-account surplus for any asset level $a < \bar{a}$. Conversely, for equity holdings $a > \bar{a}$ the expectation of depreciation and inflation lowers real wealth, raises saving, and therefore reduces the current-account deficit associated with any level of equity holdings. The perfect foresight path thus implies a slower rate of adjustment compared to static expectations.

Now consider again the disturbances already analyzed for the case of myopic expectations. Specifically, suppose that there is a decline in saving

FIGURE 13-5

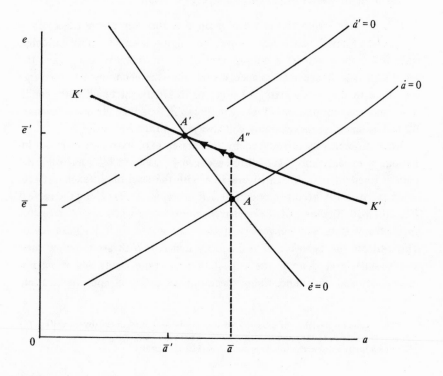

at each level of real wealth. In Figure 13-5 we show this as a leftward shift of the $\dot{a} = 0$ schedule. With reduced saving at each level of wealth we require a decline in equity holdings to restore current-account balance. Our initial equilibrium is at point A, the new long-run equilibrium is at point A'. The new perfect foresight path, appropriate to the change in saving behavior, is indicated by the line $K'K'$.

The immediate adjustment to a reduced level of saving is a depreciation of the *level* of the exchange rate to point A''. The depreciation is due to the fact that the public recognizes that the asset decumulation implied by reduced saving will imply falling wealth, falling real money demand, and hence rising prices and depreciating exchanges. The expectation of a depreciating exchange rate and rising price level reduces the demand for real balances, and therefore raises the equilibrium price level, which induces an immediate depreciation of the exchange rate. The subsequent adjustment path from A'' to A' is one of ongoing depreciation until the new long-run equilibrium is reached. The difference between the adjustment process under perfect foresight and that associated with static expectations is an important one. Under perfect foresight there is an immediate depreciation of the level of the exchange rate induced by the expectation of inflation and depreciation. That effect is not present in a model that does not emphasize expectations.

5. Anticipated Disturbances and Perfect Foresight Adjustment

In this section we extend the analysis of the adjustment process to consider disturbances arising in the future but which are fully anticipated in the present. The question is how these future disturbances affect the level of exchange rates and the current account before they actually materialize, when they occur, and after they have occurred.*

Suppose we are considering an increase in nominal money at time T in the future and suppose that this increase in money becomes known at time t_o in an economy that is initially in full equilibrium, as shown at point A_o in Figure 13-6. Once the *full* adjustment to the increase has taken place, it is clear that prices and the exchange rate will increase in proportion to the rise in nominal money and that there will be no long-run real effects. Thus the new steady state will be at A'. How does the economy move to A' over time?

Consider first a portfolio holder who contemplates the future and recognizes that on the day the money arrives the price level and exchange rate

---

*The analysis here draws on Fischer (1978), Wilson (1979), and Dornbusch and Fischer (1980).

FIGURE 13-6

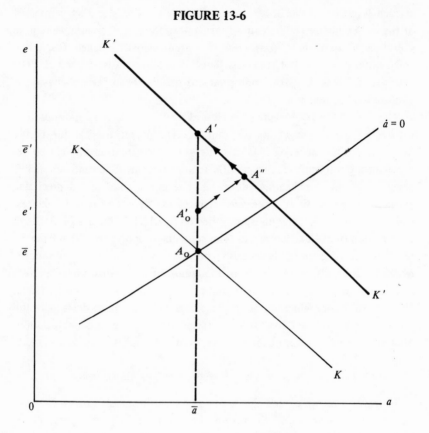

would jump, thus yielding an infinite rate of return on equities. Recognition of that jump, of course, will immediately drive portfolio holders out of money and into equity. Thus the impact effect of the announcement is to generate a jump in the price level and the exchange rate. We immediately move from A_o to A'_o.

Now at point A'_o the real money stock has declined and hence real wealth has fallen. Accordingly, there is an increase in saving or a current-account surplus. The accumulation of assets moves the economy over time from A'_o to A''. Point A'' is reached precisely at the time the nominal money stock actually rises. At that point, the real money stock increases (remember all the jumps in exchange rates and prices have been anticipated up front; there cannot be any fully expected jumps along the path), real wealth increases, saving declines, and the current account turns to a deficit and thus implies asset decumulation. Throughout the adjustment process the exchange

Exchange Rates, Assets Markets, and the Current Account

rate is depreciating. The rate of depreciation is illustrated in Figure 13-7, as derived from equation (14).

Following the initial jump in the exchange rate at time t_0 we note that (14) shows now a depreciating exchange rate ($\rho_e > 0$). Furthermore with the level of the exchange rate and the level of assets rising as the economy moves from A'_0 to A'' the rate of depreciation increases and reaches its peak at time T. At that time, again as verified from (14), the increase in nominal money reduces the rate of depreciation. The decumulation of assets, from then on, implies a decreasing rate of depreciation until the economy converges asymptotically to the steady state with zero depreciation.

The interesting aspect of this exercise is that purely nominal disturbances do have real effects. The reason is that anticipated inflation affects portfolio choices and thereby affects wealth, saving, and the current-account. The transitory real effects of anticipated monetary changes will have to be undone before the economy reaches its new steady state. Accordingly, the current account that initially moves to a surplus will then turn to a deficit.

FIGURE 13-7   *Hence, real effects are purely transitory.*

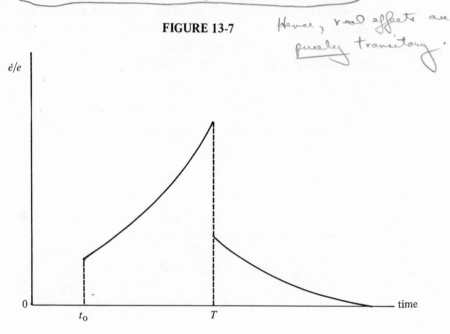

II. EMPLOYMENT, REAL WAGES, AND
THE CURRENT ACCOUNT

In this section we reintroduce cyclical considerations. The effects of external assets and wealth on saving and the current account are combined with the conventional macroeconomic adjustment process related to output and employment. We now disregard issues of expectations and instead concentrate on the interaction of wage adjustment and accumulation of assets through the current account. With wages moving sluggishly and the current account affecting the exchange rate and the real wage, we consider the adjustment process in response to a monetary expansion.

1. Wages, Assets, and the Exchange Rate

The model is that of a small country in a one-commodity world with continuous purchasing power parity. We modify, however, our earlier model in important respects. Current output now is determined by the level of real wages. A decline in real wages raises employment and output. Money wages are assumed to adjust slowly to deviations of output from full employment:*

$$Y = g(eP^*/v) \qquad g' > 0 \tag{16}$$

where v is the money wage and where we have used purchasing power parity $P = eP^*$:

$$\dot{v} = \lambda[Y - \overline{Y}] \tag{17}$$

Real money demand depends on the given world interest rate r and on real income $Y + a$. Exchange rate expectations are again static:

$$H/eP^* \equiv x = k(r)[g(eP^*/v) + a] \tag{18}$$

Saving behavior, as before, is determined by wealth and the rate of interest and is repeated here for convenience:

$$\dot{a}/r = S(x + a/r, r) \tag{19}$$

---

*This model assumes that firms are always on their demand curve for labor and that discrepancies of employment from the (long-run) vertical supply of labor lead to changes in money wages.

Exchange Rates, Assets Markets, and the Current Account

Prices and the exchange rate are fully flexible. The only adjustment processes over time derive from the slow adjustment of money wages and of assets through the current account. At any point in time, the nominal money stock, the prevailing level of money wages, and the stock of assets determine an equilibrium exchange rate and hence a level of real balances, wealth saving and output. Over time asset accumulation and money wage adjustments move the economy. We turn now to an investigation of that adjustment process.

We start with the determination of the exchange rate from the money market equilibrium condition. We can solve (18) for the equilibrium exchange rate as a function of the level of money wages and assets, given nominal money and foreign prices:

$$e = e(v,a,H,P^*) \qquad e_v > 0, \quad e_a < 0 \tag{20}$$

The equilibrium exchange rate is an increasing function of the level of money wages—it is homogeneous of degree one in money wages and the nominal money stock—and a decreasing function of the stock of assets. A rise in money wages reduces output and hence money demand. To restore equilibrium, the exchange rate and prices must rise to reduce the real money stock and raise real money demand. A rise in assets raises income, hence money demand, and thus requires a fall in prices.

The behavior of the equilibrium exchange rate in (20) implies that the real wage is a function of the level of money wages and assets:

$$\Psi \equiv v/eP^* = \Psi(v,a,H,P^*) \qquad \Psi_v > 0 \quad \Psi_a > 0 \tag{21}$$

A rise in money wages raises real wages, although proportionally less, because of the decline in income that induces a depreciation. Higher assets induce appreciation and higher real wages. Similarly, the equilibrium stock of real balances is a decreasing function of the level of money wages and an increasing function of the stock of nominal money. Equilibrium real balances are homogeneous of degree zero in nominal money and money wages. Finally, they are an increasing function of assets:

$$x = x(a,v,H,r,P^*) \qquad x_a, x_H > 0 \quad x_v < 0 \tag{22}$$

We can now study the dynamics of our model with the help of Figure 13-8. Here we show as the schedule $\dot{v} = 0$, the combination of money wages and assets such that the equilibrium real wage is equal to the full employment

FIGURE 13-8

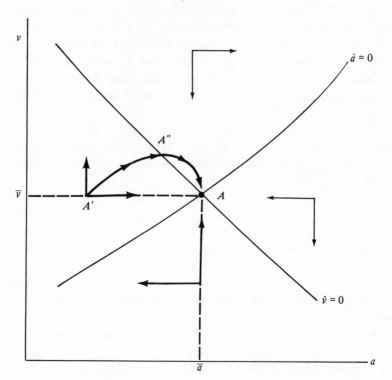

real wage. The schedule is negatively sloped in accordance with (21). Points above correspond to real wages that are too high for full employment, hence money wages are falling and conversely for points below the schedule.

Along the schedule $\dot{a} = 0$ the current account is in balance. A rise in assets raises wealth directly and through the induced change in equilibrium real balances. The resulting decline in saving would worsen the current account unless there was an offsetting rise in money wages and a resulting depreciation and decline in equilibrium real balances.

Consider now the adjustment process as shown in Figure 13-8. We only show the case where adjustment is nonoscillatory. At a point like A' there is an overemployment (boom)/surplus combination. The overemployment, by itself, leads to rising money wages, falling output, and therefore falling real money demand and depreciation. The asset accumulation, at the same time, leads to rising real money demand and hence appreciation. The net effect of money wages and the current account on the exchange rate is thus uncertain, except that real wages must be rising as the appreciation induced by the current account reinforces the effect of rising money wages on the real wage.

Over time the economy follows the path toward the long-run equilibrium at point A. On that path real wages reach the full employment level before the current account achieves balance. At this point the continuing appreciation induced by the surplus raises real wages above the full employment level. The loss of competitiveness now reduces employment, money wages will start falling, thereby inducing (partially offsetting) appreciation. The surplus continues to induce appreciation. Thus on the path from A'' to A we are in a phase of unemployment/surplus and exchange appreciation. The model thus shows the conventional cyclical behavior of exchange rates. In particular it draws attention to the fact that the current-account-induced appreciation of the exchange rate may lead to a loss of competitiveness and unemployment.

2. Exchange Rates, Money, and Wages

Suppose we start at full employment in Figure 13-9 and consider an increase in the nominal money stock. It is immediately apparent that once

FIGURE 13-9

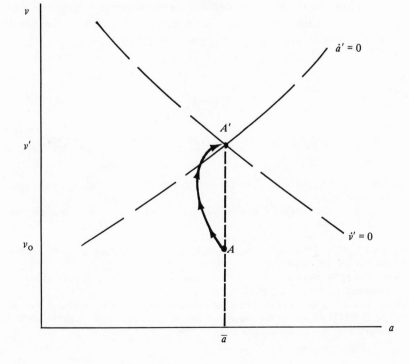

the full adjustment of money wages has taken place the economy returns to the initial *real* equilibrium at A'. In the adjustment process, because of the slow adjustment of wages, there will be transitory real effects on the current account and output.

In Figure 13-9 the increase in the real money supply initially results in a reduction of real wages and in an exchange rate depreciation which is less than proportional to the increase in money. The increase in the real money stock raises wealth, lowers saving, and thus leads to a current-account deficit. The fall in real wages leads to a gain in employment and a rise in output. The money increase thus brings about a boom/deficit situation.

The next phase, following the initial depreciation in the exchange rate, is a process of rising money wages, decumulation of assets, and exchange depreciation. The process continues until current account balance—still with overemployment—is achieved. Thereafter, money wages are still rising but the exchange rate may depreciate or appreciate depending on the relative effects of money wages and the current account. The adjustment process comes to an end when the initial real equilibrium at A' is reached.

Monetary policy thus has important, but only transitory, effects. As always, monetary policy "works" because in the short run a change in nominal money is a change in real money because wages, prices, or both, are slow to adjust. In the present formulation it is wage adjustment that is slow. Accordingly, monetary policy works on employment and on the current account through its effect on real wages and on real wealth.

REFERENCES AND SUGGESTED READING

Dornbusch, R. 1975. A portfolio balance model of the open economy. *Journal of monetary economics*, Jan. 1:3-20.

Dornbusch, R. 1976. Capital mobility, flexible exchange rates and macroeconomic equilibrium, *Recent issues in international monetary economics*, eds. E. Claassen and P. Salin, New York: Elsevier-North-Holland.

Dornbusch, R., and Fischer, S. 1980. Exchange rates and the current account. *American economic review*, forthcoming.

Fischer, S. 1979. Anticipations and the non-neutrality of money. *Journal of political economy*, April, vol. 87: 225-52.

Flood, R. 1977. A model of asset trade. Unpublished manuscript, University of Virginia.

Kouri, P. 1975. Essays in the theory of flexible exchange rates. Unpublished Ph.d. dissertation, Massachusetts Institute of Technology, Cambridge, Mass.

Exchange Rates, Assets Markets, and the Current Account

Kouri, P. 1976. The exchange rate and the balance of payments in the shortrun and in the longrun. *Scandinavian journal of economics* no. 78(2):280-304.

McKinnon, R. 1969. Portfolio balance and international payments adjustment, *Monetary problems of the international economy,* eds. R. Mundell and A. Swoboda. University of Chicago Press.

Metzler, L. 1951. Wealth, saving and the rate of interest. *Journal of political economy* vol. 59:93-116.

Rodriguez, C. 1977. The role of trade flows in exchange rate determination: a rational expectations approach. Unpublished manuscript, Columbia University, N.Y.

Tower, E. 1972. Monetary and fiscal policy under fixed and flexible exchange rates in the interrun. *Journal of money, credit and banking* 4:887-96.

Wilson, C. 1979. "Exchange rate dynamics and anticipated disturbances," *Journal of political economy* June, vol. 79:639-47.

14

Growth, the Balance of Payments, and the Exchange Rate

Chapter 13 introduced macroeconomic dynamics that concentrated on the current account. In that chapter, saving and trade in assets were at the center of analysis. In chapter 14 we widen the model to introduce investment and capital accumulation. We also broaden it by adding to the spectrum of assets that portfolio holders face. In addition to money and foreign assets we now introduce claims to domestic real capital. As always in this book, the increase in generality comes at a cost. Price flexibility and full employment are assumed throughout this chapter and we ignore expectational problems that were prominent in previous chapters.

Our purpose here is to draw attention to asset accumulation through investment and the current account as a process that influences spending, asset yields, and the exchange rate over time. With a financial structure that involves claims to real capital as well as money and bonds, the interaction of asset markets and the saving-investment balance becomes an interesting problem. Under fixed exchange rates, for example, a shift in asset preferences toward (nontraded) equity leads to a current account deficit. Under flexible exchange rates an open market purchase of money and sale of debt leads, in the short run, to capital accumulation and a current account deficit.

Chapter 14 is divided into three sections. The fairly elaborate model is laid out in section I. Section II then offers some comparative static applications under fixed exchange rates. The case of flexible exchange rates is considered in section III, where the "portfolio balance approach" to flexible exchange rates is presented.

I. ASSET MARKET EQUILIBRIUM, SAVING, AND INVESTMENT

1. An Overview

Assume a small country that produces two commodities: consumption goods (shmoo) that can be traded in the world market at a given price, and investment goods (installed machines) that are nontraded. The goods are produced by a constant labor force and the existing capital stock according to standard Heckscher-Ohlin technology.* Given these assumptions, investment and the accumulation of capital will depend on the prevailing stock of capital and the equilibrium relative price of capital or the rate of interest. Saving again depends on wealth.

There are three assets: real bonds that are internationally traded and carry a given world rate of interest r^*, domestic money, and real capital. Asset demands depend on the rates of return and wealth. Short-run equilibrium in assets markets sets the equilibrium yield on real capital, thereby determining investment and (along with wealth) saving. With saving and investment determined, we have the rate of capital accumulation and the current account and therefore the evolution of the economy over time. The economy converges to a steady state when investment equals the maintenance requirement on capital arising from depreciation and when wealth reaches a level such that saving equals investment, balancing the current account.

*See D. Foley and Sidrauski (1971) and Jones (1965).

2. The Model

In the financial markets, domestic residents face the choice between three assets: money, bonds, and equity. The demands depend on rates of return and wealth; assets are assumed to be gross substitutes:*

$$x^d = x^d(r,r^*,w) \tag{1}$$

$$b^d = b^d(r,r^*,w) \tag{2}$$

$$k^d = k^d(r,r^*,w) \tag{3}$$

where r and r^* are the yield on capital and foreign assets. Real wealth w equals the real value of asset holdings:

$$w \equiv x + k + b \tag{4}$$

The real value of money, capital, and bonds in terms of consumption goods are x, k, and b respectively. For subsequent reference, the real value of "financial assets," the sum of money and bonds, is defined as v:

$$v \equiv x + b \tag{5}$$

We turn next to the production side of the economy to discuss the relation between the interest rate and relative prices, and the equilibrium supplies of goods associated with each relative price and capital stock. The capital goods industry is labor intensive. This implies, according to the *Stopler-Samuelson theorem*, that an increase in the relative price of capital in terms of consumption goods q will raise the real wage and lower the real rental of capital in terms of both goods. But since the real rental of capital in terms of capital goods is the marginal physical product of capital, or the rate of interest on capital, there is a relation between the yield on capital and the relative price of capital:

$$q = q(r) \qquad q'(r) < 0 \tag{6}$$

In the assets market, the real value of capital in terms of consumption goods is defined as the physical stock of capital K times the relative price q and hence:

$$k \equiv qK = k(r,K) \tag{7}$$

*See Tobin (1969).

Growth, the Balance of Payments, and the Exchange Rate

Fixed exchange rates imply that the nominal money stock is fully endogenous because domestic residents can trade money for bonds at the going price, with the central bank accommodating portfolio shifts through exchange market intervention. Accordingly, we do not have to be concerned about the composition of financial assets between money and bonds. At any point in time the total of money and bonds, or real financial assets v, is given, as is the stock of physical capital. Short-run assets market equilibrium is determined by these available supplies and the asset demands in (1) through (3).

Assets market equilibrium requires that the existing stock of claims to capital be willingly held. Equilibrium in the capital market thus means that the value of the capital stock qK is equal to the demand for equities:

$$q(r)K = k^d(r,r^*,v+qK) \qquad (8)$$

where we have substituted for wealth using (5) and (7). The equilibrium condition in (8) can be solved for the equilibrium yield on capital as a function of the yield on bonds r^*, the physical capital stock K, and financial assets v:

$$r = r(r^*,K,v) \qquad r_K > 0 \quad r_v < 0 \qquad (8a)$$

Because the marginal propensity to hold capital is less than one, a rise in the capital stock creates an excess supply of capital. This situation therefore requires a rise in the equilibrium yield on capital to induce the public to hold a larger fraction of their wealth in the form of equities. Conversely, a rise in financial assets lowers the equilibrium rate of yield on capital. For a given stock of capital K_0 the right-hand panel of Figure 14-1 shows the capital market equilibrium schedule kk reflecting the negative relation between the stock of financial assets and the equilibrium yield on capital.

The equilibrium interest rate in the capital market, together with the (equilibrium) level of wealth, determines the composition of financial assets between money and bonds. In determining the composition of private portfolios they necessarily determine the level of central bank holdings of foreign assets. For the entire economy there is a stock of net foreign assets. What is endogenous is the composition of foreign assets between private sector and central bank holdings; that composition is determined by the private sector's preferences between money and bonds.

Consider next investment behavior. The relative price of capital goods q determines the allocation of factors between the production of consumption and investment goods. Given the stock of capital, a higher relative price

263

FIGURE 14-1

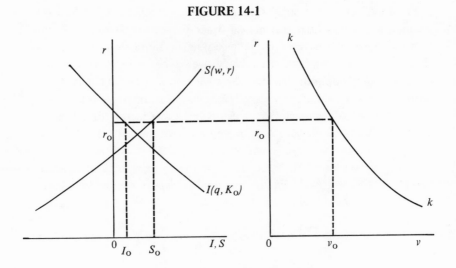

of capital implies increased supply of capital goods. With a given rate of depreciation δ, the rate of increase in the capital stock $\dot{K}$ is thus given by:

$$\dot{K} = \phi(q,K) - \delta K = \dot{K}(q,K) \qquad \dot{K}_q > 0 \quad \dot{K}_K < 0 \qquad (9)$$

An increase in the capital stock at given relative prices implies, by the Rybczinski effect, an increase in the output of the capital intensive commodity (consumption goods by our assumption) and a contraction in the output of investment goods.

While (9) gives the rate of increase in the physical stock of capital we are also interested in gross investment. Gross investment, measured in terms of consumption goods, is defined in (10):

$$I = q(\dot{K} + \delta K) = I(q,K) \qquad I_q > 0 \quad I_K < 0 \qquad (10)$$

A rise in the capital stock, in the neighborhood of the steady state (where $\phi(q,K) = \delta K$), will reduce gross investment by the Rybczinski effect.

Saving behavior is characterized by a Metzler-type wealth saving relation.* Saving, measured in terms of consumption goods, is a decreasing function of the level of real wealth and an increasing function of asset yields:

$$S = S(x + b + k, r, r^*) \qquad (11)$$

*See Metzler (1951).

Growth, the Balance of Payments, and the Exchange Rate

3. Short-run Equilibrium and Dynamics

We now have sketched our model and can turn to the determination of short-run equilibrium and to the adjustment process over time. At any time there exists a given stock of financial assets v and a given physical stock of capital K. Given these asset stocks, we determine in Figure 14-1 the equilibrium interest rate, saving, and investment. The right hand panel of Figure 14-1 shows asset market equilibrium, with the equilibrium yield on capital r_o. The yield on capital, in turn, implies a relative price of capital, a value of wealth, and an allocation of resources.

In the left hand panel of Figure 14-1 we show the equilibrium rate of investment associated with a given stock of capital K_o as a function of the rate of interest. A decline in the interest rate raises the relative price of capital, the production of capital goods, and gross investment. The investment schedule accordingly is downward sloping. At the yield r_o, the equilibrium rate of investment is I_o.

The saving schedule is shown as an increasing function of the yield on capital. Higher interest rates raise saving directly, but they also reduce the value of the capital stock, thereby reducing wealth and raising saving. The schedule is drawn for a given level of financial assets and physical capital. At a yield on capital r_o, the equilibrium rate of saving is S_o.

The current account (in the absence of a government sector) is equal to the difference between income and spending, or to the difference between saving and investment. Thus the current-account surplus in Figure 14-1 is equal to $S_o - I_o$.

The current account is equal to the balance of payments surplus less the capital account surplus. It thus equals our rate of acquisition of net foreign assets whether they be bonds acquired by the private sector or reserves acquired by the government. We therefore can write the equation describing the evolution of financial assets as:

$$\dot{v} = S(w,r,r^*) - I(q,K) = \theta(v,K) \qquad \theta_v < 0 \quad \theta_K \gtrless 0 \qquad (12)$$

We have substituted on the right hand side of Figure 12-1 to obtain the reduced form or equilibrium rate of the current-account surplus.

Consider now the effects of an increase in financial assets and real capital respectively. Increased real capital raises the equilibrium rate of interest and reduces the rate of investment. Investment declines because both the relative price of capital declines and because of the Rybczinski effect. The effect on saving is ambiguous. The increase in wealth reduces saving, but the increase in the yield on capital tends to raise saving.

An increase in financial assets reduces the equilibrium yield on capital and therefore raises investment. The effect of lower yields on capital and increased wealth is to lower saving. With investment rising and saving declining, there is accordingly an unambiguous worsening of the current account $\theta_v < 0$.

FIGURE 14-2

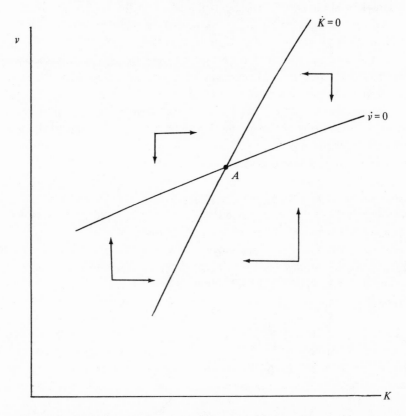

Figure 14-2 shows the dynamics of the model. Stability requires that the system of equations (12) and (9a), linearized around equilibrium, have a negative trace and a positive determinant:

$$\dot{K} = \phi[q(v,K),K] - \delta K = \lambda(v,K)$$

$$\lambda_v > 0 \quad \lambda_K < 0 \tag{9a}$$

These restrictions imply:

$$\lambda_K + \theta_v < 0 \qquad \lambda_K \theta_v - \theta_K \lambda_v > 0 \tag{13}$$

In Figure 14-2 we show the case where the stability condition is satisfied. The condition implies that the $\dot{K} = 0$ schedule be steeper than the zero current-account schedule if the latter is positively sloped.

II. COMPARATIVE STATICS

In this section three comparative statics applications are studied: an open market operation, a shift in the saving function, and a shift in portfolio preferences.

FIGURE 14-3

At r_0, $CA = 0$.

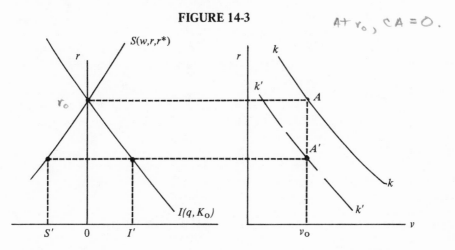

Suppose, first, that asset demands shift away from financial assets toward equities. This implies, as shown in Figure 14-3, that the equilibrium rate of return on equities declines. It now takes, with the increased preference for equities, a lower rate of return for the public to hold the existing stock. The decline in interest rates reduces saving and raises investment, thus leading to a current-account deficit.

Consider next the long-run effects and the adjustment process. The shift in asset preference implies that at each level of capital and financial assets there is a lower interest rate and hence higher investment and lower saving. In Figure 14-4 this implies that the $\dot{K} = 0$ schedule and the current-account balance schedule will shift. The $\dot{K} = 0$ schedule will shift to the right because now it takes a higher capital stock to leave zero net investment. The current-

$\dot{v} = 0$ shifts to right, at a given K, the public holds because, fewer financial assets in equilibrium (i.e., v is lower).

267

FIGURE 14-4

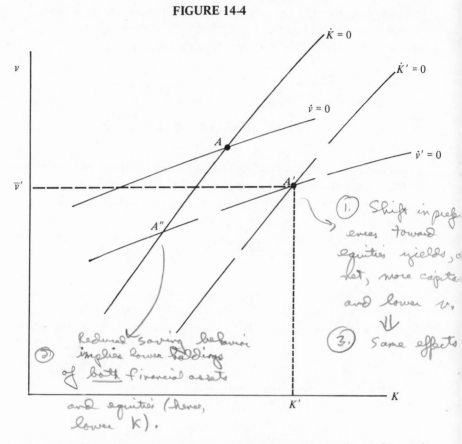

account balance shifts down to the right because it takes lower financial assets and therefore lower wealth and higher interest rates to restore the equality of saving and investment. The new long-run equilibrium is at a point like A'. The stock of capital will rise relative to financial assets—thus reflecting the shift in asset preferences. The stock of capital will rise absolutely because of the decline in interest rates in the transition period. Furthermore, since the current-account balance schedule reflects both investment *and* saving behavior, it is apparent that it must shift to the right by more than the $\dot{K} = 0$ schedule. This implies (see Figure 14-4) that financial assets must decline. In the adjustment process we run a continuing current-account deficit and decumulate assets.

We study next the adjustment to a shift in the saving function. Suppose that at each level of asset yields and wealth there is a decline in saving. In the short-run, given asset holdings, there will be no change in equilibrium interest rates, or asset prices, but there will be an immediate worsening of the current account equal to the increase in saving. This is the entire short-run effect—the absence of expectational effects bars further repercussions.

The deficit in the current account implies decumulation of financial assets. The change in the relative supply of financial assets and capital over time implies rising interest rates and will therefore start reducing investment and restoring saving. The full adjustment is readily visualized in terms of Figure 14-4 where we consider only the shift in the current-account balance schedule. The new long-run equilibrium would thus be at a point like A'', with a fall in the long-run equilibrium stocks of both capital and financial assets.

Finally, we consider an open market operation where the central bank purchases equity in exchange for financial assets. It does not matter, of course, whether the central bank sells money or bonds, since the private sector can restore their preferred portfolio composition between financial assets in the world market. What the private sector çannot undo is the change in the supply of equity relative to financial assets.

The short-run effect of a reduced supply of equity and increased supply of financial assets is a reduction in the equilibrium interest rate, increased investment, and a reduction in saving. The current account worsens, leading to a decumulation of financial assets, while capital formation rises.* It is immediately apparent that we are back to the analysis of a shift in asset preferences. The government's holdings of equity, acquired through the open market purchase, act like a private sector shift in asset demand and lead to increased physical capital formation and a reduction in financial assets.

III. FLEXIBLE EXCHANGE RATES

The previous sections looked at the fixed exchange rate case where money can be traded for securities in the world market. Exchange rate pegging implies that the central bank will accommodate security shifts between money and foreign assets at the prevailing exchange rate. The exchange rate and price level remain fixed even though there may be portfolio shifts between money and debt. Similarly, when money demand rises in the growth process, the pegging of the exchange rate implies that part of the current-account

---

*There is the question of how the government disposes of their income from the securities. We assume that the budget is balanced and that there are tax reductions, matching the equity income, that are not capitalized.

surpluses are monetized, thus providing for real balance growth at unchanging prices.

This is clearly not the case under flexible exchange rates. Without a commitment to peg the exchange rate, the authorities have full control of the money stock. Money is exogenous and portfolio shifts are now accommodated by changes in the exchange rate, the price level, and the yield on capital. Similarly, when in the growth process real money demand rises, the growth in real balances does not come about through monetization of the current account surplus, but rather through exchange rate appreciation. This section studies that adjustment process and adds an important additional aspect to the theories of exchange rate determination. This special aspect is the multiple asset feature of the present model.

1. Short-run Equilibrium

We start with the analysis of short-run equilibrium, given nominal money, foreign assets b, and the real capital stock K. Equilibrium in the assets market requires that the interest rate and the exchange rate or the price level be such that the public willingly holds the existing asset supplies. Associated with the equilibrium interest rate and price level, there are, of course, equilibrium rates of saving and investment that determine asset accumulation.

The equilibrium in the assets market is described in (14) and (15):

Money Mkt. Equil.
$$H/e = x^d(r,r^*,H/e + q(r)K + b) \tag{14}$$

Equity Mkt. Equil.
$$q(r)K = k^d(r,r^*,H/e + q(r)K + b) \tag{15}$$

which show money market and equity market equilibrium. For given asset supplies these equations determine the equilibrium interest rate and exchange rate as shown in Figure 14-5.

Probably assuming $P = e P^*$

The schedule xx shows equilibrium in the money market. Higher asset yields reduce real money demand and there must accordingly be a depreciation of the exchange rate, a rise in prices, and a decline in the real money stock to restore money market equilibrium. Along the kk schedule the equity market is in equilibrium. Higher yields on capital create an excess demand that has to be offset by a depreciation that reduces real balances, thereby reducing wealth and the demand for equity. The gross substitutes assumption implies that the xx schedule is steeper than the kk schedule. The bond market equilibrium schedule would be negatively sloped. Points along the xx schedule correspond to an excess demand for capital with a

Growth, the Balance of Payments, and the Exchange Rate

FIGURE 14-5

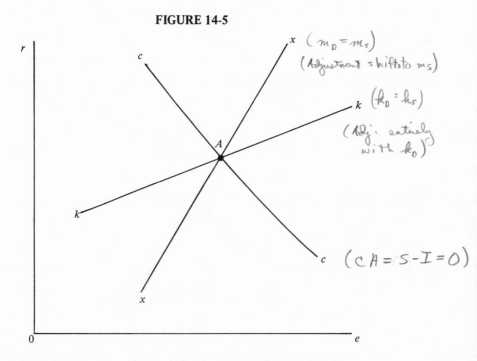

matching excess supply of bonds. Assets market equilibrium obtains at point A, where asset stocks are willingly held.

Figure 14-5 also shows the current-account balance schedule cc. For given asset supplies (H,b,K), an increase in the interest rate raises saving and reduces investment, yielding a current-account surplus. To restore balance in the current account there has to be an appreciation that raises real balances and wealth, thus reducing saving. Points above the cc schedule correspond to a current-account surplus. The equilibrium at point A shows the economy with balance in the current account.

2. Comparative Statics

What are the effects of changes in relative asset supplies or open market operations? Suppose, first, an increase in the nominal money stock. It is immediately apparent from the homogeneity of the model that an equi-proportionate exchange depreciation will take place. Consequently, money is entirely neutral because there are no other assets or prices fixed in *nominal* terms. Foreign debt, in particular, is fixed in real terms.*

*See, for comparison, Dornbusch (1978) where foreign assets are fixed in foreign currency. The latter is the standard assumption of the portfolio approach as developed in Branson et al (1977), and Isard (1978).

FIGURE 14-6

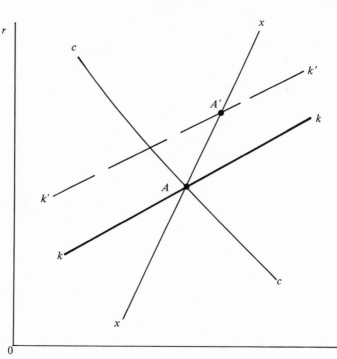

2.)

In Figure 14-6 we look at an open market operation that involves the purchase of foreign assets *b* by the central bank, and the sale of equity. Wealth is unchanged but the supply of equity rises. The *kk* schedule shifts upward reflecting the fact that it takes a higher yield on capital for the public to hold a larger share of its portfolio in the form of equity. The short-term effect of the open market operation is thus to raise the yield on capital and to depreciate the exchange rate. The exchange depreciation restores money market equilibrium, given that the higher yield on capital reduces the demand for real balances. At the new equilibrium point *A'* investment is reduced and saving rises, so that there is a current-account surplus.

To prepare for the analysis of dynamics, we examine the effect of an exogenous increase in bond holdings and holdings of capital. Consider first, an increase in bond holdings. As shown in Figure 14-7, there is an excess demand for real balances since the increase in wealth raises real money demand. Accordingly, the *xx* schedule shifts up and to the left. Likewise, there is an excess demand for capital, shifting the *kk* schedule down and to the right. The new equilibrium at *A'* involves an appreciation of the exchange rate and

FIGURE 14-7

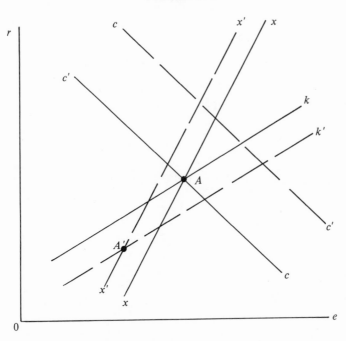

a decline in the equilibrium yield on capital. Since the increase in wealth lowers saving, the current-account balance shifts up and to the right, so that point A' corresponds to a current-account deficit. Investment rises and saving declines.

Consider next an increase in real capital as shown in Figure 14-8 where we use the money and bond market equilibrium schedules. The increase in wealth, due to higher real capital, again shifts the xx schedule up and to the left. It takes higher interest rates, or higher real balances via lower e, to restore monetary equilibrium. To restore bond market equilibrium, given the increase in wealth and bond demand, interest rates must be higher or real balances and wealth must decline. It is apparent from Figure 14-8 that the equilibrium yield on capital must rise. Whether the exchange rate appreciates or depreciates will depend on the relative shifts of the xx and bb schedules, the relative propensities to hold money and bonds out of wealth, and the relative interest responses of money and bond demands.

The effect of increased real capital on the current account is uncertain. (Figure 14-8 shows the case where increased real capital worsens the current account, thus shifting cc out.) Increased wealth per se would worsen the cur-

FIGURE 14-8

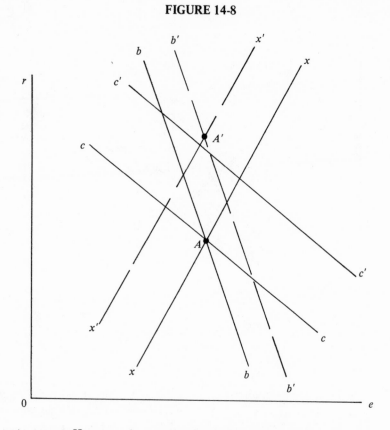

rent account. However, there is an offset from increased real capital that reduces investment and might dominate the decline in saving.

3. Dynamics

We summarize in equations (16) through (18) the effects of changes
in asset supplies on equilibrium interest rates, exchange rates, and the current
account:

$$r = r(b,K) \qquad r_b < 0, \quad r_K > 0 \tag{16}$$

$$e = e(b,K,H) \qquad e_b < 0, \quad e_K \gtreqless 0 \tag{17}$$

$$\dot{b} = \dot{b}(b,K) \qquad \dot{b}_b < 0, \quad \dot{b}_K \gtreqless 0 \tag{18}$$

Equation (18) shows that under flexible exchange rates the current account

FIGURE 14-9

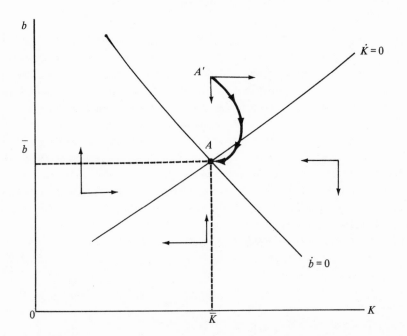

is equal to the rate at which we acquire net claims on the rest of the world. Net claims on the rest of the world in the present model take the form of bonds.

In addition to the behavior of the current account, we have to specify the evolution of the capital stock. Using (9) in combination with the equilibrium interest rate in (16) yields:

$$\dot{K} = \dot{K}q(r), K = \dot{K}(b,K) \qquad \dot{K}_b > 0 \quad \dot{K}_K < 0 \tag{19}$$

Increased bond holdings lead to a higher rate of capital accumulation since they reduce the equilibrium yield on capital, and consequently raise the relative price of capital and the rate of production of capital goods. The converse is true for an increase in the capital stock.

Equations (18) and (19) describe the dynamics of our model. In Figure 14-9 we show these dynamics for the case where an increase in the capital stock worsens the current account $\dot{b}_K < 0$. In that case the current-account equilibrium schedule is negatively sloped. Higher bond holdings, by lowering interest rates and raising wealth, lead to a deterioration in the current account: that has to be offset by the reduction in wealth arising from a decline in capital. Along the $\dot{K} = 0$ schedule the capital stock is constant.

275

The steady state equilibrium is at point A with a capital stock $\bar{K}$ and bond holdings $\bar{b}$. The adjustment process is clockwise as shown in Figure 14-9 and it may be a half-cycle or oscillatory.

We use the dynamic model to return to the question of an open market operation. Suppose the central bank reduces the money stock and sells bonds. The public holdings of bonds rise instantaneously and, in terms of Figure 14-9, we move to a point like A', where interest rates decline and real wealth rises. Capital accumulation is taking place but there is a current-account deficit. The short-run effect of the monetary contraction is thus "expansionary"— it reduces saving and raises investment. The exchange rate will appreciate proportionately more than the fall in nominal money because the yield on capital declines, thus raising real money demand.

In time the economy adjusts to the initial expansion. Bonds are decumulated and the capital stock initially rises. The reduction in bond holdings and increased capital raise interest rates until capital accumulation comes to a halt and reverses itself. Throughout the adjustment process there is a deficit in the current account. The process continues until the initial real equilibrium is reattained. At that point the exchange rate will have appreciated, since the nominal money stock is lower while all real variables are unchanged. The cumulative effect of the monetary contraction is thus clearly an equiproportionate appreciation, but only across steady states. In the adjustment process the equilibrium real money stock is affected by real wealth and interest rates.

IV. CONCLUDING REMARKS

The role of the exchange rate varies in models that we have studied. With given wages and prices, the exchange rate determines relative prices, demand, and output. In models with sluggish wages the exchange rate determines the real wage, employment, and supply. In Chapters 12 and 13 the exchange rate sets the level of prices, real balances, and real wealth. Here the exchange rate affects relative asset yields and absorption, and therefore the intertemporal choices of saving and investment, rather than allocation of expenditure between domestic and foreign goods. There is no reason to prefer one model to another; it is important, though, to recognize that the role of the exchange rate goes beyond setting the terms of trade. Even in models with full employment and price flexibility, the exchange rate retains short-run real effects.

REFERENCES AND SUGGESTED READINGS

Branson, W. 1974. Stocks and flows in international monetary analysis. *International aspects of stabilization policy*. eds. Ando, A. et al. Federal Reserve Bank of Boston.

Branson, W., Halthunen, H., and Masson, P. 1977. Exchange rates in the short run. *European economic review*, vol. 10:303-24.

Dornbusch, R. 1975. A portfolio balance model of the open economy. *Journal of monetary economics* 1:3-20.

Dornbusch, R. 1978. Monetary policy under exchange rate flexibility. *Managed exchange rate flexibility*, Federal Reserve Bank of Boston.

Foley, D. and Sidrauski, M. 1971. *Monetary and fiscal policy in a growing economy*. New York: Macmillan Publishing Co.

Frenkel, J., Rodriguez, C. 1975. Portfolio equilibrium and the balance of payments: A monetary approach. *American economic review* vol. 65, December, pp. 674-88.

Isard, P. 1978. Exchage rate determination: a survey of popular views and recent models. *Princeton studies in international finance*, no. 42, Princeton University.

Jones, R. 1965. The structure of simple general equilibrium models. *Journal of political economy* 73:557-72.

Meltzler, L. 1951. Wealth, saving, and the rate of interest. *Journal of political economy*, vol. 59, April, pp. 93-116.

Tobin, J. 1969. A general equilibrium approach to monetary theory. *Journal of money credit and banking* vol. 1, February, pp. 15-29.

Index

absorption, 7, 36, 127

accommodating transactions and debate over terminology, 15

accommodation, 162, 167-170, 172

accounting practices, 19-24

adjustment expectations, 206-207, 210

adjustment process, 104, 111, 115, 152, 245, 276; of asset accumulation and decumulation, 247-49; and asset demand, 190, 246, 267; balance of payments, 3-4, 124-25, 165; and credit creation, 217, 222-26; and exchange rate, 104, 206, 247, and high-powered money, 29; and income, 3-4; for internal and external balance, 103-108; and money flow, 124-25; and nonintervention, 226-28; and perfect foresight, 248, 249-51; and real appreciation, 111, 114; and overshooting in rate of exchange depreciation, 224; and saving shift, 268; to terms-of-trade improvement, 111; see also adjustment rate; "managed" adjustment system; monetary adjustment; price adjustment; wages, adjustment of; wage-price adjustment

adjustment rate, 136-38, 190, 204-207; perfect foresight vs. static expectations, 250, 251

aggregate budget constraints, 4

aggregate demand, 9, 57; determinants of, in the extended model, 230; and dynamic stability, 55; expansion, 42; and interest, 218, 232; and internal-external balance, 77; and monetary expansion, 176; and overshooting, 209; and relative prices, 218

aggregate spending, 35, 40, 47; equation for, 35; and income, 39, 40, 47; money as determinant of, 119; and national income identity, 20; and rate of interest, 219; and repercussion effects, 47

aggregative quality, of closed economy macroeconomics, 6

analysis: development of, 6; in macroeconomics, 4

applied research, 5

appreciation: and adjustments, 114; and credit creation, 226; of currency and the central bank, 13; and disinflation, 215; and intervention in response to credit growth, 228; and terms-of-trade adjustment, 111

Argentina, 216

asset accumulation: and current account, 242; and depreciation, 249; and hoarding, 123; and investment rate, 270; and open economy, 29; and saving, 24, 270

asset demand based on rate and yield, 187

asset level, 249, 250, 267

asset market, 5; and exchange rate level, 245; equilibrium in the short-run flexible rate model, 270; equilibrium in the Mundell-Fleming small country model, 202-205; and money supply, 177; theory of modeling, approach, 216

assets, multiple, and exchange rates determination models, 270

asset shift, and current account, 245, 261; and overshooting, 246

assets and liabilities distribution, 16

asset substitution, 189, 190-92

asset supply change, 269, 274, 275

asset yield increase, and money demand, 270

Australian model, 96-97; see also dependent economy model

automatic adjustment, and wage-price process, 77; and sterilization, 27

automatic payments adjustment mechanism, in a monetary fixed exchange rate economy, 119

autonomous expansion, 51

autonomous spending, 51

autonomous transactions, and debate over terminology, 15

balance, see external balance; internal balance; internal-external balance; real balance

balance of payments, 12-16; and borrowing, 13; domestic credit and 139-41; and exchange rate, 219; and external balance, 198; and financial policies,

balance of payments *(continued)*
192; and IMF's stabilization programs, 26; and income adjustment process, 3-4; and interest, 230; in the "managed" system, 165, 166; and monetary considerations, 5; and monetary base, 25-27; and money, 119; and money demand, 125, 139; and money level, 138; and money redistribution in a devaluation, 127; and money stock, 124, 125, 137-38; and money supply, 119; and nominal interest differential, 219; price change through adjustment process of, 127; and the price specie-flow mechanism, 148-49; in the private sector, 12; and quotas, 69; and real income, 219; in classical adjustment process, 165; and sectoral balances, 19; and surpluses, 24, 222; transfer quality of, in money redistribution, 125; in the U.S., 13; world inflation and, 141; and world patterns, 17-19
balance sheets, 4
balance of trade, 47, 48; Alexander on, 4; and incomes equilibrium determination, Harberger on, 4, 44; monetary expansion and, in the small country model, 196; and the world, 12, 37-39; *see also* trade balance
Black, Stanley, 5
bonds, 176, 178, 262, 270, 275
borderline commodity, 146
borrowing, 13, 18, 19, 21-22
Brazil, 21, 22
Bretton Woods system, 5
budget, deficit and subsidies, 74
budget surplus, 23, 65

Canada, 51-53
capital, *see* real capital
capital account, 13-15, 227; and depreciation, 277; surplus and current account, 265
capital accumulation and monetary contraction, 276
capital flow, 14, 15; and depreciation, 223; in the exchange market intervention model 219; and interest differentials, 217, 219, 221; and offset effect of credit variations, 189
capital goods and bonds, 275

capital inflow, 5
capital market, 27, 187-89
capital mobility, 4, 5, 6; and credit creation, 178; monetary and fiscal policy, 176; in the world economy, 180-86
capital stock level, 262, 263, 275
central bank, 13, 25, 26, 27; and credit, 138, 187; and deficit financing, 15; and exchange market, 13, 29; and exchange rate pegging, 269; and fiscal expansion, 179; and intervention in foreign exchange markets, 13, 14, 26; and monetary policy, 190-91; and money creation, 178; and the open market, 276
closed economy, and approach to macro-economics, 6; national income identity, 20; Taylor model of, 167
commercial banks, 15, 27
commercial policies, 66, 77, 94
commodities, *see* goods
comparative statics, 245-47, 267, 271-74
comparative statistics, 4
competitive margin, 145
competitive margin shift, 150
composite commodity, 97
composition of spending, and relative price, domestic, 58; effects of commercial policies, 77
consolidated banking system, 27
consumer price levels, 150
cost competition, 152, 155
consumption and national income identity, 20
consumption goods, 264
Cramer's rule, 55
credit, *see* credit creation; credit expansion; credit growth; domestic credit
credit creation, 27, 178, 222-26, 232
credit expansion, 27, 182, 183, 185-88 passim
credit growth, 139, 232, 234; and reduction without intervention, 228-30
credit variations: offset effect and asset substitution, 189
currency depreciation, 13, 244
current account, 5, 24, 29; adjustment of wages, and transitory effect of, 258; and assets, 24, 242, 249, 250, 261, 274, 275; and autonomous spending,

Index

51; balance, 17-19, 271; and balance of payments, 13-14, 265; and capital stock, 275; and comparative statics, 245, 268; and depreciation-inflation expectation, 247, 250; deterioration and monetary contraction, 199; and disposable income, 49; and exchange rate, 239, 247, 256; and exchange rate dynamics theory of modeling, 216; future disturbance and effect on, 251-53; factors contributing to, 14; and income and spending, 265; and interest rate, 267; and international interdependence, 51-52 and money accounting, 27, 28; in national income accounting, 19; and open market money purchase, 261; and real balance, 246; and saving rate of, 250; and the small open economy, 241, 242; spending influence on, 261; and the transfer problem, 49-50; *see also* current-account deficit; current-account induced appreciation of the exchange rate; current-account surplus

current-account deficit: and decumulation of financial assets, 269; and depreciation, 245; and financing of, 18, 19; and saving level, 269; and undereffected transfers, 50

current-account-induced appreciation of the exchange rate, 257

current-account surplus, 23; and asset preference shift, 245; and balance of payments, 24

current balance and capital account, 265

current value and rate of depreciation, 206

cycles in economics, 5, 23

deficit, 14, 15; demand shift effect on 48, 135; finance, 5, 27-28; and international interdependence, 52-53; and international net purchases, 13; and repercussion effects of demand shift, 48; *see also* deficit countries; deficit/unemployment balance and conflicts

deficit countries: and money supply, 27-28; price patterns in, 129

deficit/unemployment balance and conflicts, 42-43

deflation and real balances, 229, 230

deflation abroad and fiscal expansion, 186

deflationary fiscal policy, and tariffs, 65

deflation and appreciation expectation and perfect foresight adjustment process, 249

demand: composition of, and fiscal expansion, 199; conditions of, 100; and credit creation, 225; and depreciation, 195; for domestic goods, 39-40, 155, 197; for domestic output, 34-35; and employment level, 162, 163; expansion of, 42, 65; and fiscal expansion, 179; and income, 109, 163; income effect of terms of trade deterioration, 90; and interest rates, 179, 195, 231; money balances and, 163; and output, 34, 168; and prices, 91, 106, 163, 204-205; production adjustment, and, 111; and range of goods, 147; and redistribution of money in the price specie-flow mechanism, 149; relative price adjustment effect on, 106; and schedule for domestic output and net exports, 36; for securities, 186-87; substitution, 100, 109; and terms of trade deterioration on, 90; and wages, 147; *see also* demand for goods; demand shift

demand for goods: and devaluation, 127; and productivity growth, 151, 152; and trade balance deterioration, 107; and the transfer problem, 49

demand shift: and repercussion effects, 47-49; and terms of trade monetary model, 134-35

dependent economy model, 97-103, 109-11

depreciation: and asset accumulation, 249; and balance of payments, 227; and balance of trade, 4; and capital account, 277; and capital flow, 223; and commodity and labor intensive goods, 89; condition necessary for success of, 64; and credit creation, 222, 224, 225, 226; and credit growth, 230, 234; of currency and the central bank, 13; and current-account deficit, 245; and demand, 195; and direct effect on inflation model, 234; effects

depreciation *(continued)*
of, 156-57; and employment, 88; and
equilibrium output, 77; and exchange
rate, 87-89, 206, 227, 248; expectation
of, 203, 204, 250; in the flexible rate
system, 229; and foreign expenditure,
157; on imports and exports, 157;
and interest differential, 221; and
intermediate goods, 87, 89; and
internal-external balance, 77; in the
managed system, 166; and monetary
expansion, 201; and monetary growth
over credit creation, 220; and output,
167, 195, 230; rate of, in the complete
extended model, 223; and real income,
88; and spending composition, 77; and
trade balance, 88; and wages, 156-57,
166; *see also* devaluation; exchange
depreciation
devaluation, 7, 87-89, and absorption,
127; and employment, 91; and expansionary effect of, 81; and export
subsidy, 67-68; in home extended
monetary model, 130-31; implications
of, 126-27; and intermediate goods,
88-89, 90; and internal balance control, 42; in the monetary model,
125-27; as policy tool, 57, 62-64;
and tariff, 65, 67-68; and trade balance,
63, 89, 126-27; and real-wage resistance, 73-74; transitory nature of, 127,
131; *see also* depreciation; exchange
depreciation
developing countries, 17-19
dirty floating, 6, 13
dishoarding, 123; and foreign countries,
123
disinflation, 215, 216
disposable income, 49, 50-51
distribution of reserves and money supply, 181
disturbance persistance and accommodation, 170
dollars, buying of, 14
domestic credit: as an asset, 25; and balance of payments, 139-40; and capital
flow, 189; central bank and, 26, 138;
and credit ceilings, 26; and endogeneity, 190; expansion in the world
economy, 139-41; and money demand
growth, 139-40; and money growth,
222; and offset coefficient, 191; and

policy reaction function, 190; and
reserves, 26, 177-78; and settlement
balance, 25-26
domestic demand for goods, and balanced
budget export subsidies, 67
domestic demand for imports, and price
elasticity, 59
domestic expansion, 46, 155-56
domestic goods, 39-40, 45, 46, 194
domestic income: contraction of, and
import spending, 40; and credit expansion, 185; and export expansion, 47
domestic money reserves, 182
domestic output, 34, 45, 46, 80, 134
domestic security supply and interest
rates, 188-89
domestic spending, 45-47, 58, 59
dynamic stability of the OECD model,
determination of, 53-56

economists, international, of the 1950s and
60s, *ix*
elasticity, 64-67 passim, 138; and demand,
91, 138; and devaluation, 7, 89; and
exchange rate depreciation, 88; and
expenditure, 80; and income expansion, 52; and overshooting, 209; in
perfect capital mobility country, 180;
of relative price and demand for
domestic goods, 135, 136
empirical research and testing, 5
employment, 163; in classical adjustment
system, 165; and demand expansion,
42; and demand relationship, 162,
163; and depreciation, 88; and domestic increase, 155; and expectations of
relative wage, in adapted Taylor model,
169; and export subsidy, 66; and
foreign money, 158; and foreign wage,
155, 156, 158-59; income effect of
terms-of-trade deterioration on, 90;
and income redistribution, 87; and
intermediate goods price rise, 90, 91;
in the managed system, 166; and
monetary contraction, 199; and
monetary expansion, 196, 202; and
monetary policy, 161-62; and money
holdings, 153; and multiplier effect,
86; and quota, 69; and real income,
85; and real money supply, 157-58;
and real wages, 71, 73, 74, 85-86,

Index

98; and relative price, 164; and sticky wages, 153-155; and wage change patterns in the "managed" system, 165; and wage-price change, 86

equilibrium and repercussion effects, 46; interdependence, 4

equilibrium income, 34-35, 43-45, 63, 64; and relative price, 61; and spending, 35, 37, 39-40

equilibrium interest rates, 182, 187

equilibrium output, 57-81; and commercial policies, 77; and demand, 34, 48, 168; and depreciation, 77; and interest rate, 179; money holdings and, 154; in the Mundell-Fleming model, 199; and price, 57-81, 99, 168; and real exchange rate, 218; and terms of trade, 75; and trade balance, 34-37; and transfer problem, 49; and world demand, 37-39

equilibrium stock of real balances, 242

equilibrium in supply and demand, 128

equilibrium supply of goods, 262

equilibrium terms of trade, 199

equity, 262, 267

equity market short-run equilibrium, 270

equity values and price level, 243

excess cash balance, 124

exchange appreciation, 178, 199

exchange equalization account, 13

exchange depreciation, 64; and employment, 163; and equilibrium income, 63, 64; and external balance, 163; and inflation, 228-29; and monetary expansion, 196, 198; rate of, 223; in the Mundell-Fleming 2 country model, 200; and saving shift, 247; and wage-price adjustments, 77

exchange intervention, 217, 220, 222-26

exchange rates, 6, 245, 251-253, 276; and accomodation policies, 167, 170, 172; and adjustment process, 104, 206, 247; and aggregate demand in the extended model, 230; and appreciation, 228, 246, 270; and asset supply change, 247; and balance of payments, 219; and central bank intervention, 13; and competitiveness, 257; and credit creation, 225; cyclical behavior of, 257; and depreciation, 206, 248; devaluation and, 130; and disequilibrium, 102; equilibrium level of,

244, 247; expectations about, 202, 203, 247; fixed vs. flexible, 159; and floating, 5; and income, 221-22; and intermediate goods price policies, 90; in the "managed" system, 165, 166; and monetary contraction, 199; and money expansion, 193, 201; and money stock increase, 208; and output, 210; and overshooting, 224; pegging of, 269-70; and perfect foresight, 248; and portfolio shift, 270; and price of goods, 218; and real balance, 221-22; and relative prices, 4, 157; and relative wage, 156, 157; and stabilization policy, 4-5, 167; and standard analysis, 4; and trade balance, 163; *see also* exchange rate depreciation; exchange rate intervention model; real exchange rate

exchange rate depreciation: and accommodation policy rules, 168; and capital yield, 272 and expectation of, 251; and imports and exports, 157; and interest rates, 245; and money demand, 246; and price, 205, 246; and wage-price adjustments, 77

exchange rate intervention model: and adjustment to credit creation change, 222-26; dynamics of, 220-22; and structural equations, 218-20

exchange stabilization and monetary authority, 25

excise tax, 74

expansion, 47, 51-52, 185, 195, 276; *see also* credit expansion; demand, expansion of; domestic expansion; fiscal expansion; income expansion; monetary expansion; output expansion

expenditure, 80, 121n, 150; balances in goods and services, 51, 52 income and, in relation to hoarding, 122-23; internal-external balance and, 100; pattern shifts in and equilibrium income, 39-40; and real income, 79-80;

expenditure-switching effect, 60

exportables, 90, 94, 109

export disturbances, 36, 37-38

exports, 6, 14, 20; expansion of, 47, 185, 195; increase of, 38; market equilibrium and, 112

export subsidies, 66, 67-68

external assets, banking system's acquisition of, 27
external asset accumulation and distinction between GNP and GDP, 22
external balance, 4, 22; adjustment mechanism, 26, 75-77, 96; and balance of payments equilibrium, 198; as current-account equilibrium, 104-105; and devaluation, 127; and developing non-oil producing countries, 17, 18, disaggregated view of, 14-16; and exchange depreciation, 163; and financial and monetary sectors, 27-29; and government budget, 27; and income expansion, 42; and monetary expansion, 199; money redistribution and, 138; official financing of, 13; and policy instruments, 62; Mundell's theory and emphasis on, 5; and real-wage resistance, 71, 74; and tariffs, 42, 66; and terms of trade, 75
external debt, 14, 26
external public debt reduction, 24
external surplus, 23

Federal Reserve research on economic theories, 5
Federal Reserve Credit Outstanding, 25
financial assets, 263, 266
financial policies and balance of payments vs. price adjustment, 192
financial programming, 26
financial sector, 27-29
financial transactions and accounting, 14-15
financing balance of payments, 14-15
financing current account deficits, 18
fiscal expansion, 179, 186; and asset substitutability, 191; and income, 176, 179, 186; and interest rates, 186, 191; in Mundell-Fleming flexible exchange rate models, 193, 195, 197, 199, 201; offset coefficient and effectiveness of, 191; and world economy, 193, 196; see also fiscal policy
fiscal policy: and capital mobility, 176; and imperfect substitutability, 190-92; and internal-external balance, 77; in perfect capital mobility country, 178-80; and repercussion effects,

186; and wage-price adjustments, 75-77
fiscal policy, monetary policy vs., in the imperfect asset substitution model, 190-91
fixed exchange rate, flexible vs., 159
fixed rates and money stock, 195
flexible exchange rate: fixed vs., 159; and adjustment process, 229; and foreign wage-price disturbance effects, 159; and money stock, 195; and the Mundell-Fleming flexible exchange rate model, 193, 194, 199, 269-76; in the Ricardian model, 156-60
flexible real wages, and the managed system, 166
floating exchange rate, and economic modeling, 5
foreign assets, 14, 24
foreign currency, 13, 201
foreign demand: and income, 47; and price elasticity equation, 59, 86; and increased spending, 46; and relative price, 58; and terms of trade, 111-14; equilibrium; and wage-price relationship, 86
foreign elasticity, 59, 88
foreign employment and wage patterns, 156
foreign exchange, 13, 14
foreign expenditure and exchange depreciation, 157
foreign income, 156, 185
foreign income expansion, 46-47
foreign money and hoarding, 123
foreign output and equilibrium, 46
foreign price and exchange rate, 244
foreign trade balance deterioration, 156
foreign trade multiplier, 3-4
foreign wages: cause and impact of an increase, 155-56; and the flexible rate Ricardian model, 158-59
full employment and internal balance, 198
future disturbance and the perfect foresight adjustment process, 251-53

Gastarbeiter, 22
geographic specialization, 146
Germany: and international interdepend-

Index

ence, 51-53; as net external creditor, 21, 22

goods: commodity intensive and depreciation, 89; for consumption, 264; export of, as credit item, 14; nontraded, and traded, 6; labor intensive, 87, 90; real price and expenditure, 80; in Ricardian production model, 144; supply of and relative prices in the monetary model, 128; would excess of and equilibrium output, 48

goods market equilibrium, 121-22, 123

government absorption and national income identity, 20

government budget, 19, 27

government budget deficit, 23, 28

government spending increase, 42, 45, 46

gross domestic product (GDP), 19, 21-22

gross investment, 264, 265

gross national product (GNP), 19, 21-22

gross national product deflator and productivity growth, 152

Hecksher-Ohlin technology, 261

high-powered money, 25-26, 29

hoarding, 122, 123

home goods, *see* nontraded goods

identities, 4

imperfect substitutability, and capital market equilibrium, 186-89; and fiscal and monetary policy, 190-92; and offset coefficient estimates, 189-90

imports: criteria for, 94; as deficit item, 14; and demand, 39-40, 58; elasticities and income expansion, 52; and external balance, 42; and international interdependence, 52; and price, 6, 58, 87, 109, 194; tariffs and expansion in output, 65; trade balance, 40, 47

imports and exports, 150, 157

income, 4, 29, 241; and aggregate spending, 39, 47; and balance of payments, 3-4, 219; and credit, 139, 228; and demand, 42, 47, 109, 163, 177, 178; in the dependent economy model,
102; open economy and determination of, 33-57; determination of, 34, 37-39; and employment, 91; and exchange depreciation, 200; and exchange rate, 221-22; and expenditure, 121n; and exports, 38, 39; and fiscal expansion, 176, 186, 201, 202; from foreign assets, in OECD countries, 17; and foreign trade multiplier, 4; and hoarding, 122-23; interdependence and determination of, 184; integration with relative prices and determination of, 4; and monetary expansion, 194, 199, 201, 202; and money holdings, 121, 153; and money supply, 177; and nominal definition equation of, 120-21; and output, 59; and quota, 69; and real balance, 221-22; and real wages, 87; redistribution and employment, 87; and relative price of exportables, 112; and reserve inflow, 177-78 and saving, 36-37; and trade balance, 37, 184; world inflation and, 139; *see also* income expansion; income and spending; real income

income expansion, 42, 46, 52

income and spending: balance between, and adjustment process, 115; and current-account surplus, 265; devaluation and, 127; equilibrium for, 133; and money flow adjustment, 125; redistribution of money and, 138; in terms-of-trade monetary model, 133

inflation: and credit creation, 223, 225, 226; and deflation, 234; and depreciation, 222, 228-29, and exchange rate, 229; and equilibrium rate change, 224; expectations of, and saving, 250; and high-powered money, 26; and intervention, 225; and monetary growth, 218; and money growth, 228, 229, 232; Mundell's theory and emphasis on, 5; and output, 217, 218; and productivity growth, 132, 152-53; and real balances, 234; and real growth, 139; world economy inflation rate, 138-41

instability, sources of in monetary model adjustments, 136

instruments of policy and adjustment, 57

insurance and OECD countries, 17

instantaneous adjustment and perfect capital mobility, 176

integration of open and closed economy, 4

interest rate, 179, 217, 218; and aggregate demand, 218, 230, 232; and asset changes, 267, 274, and balance of payments, 230; and capital, 265; and credit creation, 178, 225; and credit expansion, 185, 187; and credit growth reduction, 228; and current-account deficit, 267; and demand, 179, 194, 195, 231; differential, 219, 221, 223; and domestic securities supply, 188-89; and exchange depreciation 200; and expenditure, 121n; and fiscal expansion, 186, 191, 202; and foreign income and expansion, 185; and gross investment, 265; and money supply and demand, 177, 179; and offset coefficient, 183; open economy model, 245; output, 179, 195, 210; and production, 179, 265; and real balances, 227; and real capital, 265; and real income, 221; and real money, 217, 276; and price, 204, 205, 262; response to expectations, 206-207; and spending, 219; and sterilization monetary policy, 27; interest response to demand and speed of adjustment of expectations, 206, 207

intermediate goods, 82, 85, 87; price increase, 90; and response to depreciation, 89

internal balance, 4, 77; and demand expansion, 42; and full employment, 41, 198; and income expansion, 42; and policy instruments, 62; and real-wage resistance, 71, 74; and tariff on, 66

internal-external balance: and the adjustment process, 103-108; and commercial policies, 77, 78; and the dependent economy model, 100; and equilibrium price, 111; in the managed system, 165, 166; and policy instruments, 62; and real-wage resistance, 71; and relative price adjustment of nontraded goods, 93-95

international economics, 3, 4, 6

international interdependence, 51-53

International Investment Position of the United States, 16

International Monetary Fund (IMF), 5, 14-15, 26

intervention, 216, 223-25, 229

intervention coefficient, 219, 232

intervention policy of "leaning against the wind," 218-19

investments: behavior and, 264; and asset demand shift, 267; determination of, in two-commodity model, 261; level of and financial assets, 266; and national income identity, 20; and real capital, 265

investment, direct foreign, and financing current-account deficits, 18, 19

Israel, 21, 22, 215, 216

Japan, 51-53

Johnson, Harry, ix, 4

joint-expansion, and international interdependence, 52, 53

Keynesian income determination, 34, 35

labor: demand for, and range of goods, 147

labor derivation, 98

labor-intensive capital goods industry, 262

labor-intensive commodities and wage-price relationship, 84

labor-intensive goods: and employment patterns, 87; price of, and real wages, 87; and substitution in intermediate goods price rise, 90; wage-price relationship, 86

labor productivity, 151, 152; growth in, 151, 152

labor share in exportables, and effects of depreciation, 88

labor, value of services, output and, 147

Latin America, 215, 216; and disinflation, 215, 216

Laursen-Metzler, 4; on balance of trade, 4

"leaning against the wind" intervention policy, 218-19

Index

least cost location and geographic specialization, 145
lending countries, 21, 22
liability, and high-powered money, 25
log-linear macroeconomic model, 167-68
long-run adjustments of money stock increase, 207, 209
long-run equilibrium levels of wages, and price specie-flow mechanism, 148-50

macroeconomics, 3-5
macroeconomic stability and accommodation, 167-70
"managed" adjustment system, 165-66
marginal properties, and payments adjustment process, 132
market equilibrium: in goods added monetary model, 128-29; and exchange depreciation, 200; and monetary expansion, 201; and output with total planned spending, 36; and the Ricardian model, 147-48; in terms of trade monetary model, 132-33
Marshall-Lerner condition, 61, 63, 64, 88, 89; derivation of, 59; and elasticity, 91; stability dependent on variant of, 136
material intensive goods, 85
Meade, James, and integration of value and income theories, 4
Metzler-type wealth saving relation, 264
Metzler, Lloyd, ix, 4, 5
models, 5 7, for labor economy, 83-87; and macroeconomic analysis, 115
monetary adjustment, 151
monetary base and balance of payments, 25-27
monetary contraction, 199, 276
monetary disinflation, results of, 215
monetary disturbance, adjustment process, 150; in monetary model with goods, 129
monetary equilibrium, 177-79, 181-83, 195, 200, 241
monetary expansion: and aggregate demand, 176; and balance of trade, 196; and foreign currency, 201; and foreign income, 194, 201; and intervention, 224; and output, 176, 193, 195,

210; in the Mundell-Fleming small country model, 193, 195-96, 198-99; in the Mundell-Fleming two-country model, 201
monetary growth, 218, 220, 224
monetary interdependence, Mundell's theory, and emphasis on, 5
monetary mechanism and terms of trade, 132-38
monetary model, 120-26, 127-32
monetary policy; and accommodation, 172; and asset substitutability, 190-92; and capital mobility, 176, 178; and effectiveness of, in flexible exchange rate model, 193, 198-99; and the Mundell-Fleming small country model, 198; and repercussion effects, 186, transitory effects of, 258
monetary sector and external balance, 29
monetary stabilization, 229
money: accounting of, and balance of payments, 25-29, 125; aggregate expenditure and, 119; as an asset, 262; contraction of 276; and exchange-rate level, 245; expansion of, 27, 178; flow of, 123-25, 135; and price level influence, 119; see also redistribution of money; real money
money adjustment process, see price specie-flow mechanism
money balance, 163, 170
money creation: and disinflation, 215; and exchange intervention, 222; and exchange depreciation rate, 223; Mundell's model and emphasis on, 5; and reserve change, 26; and stabilization, 216
money demand: and asset yield increase, 270; and change induced by credit expansion, 183n; and exchange rate depreciation, 246; expenditure influenced by, 121n; and income, 177, 178; and interest rate, 177, 179, 254; and monetary expansion, 178, 201; and offset coefficient, 183; and overshooting, 209; and perfect capital mobility, 177; and the purchasing power parity model, 254; and real balance growth, 270; and world interest rates, 183, 185; in the Mundell-Fleming model, 207-209
money growth: and credit, 222, 232;

money growth *(continued)*
and inflation, 228, 229, 232
money holding, 121, 147, 153, 154
money purchase and current account, 261
money stock: and accommodation policy
rules, 168; and adjustment expectations, 207; and balance of payment,
137-38; and capital market equilibrium, 186; control of, 270; and depreciation, 230, 244; devaluation and
effect on, 130; employment, and
change in, 163; and exchange rate,
195, 244; expansion of, and world
interest rate level, 183; and monetary
contraction, 199; and output expansion, 210; and the price specie-flow
mechanism, 149-50; and spending in
terms-of-trade monetary model, 133
money stock-oriented monetary policies
and sterilization, 27
money supply, 177; balance of payments,
and effect on, 119; change in, and
classical adjustment process, 165; in
deficit countries, 27; in the managed
system, 165, 166; in surplus countries,
27
money wage adjustment process and equilibrium exchange rate, 255, 256
multiplier effect in real income, spending
and employment, 86
Mundell, Robert, *ix*, 4-5
Mundell-Fleming model, 194-202; adjustment of expectations, 206; and exchange rate expectations, 202, 203;
and monetary equilibrium for income
levels, 200; of the small country,
194-99; of two countries, 199-202

national domestic product (GDP), as
distinct from gross national product,
19, 21-22
national expectations, in the exchange
market intervention model, 219
national income accounting, 19-20
national income identity, 20-21, 22
net exports, 29, 35-36
net external assets, 16, 28
net external creditor, *see* lending countries
net factor receipts from abroad and GNP,
21
net foreign assets, NFA, 25, 26, 27, 29

net foreign investment, 23, 24, 36-37
net official assets and current-account
surplus, 24
net purchases and international payment
of, 13
net reserves, change in, 26
net saving and asset acquisition, 24
net taxes and external surplus, 23
nominal interest differential and balance of payments, 219
nominal money increase abroad, 158
nontraded goods, 93, 94-97; categories
of, 83; and effect of money redistribution on demand, 149; expenditure
on and money holdings, 147; introduction of, 82; monetary model and
effect of, 131; money holdings and,
147; and relative price level, 151; and
productivity growth, 151; and transport, 94-95

offer curves, 6
official aid, and financing current-account
deficits, 18, 19
official monetary authorities, 13
official reserves, increase in, 24
official sector vs. international investment position, 16
official settlements, 13, 14-15, 25-26
official transfer and capital account, 14,
15
offset coefficient, 17, 183, 188-90
oil shock, influence on external balance,
17-18
open economy: and assets market, 5;
and capital mobility, 5; and comparative statics, 267; complexity of, 6;
Dornbusch's approach to, 6; and income determination, 29, 33-57; and
macroeconomic approach, 4; modeling
of, 6-7; and national income accounting, 19-24; and national income identity, 20; and nontraded goods, 95; and
sectoral balances, 29; and trade balance, 33-57; *see also* open economy
multiplier
Open Economy Macroeconomics, over-
view of, 7-10
open economy multiplier, 38
open market adjustment, 269

Index

Organization for Economic Cooperation and Development (OECD) countries: and financing current-account deficits, 18, 19; and international interdependence, 51-53; oil shock influence, 18; and service balance surplus, 17, 18; and world payment patterns, 17-19

OECD International Linkage Model, 51-53

Organization of Petroleum Exporting Countries (OPEC), 17-18

output, 34, 99, 233; and adjustment expectations, 209, 210; or capital intensive commodities and capital stock, 264; and credit, 185-86, 225, 230, 232; demand in adjustment of, 53; and depreciation, 195, 230; and dynamic stability, 56; and export subsidy, 66, 67; and expenditure, 80; and fiscal expansion, 179, 199; and foreign wage increase, 155; and government spending, 45, 46; and income and spending, 59-60; and inflation, 217, 218; and interest rate increase, 195; and labor services value, 147; and monetary contraction, 199; and monetary expansion, 176, 193, 196, 199; and net exports, 36; and price adjustment, 209-210; stability and exchange rates, 167, 170; in terms-of-trade monetary model, 134; and trade surplus, 60; and traded goods, 100; and wages, 71, 155, 158-59, 254, 258; *see also* output expansion

output expansion, 50, 210; and exchange depreciation, 64; and money holdings in the adjustment process, 154; and real balances, 225; and recession, 232; and tariffs, 65, 66; and wage-price adjustment process, 77

overshooting, 5, 208, 209, 224, 246

overeffected transfer and current account surplus, 50

overlapping wage contracts, Taylor model and the accommodation policy, 168-69

partial equilibrium analysis, 4

Pakistan, 21

payments adjustment, 5, 132, 150-51

pegging, 269-70

perfect capital mobility, 199; and fiscal expansion, 179; and instantaneous adjustment, 176

perfect foresight, 210-13; in the adjustment process, 248, 249-51; and anticipated disturbance, of adjustment, 251-53

perfect substitution, 176

Peru, budget deficit in, 28

policy choices, Meade on, 4

policy disturbance and spreading through exports, 199

policy instruments, 57, 62

policy intervention, 77, 94; and quotas, 68-69; and tariffs, 65-66

policy issues and balance, 41-43

policy reaction function for domestic credit, 190

portfolio shifts and exchange rate, 270

Portugal, 21

price, 70-71, 245, 246; absolute, 127; accommodations to disturbances of, 162, 167, 170, and adjustment process, *see* price adjustment; of capital and interest rates, 265; deficit countries pattern of, 129; and demand, 163, 194; and depreciation, 246; elasticity of, 136, *see also* price elasticity of demand; equilibrium, 111, 122, 123, 243; and exchange-rate level, 218, 245, 246; of imports in small country model, 194; intermediate goods' response to increase, 90; and money redistribution, 149; and profit markup, 70-71; and saving shift, 247; of traded goods and devaluation, 130; wages' effect on, 163; *see also* price index; price level; price specie-flow mechanism; price taker; relative price

price adjustment, 274; and balance of payments, 127; elasticity of demand, 138; and external balance problems in the nontraded goods model, 96; and financial policies, 192; to output, 209-210; of productivity, 107; rate of, 136-38, 204-207

price elasticity of demand, 136, 138; for exports by foreign countries and imports at home, 59; and inflation rate in the adjustment process, 206-207; for output and speed of adjustment expectations, 206

price index, 70, 79-80

price level, 6, 204, 205; and accommodation policy, 168, 170; and demand, 204-205; and devaluation, 127; and equity values, 243; and exchange rate appreciation, 246; money and influence on, 119; and money stock, 124, 125, 208; and portfolio shifts, 270; and supply, 205; purchasing power parity and instability of, 170; and wage settlements in the adapted Taylor model, 169; *see also* computer price level
price specie-flow mechanism 148-50
price taker, 97
production: adjustment of, 111; of capital goods and bond holdings, 275; and geographic specialization, 146; and interest rates, 179, 265; real wages and level of, 70-71, 74; relative price and level of, 107, 151-53; Ricardian model of, 144-46
productivity growth, 131-32, 151-53
product wage, 98
project LINK, 51
purchasing power parity, 150-53

quotas, 68-69

range of traded goods, 146, 147
rate of interest, *see* interest rate
real balances, 221-22, 241; and capital account, 227; and credit creation, 225; current account, 246; and deflation, 229, 230; exchange rate, 221-22, 244, 247; growth of, 270; and interest rates, 221, 227, 245; and inflation, 234; and price level, 204, 205; and real income, 177
real capital, 265
real disturbance, 159
real exchange rate, 102; appreciation and partial accommodation, 168; and credit growth, 234; and depreciation without intervention, 227; and relative price, 107-108
real income: and demand for exportables, 87; definition of, 78; and depreciation, 88; and employment, 85; and expendi-

ture, 78-80; and interest rate, 217, 218; and multiplier, 86; and price index, 79-80; and real balances, 177; and real wages, 85; *see also* real income transfer
real income transfer, 67
real money balances and credit creation, 225
real money demand and inflation, 139
real money stock, 127, 210, 217, 276
real money supply and employment, 157-58
real variables and the exchange rate, 245
real wage, 70-71; adjustment of, 75-77; and asset level, 255; and depreciation, 87; and employment, 85-86, 87, 98; and excise tax, 74; flexibility in the managed system, 166; labor's response to, 71, 72; and money wages, 255; and output, 71; and price of capital, 262; and relative prices, 70, 84; and real income, 85; *see also* real-wage resistance; wages
real-wage resistance, 5, 64, 71-74, 77
redistribution of money, 135, 138, 149, 150
relative prices, 58-62; and balanced budget export subsidy, 66-67; and demand, 91, 106, 163, 194, 218; in domestic economy and factor prices, 84-85; and elasticity effect on demand, 135; and employment, 99, 164; and exchange rate, 107-108, 157, 159; and expenditure, 136; of exportables, 109, 111-12; and goods supply, 128; and intermediate goods price rise, 90; and interest rate, 262; and internal-external balance, 93, 100, 104; and money, 119; and monetary adjustment, 151; and nontraded goods, 93, 131, 151; and output, 61, 97, 99; and payments adjustment, 150-51; and productivity, 107, 151-53; role of, in monetary model, 136; and spending level of, 78; and tariff, 65; and technology, 96; and trade balance, 115, 163-64; and trade deficit, 107; of traded goods, 98, 100; transfer and 104-105; and wages, 70, 84-87, 151; *see also* terms of trade
relative unit labor requirement, 144
relative wage: and demand for labor, 147; and depreciation, 156-57; effect

of change on imports and exports, 150; and employment expectations, 169; equilibrium specialization pattern, 148; and the exchange rate, 156, 157; and foreign money increase, 158; and foreign wages increase, 155; geographic specialization pattern and, 146; and monetary adjustments, 151; and range of goods, 146, 147; and productivity growth in traded goods, 151, 152; and relative price levels, 151; spending and, 147

repercussion effect: and balance of trade, 47; of demand shift on deficit, 48; of fiscal expansion, 201; and foreign income expansion, 46; of income and interest rate change, 185; and income expansion, 43-51; of monetary policy, 186; in the Mundell-Fleming two-country model, 200

reserves, 13, 18-19, 26

reserve level, 14-15, 177, 179, 183, 188; see also offset coefficient

reserve outflow and credit creation, 178

reserve stock, 186

Ricardian Model, 144-50; description of, 96; market equilibrium conditions, 147-48; and production, 144-46; and the Scandanavian variant, 96

royalty: receipts of, as services, 14

Rybczinski effect, 264, 265

saving: asset demand shift, 267; and current account, 245, 250, 269; determination of in two-commodity model, 261; and inflationary expectations, 250; and interest rate in the purchasing power parity model, 254; savings and investment in monetary contraction, 276; reduction in, 40-41, 45, 46; restoration of in the adjustment cycle, 269; in the small open economy, 241; and wealth in the purchasing power parity model, 254; and yield on capital, 265

savings-investment balance, 19, 23

Scandinavian model, 96

sectoral balances, 19, 22-24, 29

sectoral labor shares, 88

securities, and distribution of assets and liabilities, 15

services, 12, 14, 95

sheltered goods, see nontraded goods

short-run adjustments, 209

short-run monetary policy effectiveness, 258

statistical error in capital account, 14-15

slow adjustment of wages, 258

small country model, 33-43

Spain, 215, 216

spending: and absorption, 36; contraction and transfer problem, 49; and devaluation, 127; and demand, 45-46, 135; and depreciation, 64; and disposable income, 49; and income, 22, 35, 37; money holdings and levels, 128; and multiplier effect, 86; and output, 39-40, 80; and price index, 80; and the price specie-flow mechanism, 149; and relation to, 22; and relative prices, 78, 128; terms-of-trade deterioration and income effect on, 90; and wage-price change, 150; see also income and spending

spot rate, 204

stability and accommodation, 167-70; and money redistribution adjustment, 135-38; price elasticities and, 138; requirements for, 233

stabilization: and capital mobility, 4; and external balance considerations, 43; International Monetary Fund programs and, 26; and intervention, 216; shift in, 247, 268

sterilization, 27

sticky wages, 153-56

Stopler-Samuelson theorem, 262

strategic use of assumptions, 160

structural policies, 78

subsidies, and excise tax, 74

substitutability, 88, 186-89

substitution: and balanced budget export subsidy, 67; and demand, 100, 109; and employment, 87, 91; and exchange rate depreciation, 88; and intermediate goods price increase, 90; and relative price of exportables, 111-12; and wage-price change, 86

supply and demand, 130, 145

supply shocks, 5

surplus, 13, 14, 17, 18

surplus countries and money supply, 27
surplus/overemployment balance, 42-43
Swan, Trevor, 4
Switzerland, 21-22

tariff, 42, 57, 65-66
tariff, equal rate and relation to devaluation, 67-68
tariff subsidy combination and transfer, 68
Taylor's model, 167-70, 171-72
taxes and financing export subsidies, 66
tax cut and aggregate expansion, 42
technical efficiency, 144
technology, 17, 146
terms of trade, 58, 60, 132-34; and depreciation, 62; and deterioration, 90; and elasticity of expenditure, 80; and equilibrium income, 63; exogenous change, 109-11; and fiscal expansion, 202; improvement of, and adjustment process, 111; and monetary expansion, 201; and payments adjustment process, 132; and price taker, 97; and the real wage, 71-72; and trade balance, 59; and wage-price adjustment process, 77
testing of theories in the 1970s, 5
total adjustment, 219
total planned spending and market equilibrium output, 36
tourist receipts, as services, 14
trade adjustments and applied research, 5
trade balance, 33-57, 88, 128-29, 160; and aggregate spending, 40, 47; and commercial policies, 77 and current account 14; and demand, 40, 163; and depreciation, 64, 77, 88; and deterioration, 106-107, 193, 196; and devaluation, 63, 89, 126-27, 131; and disequilibrium, 102; and exchange rate, 163; and export disturbances, 37-38; and export subsidy, 66, 67; and fiscal expansion, 193-94; and foreign income expansion, 46-47; and import price, 61; and improvement, 36, 38, 88; income and spending, 37, 102; and income, 35, 37, 184; and interest rates, 179; and international interdependence, 52; and equilibrium output,

34-37; relative prices and effect on, 57-81; and quota, 69; and savings reduction, 40-41; and spending shifts, 40; stability, 56; and substitutability, 88; and tariffs, 66; and terms of trade, 59; and transfer, 106-107; and wages, 163
trade deficit, and relative price, 107
traded goods, 97; and expenditure, 146, 147; and productivity growth, 131-32, 151, 152; and trade balance deterioration, 106-107
traded and nontraded model, 83-84
trade improvement and increased expenditure, 81
trade, international, 12, 13
trade surplus, 60, 102, 123
transfer, 12, 14, 49-51; balance of payments, 125; as credit item, 14; and current accounts, 14; and deficits, 49; and tariff-subsidy combination, 68; and trade balance, 106-107; see also official aid, and financing current-account deficits
transport, 17, 94-95
transitory effect of wage adjustment, 258
treasury as official monetary authority, 13
trend price level and accommodation effect, 170
two-commodity models, 43-51, 83

undereffected transfer and current-account deficit, 50
unemployment: and competitiveness, 227; and credit creation, 226; and disinflation, 215; and monetary stabilization, 229; and real balances, 225; and real wage resistance, 74
unemployment shock, 229
unit labor cost and pricing, 70
unit labor requirement, 144, 151
United States asset position, 16
United States balance of payments, 13-14, 15 (table); expansion and spill-over effect in, 51-52; and interdependence, 51; and international investment position, 16 (table); as a net external creditor, 21-22; sectoral balance in, 23

Come up with <u>Outline</u>

for Mundell-Fleming

~~Ideas~~

Index

value theory, Meade on, 4
velocity, money flow adjustment process and, 125

wage-price adjustments, 75-77
wage-price behavior, 168-70
wage-price change, 86, 150
wage-price disturbance persistence, 167, 169-70, 172
wage-price relationship, 86
wage-price stickiness and accommodation stabilization policies, 170
wages: and accommodation process, 171; adjustment of, and output, 258; and competitiveness, 85; and depreciation, 166; and disturbance of, 167; and exchange rate relation to foreign wages, 158; home goods price level, and level of, 151; and price, 70-71, 163; rate of, in dependent economy model, 98; and real demand, 147; redistribution of money and effect on, 149; and relative price, 84-87; and settlements, 169; and trade balance, 163; and unemployment, 165; *see also* real wage; real-wage resistance
wealth, 242, 276

Wealth, Saving and the Rate of Interest (Metzler), 5
world demand, 37-39, 46
world "domestic" credit, 139
world economy, 180-86; asset substitutability and fiscal expansion in, 191; and current-account balance payment pattern, 17-19; and equilibrium income and spending, 138; and goods market equilibrium, 122; and inflation rate, 138-41; interdependence and expansion in, 51-52; and interest rates, 183, 185, 199; monetary and fiscal policies in, 183-86; money flow adjustment process in, 124; and money stock defined, 122; and money supply, and interest rates, 185; and price level equation, 138; reserves as outside assets in, 181; and world "domestic" credit, 139
world quantity theory, 138-41

yield on assets and demand, 187
yield on capital: and financial asset increase, 263; and portfolio shift, 270; and saving, 265
yield on securities, 186